SUBREGIONAL COOPERATION IN THE NEW EUROPE

Subregional Cooperation in the New Europe

Building Security, Prosperity and Solidarity from the Barents to the Black Sea

Edited by

Andrew Cottey
Lecturer, Department of Peace Studies
University of Bradford

Foreword by

Thorvald Stoltenberg
former Foreign Minister of Norway

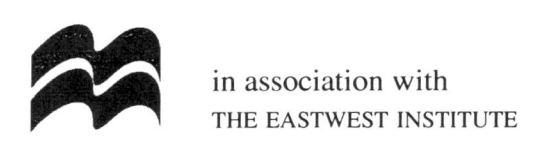

in association with
THE EASTWEST INSTITUTE

First published in Great Britain 1999 by
MACMILLAN PRESS LTD
Houndmills, Basingstoke, Hampshire RG21 6XS and London
Companies and representatives throughout the world

A catalogue record for this book is available from the British Library.

ISBN 0-333-73360-6

First published in the United States of America 1999 by
ST. MARTIN'S PRESS, INC.,
Scholarly and Reference Division,
175 Fifth Avenue, New York, N.Y. 10010

ISBN 0-312-22072-3

Library of Congress Cataloging-in-Publication Data
Subregional cooperation in the new Europe : building security,
prosperity and solidarity from the Barents to the Black Sea /
edited by Andrew Cottey ; foreword by Thorvald Stoltenberg.
p. cm.
Includes bibliographical references and index.
ISBN 0-312-22072-3 (cloth)
1. National security—Europe, Central. 2. National security-
-Europe, Eastern. 3. North Atlantic Treaty Organization-
-Membership. 4. European cooperation. I. Cottey, Andrew.
UA646.S86 1999
355'.033043—dc21   98-37391
                                                                    CIP

Selection and editorial matter © EastWest Institute 1999
Foreword © Thorvald Stoltenberg 1999
Introduction and chapters 5, 10 and 12 © Andrew Cottey 1999
Chapters 2-4, 6-9 and 11 © Macmillan Press Ltd 1999

All rights reserved. No reproduction, copy or transmission of this publication may be made without written permission.

No paragraph of this publication may be reproduced, copied or transmitted save with written permission or in accordance with the provisions of the Copyright, Designs and Patents Act 1988, or under the terms of any licence permitting limited copying issued by the Copyright Licensing Agency, 90 Tottenham Court Road, London W1P 9HE.

Any person who does any unauthorised act in relation to this publication may be liable to criminal prosecution and civil claims for damages.

The authors have asserted their rights to be identified as the authors of this work in accordance with the Copyright, Designs and Patents Act 1988.

This book is printed on paper suitable for recycling and made from fully managed and sustained forest sources.

10 9 8 7 6 5 4 3 2 1
08 07 06 05 04 03 02 01 00 99

Printed and bound in Great Britain by
Antony Rowe Ltd, Chippenham, Wiltshire

Contents

List of Figures   vii

Foreword: Stellar Moments   viii
Thorvald Stoltenberg

Preface   x

List of Abbreviations and Acronyms   xii

Notes on the Contributors   xiii

PART I: INTRODUCTION

1 Introduction   3
   Andrew Cottey

2 European Security at the End of the Twentieth Century: 8
   The Subregional Contribution
   Anders Bjurner

PART II: SUBREGIONAL COOPERATION:
FROM THE BARENTS TO THE BLACK SEA

3 The Barents Euro-Arctic Council   23
   Pertti Joenniemi

4 The Council of Baltic Sea States   46
   Carl-Einar Stalvant

5 The Visegrad Group and Beyond: Security Cooperation   69
   in Central Europe
   Andrew Cottey

6 The Central European Free Trade Agreement: 90
   Problems, Experiences, Prospects
   Andrzej Kupich

7 The Central European Initiative   113
   Christopher Cviic

8 The Black Sea Economic Cooperation: 128
    Will Hopes Become Reality?
    Oleksandr Pavliuk

PART III: SUBREGIONAL COOPERATION AND THE NEW
EUROPEAN SECURITY ORDER

9 The Role of Subregional Cooperation   153
    in Post-Cold War Europe: Integration, Security, Democracy
    Alyson JK Bailes

10 Subregional Cooperation and the New European   184
    Security Architecture
    Andrew Cottey

11 Emerging Subregional Cooperation Processes: 213
    South-Eastern Europe, the Newly Independent States
    and the Mediterranean
    *Ian Bremmer, Sophia Clement,
    Andrew Cottey and Thanos Dokos*

PART IV: CONCLUSION

12 Conclusion   243
    Andrew Cottey

Appendices

Appendix 1. Membership of the Barents-Black Sea   255
Subregional Group (August 1997)

Appendix 2. Members of the Steering Board of   256
the EastWest Institute Project
'Multi-Layered Integration: The Subregional Dimension'

Notes and References   257

Index   277

List of Figures

Figure 9.1. The 'Down-Side': 154
Possible Reasons for States to Resist Subregional Cooperation

Figure 9.2. The 'Security Spectrum': 170
The Spectrum of Security Roles Open to Subregional Groups

Foreword: Stellar Moments

The end of the Cold War represents what Stefan Zweig called 'Stern Stunden' or stellar moments of history. These stellar moments have given us new opportunities in international relations. We do not know how long these opportunities will last. It is our responsibility to grasp the present opportunities in order to safeguard the future.

The expansion of the European integration process to some countries from Central and Eastern Europe will hopefully be completed with the integration of all of Europe. An important by-product of the integration process is the subregional cooperation that we now see in central parts of Europe, from the Barents area in the north to the Barcelona process in the Mediterranean in the south. This development may prove to be of decisive importance for the future security of Europe.

I believe that peace will prevail in the Balkans. Peace in Bosnia is not only a question of the future of the people in that region, but also of NATO. Our most important security organization cannot afford to fail in its first ever international operation. NATO cannot leave the area before we know that the peace will last and that the operation has been successful.

If peace is secured in the Balkans, we may in the next century have a zone of subregional cooperation through all of Europe, from the Barents in the north through the Baltic Sea and the Balkans, and with luck also in the Black Sea area and the Mediterranean. This zone represents the very areas of Europe where there have historically been tension, violence and war. Successful subregional cooperation in this zone will reduce the chances of new tensions. This zone is also where we may experience a new curtain through Europe – this time not an iron curtain, but a division between the rich and poor countries. Subregional cooperation will reduce this danger and contribute to stability. Subregional cooperation may change this zone from one of tension, violence and war to one of stability and more evenly spread prosperity.

In our tedious day-to-day work with subregional cooperation it is important not to lose sight of this vision and the enormous opportunities it offers. With the end of the Cold War one order came to an end – an order dominated by fear. The integration process and subregional cooperation may for the first time ever contribute to a new and stable order without the preceding ravages of wars. The five 'Bs' – the Barents, the Baltic, the

Balkans, the Black Sea and the Barcelona process – will stand for peace. If so, we will have used the opportunities offered us at the present stellar moments.

THORVALD STOLTENBERG
*Former Defence Minister, Foreign Minister
and Ambassador to the United Nations of
Norway, former United Nations High Commissioner
for Refugees and former United Nations Peace
Mediator in the former Yugoslavia.*

Preface

This book is the product of a research and policy-forming project undertaken by the EastWest Institute (EWI) in 1996-97, entitled 'Multi-Layered Integration: The Subregional Dimension'. The project examined the roles played by subregional groups of states – specifically the Barents Euro-Arctic Council, the Council of Baltic Sea States, the Visegrad group, the Central European Free Trade Agreement, the Central European Initiative and the Black Sea Economic Cooperation – in post-Cold War Europe. The project was funded by the Carnegie Corporation of New York, to which EWI wishes to express its grateful thanks. During 1997-98, again supported by the Carnegie Corporation, EWI will be undertaking a further project examining the prospects for subregional cooperation in South-Eastern Europe, the western former Soviet Union and the Caucasus and Central Asia. Further information and reports from both of these projects can be obtained from EWI.

The project, of which this book is the concluding product, was very much a collaborative effort, bringing together representatives of governments, international organizations, non-governmental organizations and the academic community. The project was guided by an international advisory Steering Board (whose members are listed in Appendix 2), which met in Warsaw in June 1996 and in Stockholm in January 1997. The project involved two international conferences, in Bucharest in October 1996 and in Bratislava in April 1997, which brought together governmental and non-governmental experts. Representatives of EWI also benefited greatly from the opportunity to participate in an official Organization for Security and Cooperation in Europe (OSCE) seminar on 'Regional Security and Cooperation' held in Vienna in June 1997 and a project, sponsored by the Government of Norway, examining the Barents Euro-Arctic Council, the Council of Baltic Sea States and the Black Sea Economic Cooperation.

EWI and the editor wish to express their thanks to all those who participated in and supported this project. In particular, thanks are due to the following people and organizations: the members of the project Steering Board, especially its Chair Anders Bjurner of the Swedish Ministry of Foreign Affairs, for their support and advice; the authors of the chapters contained in this volume; the Polish, Romanian, Slovakian and Swedish authorities for their generous support in hosting the project Steering Board meetings and conferences; the Institute for Security Studies of Western European Union; Ambassador Arnt Rindal of the Norwegian Ministry of

Foreign Affairs and Arne Olav Brundtland of the Norwegian Foreign Policy Institute; the participants in the two project conferences; representatives of the various subregional groups and of the European Union, the North Atlantic Treaty Organization, the Council of Europe and the OSCE (in particular, the Foreign Ministries of Switzerland and Denmark, as Chairmen-in-Office of the OSCE in 1996 and 1997, and their permanent delegations to the OSCE in Vienna). Within EWI, particular thanks are due to John Mroz, Stephen Heintz, Vasil Hudak, Oleksandr Pavliuk, Ian Bremmer, Rachel Lutz, Tomasz Chojnecki, Lydia Moleros, Scott Rogers and Rick Robison. The editor would like to express especial gratitude to Alyson Bailes and Maeve Lankford for their support throughout the project and their assistance in the editing of this book. The contents of this book are solely the responsibility of the editor and the authors. They should not be construed as reflecting the views of the Institute for EastWest Studies, the Carnegie Corporation of New York, or any of the governments, organizations or individuals mentioned above.

ANDREW COTTEY

List of Abbreviations and Acronyms

BEAC *Barents Euro-Arctic Council*

BSEC *Black Sea Economic Cooperation*

CBSS *Council of Baltic Sea States*

CEFTA *Central European Free Trade Agreement*

CEI   *Central European Initiative*

CFE   *Conventional Armed Forces in Europe Treaty*

CIS   *Commonwealth of Independent States*

EAPC *Euro-Atlantic Partnership Council*

EU   *European Union*

NATO *North Atlantic Treaty Organization*

NIS   *Newly Independent States*

PFP   *Partnership for Peace*

OSCE *Organization for Security and Cooperation in Europe*

SECI *Southeast European Cooperation Initiative*

WEU   *Western European Union*

Notes on the Contributors

Andrew Cottey is a lecturer in the Department of Peace Studies at the University of Bradford. During 1996-97, he was European Security Programme Project Manager in the Warsaw office of the EastWest Institute. He has previously worked for Saferworld and the British American Security Information Council and is a 1996-98 NATO Research Fellow. He is author of *East-Central Europe after the Cold War: Poland, the Czech Republic, Slovakia and Hungary in Search of Security* and is currently writing a book on Western security policy towards post-communist Europe.

Alyson JK Bailes is a career member of the British Diplomatic Service. During 1996-97, she served as Vice-President responsible for the European Security Programme at the EastWest Institute. Her previous experience included postings at Budapest, NATO headquarters in Brussels, Bonn, Peking and Oslo, an attachment to the British Ministry of Defence and a sabbatical at the Royal Institute of International Affairs (Chatham House), London. She is currently Political Director of Western European Union.

Anders Bjurner is Deputy State Secretary for common security policy issues in the Swedish Ministry for Foreign Affairs. He has previously been Chairman of the Committee of Senior Officials of the Organization for Security and Cooperation in Europe (OSCE), Chairman of the OSCE Minsk Group on the Nagorno-Karabakh conflict, Special Assistant (Diplomatic Adviser) to the Minister for Foreign Affairs on the Middle East peace process, and Counsellor (Political Affairs) at the Swedish Permanent Mission to the United Nations. Before this he worked on Africa, in the region, in Stockholm and at the United Nations.

Ian Bremmer is Senior Fellow at the World Policy Institute and President of the Eurasia Group. An expert on nation- and state-building in the Newly Independent States, he has published widely on issues of post-communist transitions, including most recently *New States, New Politics: Building the Post-Soviet Nations* (with Ray Taras) and articles in *International Affairs, World Policy Journal, Security Dialogue, Journal of Democracy, The New Republic* and *The Los Angeles Times*.

Sophia Clement is a Research Fellow at the Institute for Security Studies of Western European Union in Paris, working on South-Eastern European security issues. Previously, she worked for the Centre d'Etudes et de Recherches Internationales (CERI) in Paris. She is author of the Chaillot Paper *Conflict Prevention in the Balkans: the Case of Kosovo and the FYR of Macedonia*.

Christopher Cviic is Associate Fellow, European Programme, the Royal Institute of International Affairs (Chatham House), London and former Editor (1984-1995) of *The World Today*, the Institute's monthly journal. He worked for the BBC World Service from 1954 to 1959 and again from 1964 to 1969 and was from 1969 to 1990 leader-writer and correspondent on Central and Eastern Europe on the staff of *The Economist*. He is author of *Remaking the Balkans* and is currently writing a book about Central European politics and security.

Thanos Dokos is the Director for Research at the Strategic Studies Division of the Hellenic Ministry of Defence and a 1996-98 NATO Research Fellow. He has held posts at the Hessische Stiftung Friedens und Konfliktforschung in Frankfurt (1989-90), the Center for Science and International Affairs at Harvard University (1990-91), and the Hellenic Foundation for European and Foreign Policy (ELIAMEP) in Athens (1994-95). His most recent publications include *Negotiations for a CTBT: 1958-1994* and *Security Problems in the Mediterranean* (in Greek).

Pertti Joenniemi is a Senior Research Fellow and Project Director of Nordic-Baltic Studies at the Copenhagen Peace Research Institute. His recent publications include an edited volume on *Neo-nationalism or Regionality? The Restructuring of Political Space*.

Andrzej Kupich is adviser to the Minister in the Department of Studies and Planning, Ministry of Foreign Affairs, Warsaw. He has previously worked in the Polish Institute of International Affairs, is an expert on economics and economic cooperation in Central and Eastern Europe, and is author of, inter alia, *Partnership for Transformation* (in Polish).

Oleksandr Pavliuk is the Director of the Kyiv Centre of the EastWest Institute, and Associate Professor at the University of 'Kyiv-Mohyla Academy'. An expert on European security and international relations in Central and Eastern Europe, he has published articles on regional cooperation and Ukraine's foreign policy, and is the author of *Ukraine's Struggle for Independence and the US Policy*.

Carl-Einar Stalvant is the Research Director of the newly established Sodertorns Hogskola south of Stockholm. Its research, supported by a special foundation, will concentrate on the Baltic sea region and Central and Eastern Europe. He has been lecturer at the Department of Political Science, Stockholm University and a fellow of the Swedish Institute of International Affairs. He has editorial responsibilitites for the North European and Baltic Sea Integration Yearbook and Nordeuropaforum. His latest works includes *Baltic Sea Politics: Challenges and Achievements* and *Creating a Baltic Sea Agenda 21*.

Part I
Introduction

1 Introduction

Andrew Cottey

Since the late 1980s, a belt of new subregional groups has emerged in Europe, stretching from the Barents area in the far north to the Black Sea in the south. The Barents Euro-Arctic Council (BEAC), the Council of Baltic Sea States (CBSS), the Visegrad group, the Central European Free Trade Agreement (CEFTA), the Central European Initiative (CEI) and the Black Sea Economic Cooperation (BSEC) – though diverse in membership and character – are an important, new dimension of Europe's post-Cold War international relations. Compared to the larger European security organizations – the European Union (EU), the North Atlantic Treaty Organization (NATO), the Western European Union (WEU) and the Organization for Security and Cooperation in Europe (OSCE) – however, these subregional groups have received relatively little attention and are often perceived as weak. They lack the economic power of the EU, the military power of NATO or the normative, standard-setting role of the pan-European OSCE. The diversity of their members, their largely consensus based decision-making and their sometimes limited agendas constrain the areas in which they can act.

It is too easy, however, to dismiss these subregional groups. In a wide variety of subtle and complex ways they contribute to overcoming the Cold War, East-West division of the continent and to building security in the new Europe. The larger of these groups – the BEAC, the CBSS, the CEI and the BSEC – bring together NATO and EU members, Central and Eastern European states aspiring to join NATO and the EU, neutral and non-aligned countries and former Soviet states (including Russia in the cases of the BEAC, the CBSS and the BSEC). By their very existence, therefore, these groups provide frameworks for cooperation amongst states in very different geo-strategic and security circumstances and with very differing views on Europe's post-Cold War order. Although these groups have had little or nothing to do with 'hard' security issues (defence policies, security guarantees, peacekeeping and peace enforcement, military cooperation), they have facilitated practical cooperation in a number of non-security or 'soft' security areas (economic development, the management of environmental problems, the management of borders, the promotion of transfrontier cooperation between regions of states). Such cooperation helps not only to address the specific practical problems involved, but also to promote a wider sense of shared interests and common identity. The smaller and more homogenous of these subregional groups (the Visegrad group and CEFTA), while promoting cooperation amongst their members, have also assisted those states in dismantling their old Soviet bloc ties, putting the issue of their membership of NATO and the EU on the political agenda and preparing for integration with NATO and the EU.

As plans for NATO and EU enlargement moved forward in the mid-1990s, interest in the role and potential of European subregional groups grew. There were fears that NATO and EU enlargement might create new 'dividing lines' between those states joining NATO and the EU in first or subsequent waves of enlargement, those states excluded (whether from first phases of enlargement or entirely) and those states opposed to the enlargement processes (particularly Russia). The members of NATO and the EU sought to avoid the emergence of new 'dividing lines' by strengthening their own eastern outreach and cooperation policies and by developing special relationships with Russia and Ukraine in particular. In this context, the cooperative, bridge-building function of subregional groups became increasingly important. By bringing together existing NATO/EU members, states invited to join NATO/EU, those states excluded from or not seeking NATO/EU membership and those states opposed to NATO or EU enlargement, subregional groups had the potential to sustain cooperation and help to avert the development of potentially dangerous divisions in the new Europe. At the same time, some of the subregional groups appeared to be entering new phases in their own development in the mid and late-1990s. Having been established and having developed basic institutional frameworks in the early 1990s, they began to explore how their cooperation could be given more substance and whether – and how far – they should engage in more directly security related activities. As a result of these two dynamics – the integrative processes of NATO and EU enlargement and the further evolution of the subregional groups themselves – the larger organizations (the EU, NATO the WEU and the OSCE) began to show an increasing interest in promoting subregional cooperation and developing cooperation and practical 'divisions of labour' with the existing subregional groups. By 1996-97, therefore, the subregional groups in the Barents-Black Sea belt seemed likely to play an important role in the wider context of the integrative processes of NATO and EU enlargement and the development of cooperation with those countries not joining NATO or the EU.

In the longer term, how far and in what ways the subregional groups – and the broader dynamic of the subregionalization of European security which they reflected – would develop was less clear. By 1996-97, the Visegrad group had already fallen into disuse, as its primary goals of dismantling its members' Soviet bloc ties and facilitating their integration with NATO and the EU had been – or were near to being – achieved. If the majority of CEFTA and CEI members joined the EU in the medium term (over the next ten to fifteen years, for example), these groups might also fall into disuse – although 'echoes' of them might remain in the form of loose Central European caucuses within the EU and NATO. The BEAC, the CBSS and the BSEC seemed more likely to have longer term roles because they included former Soviet states, above all Russia, unlikely to join NATO or the EU (except perhaps in the very long term). As NATO and the EU enlarged, however, other subregions – South-Eastern Europe, the western former Soviet Union, the Caucasus, Central Asia and, in the south, the Mediterranean – seemed likely to assume increased importance as the 'boundary zones' of a larger NATO and EU. By the mid/late-1990s, new cooperation processes were beginning to be established in these subregions. As NATO and EU enlargement proceed, therefore, the most politically critical zone for judging the evolution of subregional cooperation may shift further to the south and east.

This book examines the role of subregional cooperation in the new Europe, focusing on the six groups in the Barents-Black Sea belt, but also examining their relations with the larger European security organizations and the lessons from these groups for attempts to establish similar processes elsewhere. Before summarizing the structure of the book, it is important to clarify how the term subregional is used. The term 'region' is used by many people, but its meaning may vary, creating some confusion. The term 'region' may refer to an entire continent, seaboard or other very large geographically defined area (Europe, the Asia-Pacific region, the Middle East), a somewhat smaller geographic space nevertheless comprising several whole states (East Asia, the Baltic Sea region, the Persian Gulf), or at a lower level a part of a state or a single territory covering parts of several states (as in the various 'Euro-regions'). The definition used here is derived from the United Nations (UN) Charter, which refers to the possibility of 'regional arrangements' below the global level of the UN itself.[1] From this perspective, Europe is a 'region' of the world. This definition of Europe as a region was reaffirmed in 1992 when the members of the then Conference on (now Organization for) Security and Cooperation in Europe declared their 'understanding that the CSCE is a regional arrangement in the sense of Chapter VIII of the Charter of the United Nations. As such, it provides an important link between European and global security.'[2] In this context, 'subregional' refers to a geographically and/or historically reasonably coherent area within the OSCE space as a whole. The term is not exact, since it is clear that the definition of any subregion (like that of a region) reflects not only geography, but also history and politics – often making the issue contentious. Nevertheless, in this sense the BEAC, the CBSS, the Visegrad group, CEFTA, the CEI and the BSEC may reasonably be defined as subregional groups.[3]

The BEAC, the CBSS and the BSEC are defined by reasonably discrete geographic factors (their members' location in the Barents, Baltic Sea and Black Sea geographic areas), as well as by elements of shared history resulting from their geographic location. The Visegrad group, CEFTA and the CEI are less clearly delineated by geography. Nevertheless, their members share a certain common geographic and historic sense of being Central European states – as the names CEI and CEFTA indicate. More generally, these groups recognize each other as peers and are recognized as a distinct category by the OSCE itself and by other larger institutions such as the EU. Although other European organizations (the EU, NATO, the Commonwealth of Independent States (CIS)) are also composed of sub-groups of the OSCE as a whole, they are too large and have little in terms of common geography or history – beyond the fact that their members are members of the given organization – which might define them as subregions. There is sufficient distinction between larger groups such as the EU and NATO on the one hand, and subregional groups such as those in the Barents-Black Sea belt on the other, to consider them as different entities.[4]

It is also worth noting that subregional groups are not entirely new in recent European history. The post-war cooperation among the Benelux countries and the Nordic countries may reasonably be described as subregional in the sense used here. The groups in the Barents-Black Sea belt, however, share the common elements of having been made possible by the end of the Cold War and, as suggested above, of playing an important role in helping to overcome the Cold War division of Europe. Thus, while the groups in the Barents-Black Sea belt are comparable with post-war Benelux or Nordic cooperation, their historical and geo-political contexts are obviously very different. It might be argued, however, that there are broad similarities between the roles played by Benelux and Nordic cooperation in the post-second World War political reconstruction of Western Europe and those played by the Barents-Black Sea groups in the post-Cold War political reconstruction of a larger Europe.

A number of other consequences for this volume's terminology flow from the definition of the term 'subregion' used here. The larger European organizations – the OSCE, but also the EU, NATO, the WEU, the Council of Europe and the CIS are referred to as 'regional' or 'European' organizations to denote their broader European character. Areas covering only part of a single state are referred to as 'provinces', 'zones' or 'substate regions'. Cooperation between such 'substate regions' of two or more adjacent states is referred to as 'transfrontier' or 'cross-border' cooperation.

In terms of the structure of this book, the following chapter by Anders Bjurner introduces the subject in more detail, emphasizing the contribution of subregional cooperation to post-Cold War European security. The six chapters in the second section of the book then examine each of the groups in the Barents-Black Sea belt in more detail. Each chapter explores the emergence and evolution of the group concerned, its contribution to European security and cooperation, its relations with the larger European organizations and its future prospects. The third section of the book places the Barents-Black Sea groups in the wider context of the emerging post-Cold War European security order. Alyson Bailes analyses the nature of the contribution of the Barents-Black Sea groups to post-Cold War European security, arguing that they help in the management of the integrative processes of NATO and EU enlargement, promote security in a spectrum of ways particularly in 'soft' security areas and promote democracy by facilitating 'bottom-up' non-governmental and transfrontier cooperation. Andrew Cottey addresses the relationship between the larger European organizations and subregional cooperation, arguing that there are significant opportunities for fruitful cooperation between the larger organizations and subregional groups and suggesting a number of ways in which such cooperation might be developed. Ian Bremmer, Sophia Clement and Thanos Dokos then examine the prospects for subregional cooperation in Europe's new 'boundary zones' – South-Eastern Europe, the Newly Independent States of the former Soviet Union and the Mediterranean. The final chapter summarizes the conclusions of the book and raises some wider questions about the longer term future of the groups in the Barents-Black Sea belt, the possible implications of a broader subregionalization of European security and the global relevance of European subregional cooperation.

2 European Security at the End of the Twentieth Century: The Subregional Contribution

Anders Bjurner

As in previous post-war periods, the end of the Cold War initiated a dynamic and creative process of reorganizing international security structures. That process is still in an intense, formative stage at the global and regional, as well as subregional, levels. In Europe, the creation of subregional structures from the Arctic in the north to the Black Sea in the south-east is a fascinating – yet very down-to-earth – security enhancing process. Across the old dividing lines we have today the Barents Euro-Arctic Council, the Council of Baltic Sea States, the Central European Free Trade Agreement, the Central Europe Initiative and the Black Sea Economic Cooperation, as well as emerging cooperation processes in South-Eastern Europe. These 'children of the post-Cold War era' are actively contributing to welfare, security and solidarity both between and within the states of Europe.

Along the old European dividing lines between 'East' and 'West' we have moved away from ideological and bloc confrontation to a common belief in democracy, respect for human rights and the rule of law. Militarily we have moved from armaments and nuclear deterrence to mutual disarmament, arms control, confidence-building, joint peacekeeping and military cooperation. On the individual, human level we have in these subregions moved from alienation, government control and few and sterile official contacts to a myriad of contacts between individuals, professionals, non-governmental organizations, cultural associations, political communities, municipalities and private companies. Subregional cooperation is a vital product of and force behind these changes. The new subregional groups are not only products of but also significant contributors to the positive changes in Europe's security environment in recent years.

NEW CHALLENGES, NEW OPPORTUNITIES

European security has changed and is changing in two fundamental aspects. These two aspects – new challenges and new opportunities – are (and should be) closely linked. First, the types of security threats and risks we face have changed radically. Today, armed conflicts have almost exclusively domestic and internal roots. Their sources are mainly internal strife and tension, but with the risk of spill over into neighbouring states. During the Cold War the threat of a bloc confrontation and nuclear war was our dominant security concern. Security was defined rather narrowly and almost exclusively in military terms. Military security is by no means irrelevant today. However, the main contemporary threats to security do not stem primarily from military conflict and confrontation. When armed conflict occurs today it is normally between groups within states and with a limited reach. The security concerns of people in Europe today largely focus on such issues as transnational organized crime, nuclear power disasters, illegal mass migration and environmental degradation. These transnational threats have to be tackled by 'trans-state' action.

The roots of violent confrontation and potential armed conflicts are to be found today – directly or indirectly and in varying degrees – inter alia in:
- historical injustices (real or perceived) with implications for inter-ethnic/majority-minority relations and inter- and intra-state borders;
- weak societal, judicial and democratic structures, especially in 'transitional societies';
- economic and social differences between and within countries (aggravated by inadequate social welfare systems);
- the collapse or weakening of national security structures (armed forces, police, frontier guards, customs systems and so on);
- porous frontiers which increase the risks of the smuggling of hazardous goods, terrorism, organized crime, illegal immigration and refugee 'smuggling'.

While the new order has brought new security challenges, however, it has also opened up new, much wider opportunities to tackle these challenges. The second new aspect of the contemporary security order is the greatly expanded potential for crisis management and, in particular, for the prevention of violent conflicts. The Cold War prohibited cooperative action across the blocs to tackle security problems and prevented the effective functioning of multilateral security institutions both globally and regionally. Before 1989, the possibilities for peacekeeping and other peace support operations were severely constrained by the East-West conflict and the associated risks of 'competitive intervention', proxy conflicts and escalation. With the growth of shared values and common principles and commitments, the ability of inter-governmental institutions to act is being enhanced, not least in relation to what used to be called domestic matters and internal disputes. Furthermore, there is today not only greatly reduced tension between states. There is also a great potential for the development of inclusive policies and approaches and the involvement of new members in old cooperative structures. Not least, there is open space for the development of new, cooperative international structures.

In Europe, all the old, existing institutions are affected by these developments. They are broadening their memberships, adapting their norms and guide-lines and reforming their instruments and mechanisms. Today, both old and new institutions are working with a wider agenda, involving an integrated multi-dimensional approach to security and a greater readiness for earlier and more rapid involvement with security problems. In short the European security structure – or 'house'– has been drastically remodelled, amended and extended. Considering both these new aspects – a new concept of security and new opportunities to enhance security – subregional structures are important producers of and contributors to security in its broadest sense.

THE SUBREGIONAL CONTRIBUTION

The historical background, economic situation, political geography and number of actors vary greatly in the different subregions of Europe. Similarly, and as a consequence, the security problems and risks vary in different subregions. The agendas, instruments and norms of the various subregional structures are consequently diverse and multi-faceted. In my view, the flexibility and adaptability of subregional structures to the specific needs (and different roots of conflicts) is in itself a vital asset.

Subregionalism, as defined here, is certainly not a new, post-Cold War phenomenon. In Western Europe, for example, we find long-standing subregional cooperation processes among the Nordic countries and the Benelux countries. These cooperation processes served and continue to serve useful purposes in relation to European integration and cooperation, including their security dimensions. Many important experiences could be drawn from these examples, with relevance for the new subregional structures in Europe. However, the new structures have their specific origins and features. In general, they share the experience of having been developed along the old 'East-West' dividing line. When the 'iron curtain' was lifted, individual contacts, trade and inter-governmental cooperation began to flourish across the borders in these zones. Institutions and mechanisms to handle this new trans-border interchange were created. In some subregions, for example Northern Europe, new structures were developed rapidly. In other subregions the process has been slow or even non-existent from an institutional point of view.

The degree of success of such structures, as measured in their contribution to European security, depends on a number of factors. History is one powerful factor. Experiences in institution building are another. The availability of human and material resources play their part. To be successful, I would argue, subregional cooperation should be part of the general process of building a pan-European security order. Second, subregional institutions must operate in accordance with and respect the principles and commitments of the United Nations and the Organization for Security and Cooperation in Europe (OSCE) – including the right of each state to freely choose its own security arrangements as long as it does not undermine the security of another state. Third, their agendas should be comprehensive, integrated and flexibly adapted to the specific needs of the subregion in question. Fourth, they should be based on the democratic consent of the peoples concerned and governments at all levels should respect and encourage local and non-governmental engagement in subregional cooperation.

While the contribution of subregional groups to European security obviously differs from case to case, the various subregional groups all have – albeit in different degrees – certain comparative advantages over the larger European structures. In my view, subregional structures all contribute (or have the potential to contribute) to security in the following ways:

1. Interdependence and economic cooperation helps to build security within and between states, the extent of its impact being dependent on the depth of cooperation. The Cold War severely limited the possibilities in this area. Artificial obstacles to trade and cooperation were erected. Thus, transfrontier cooperation, in particular on a sub-state and non-state level, is an area which has benefited greatly from the end of the Cold War. Subregional cooperation has great potential to support the development of trade, investment and common infrastructure (for example, in transport and communications). Subregions are, for geographical reasons, particularly dependent on common infrastructures. In turn, joint infrastructures are a vital contribution to wider economic cooperation and trade.

2. Subregional structures are by their nature close to the specific common problems of each subregion. Their smaller size enables them to rapidly address problems more easily than larger organizations such as the OSCE, the European Union (EU) and the Council of Europe. The common interests of member states makes subregional groups well-suited to addressing specific problems in their subregions. Efforts to address organized crime, illegal (mass) migration and environmental problems (such as nuclear reactor safety) are typical examples of areas where specific and concrete common interests have resulted in collective action at a subregional level.

3. Democracy and respect for human rights are indispensable to security. History suggests that wars are not waged between democracies. Subregional contacts and cooperation between 'democracies' and 'emerging democracies' are one vital element in democracy building. Contacts between civil societies are of special significance. The many contacts between individuals across borders support democratization. Again, the relatively small size of subregional groups and the proximity of states within subregions facilitates the development of networks between individuals and various democratic institutions and organizations.

4. A sense of common destiny – and shared history – within a subregion can also be an important basis for mutual understanding and confidence. Personal contacts, exchange and scholarship programmes, town-twinning, joint chambers of commerce are, in fact, confidence-building measures and, indeed, help to produce peace (although the actors involved in these efforts do not necessarily see themselves playing that role). These small contributions to the new European security architecture are all too easily forgotten.

The OSCE's 1990 Vienna Document, with its military Confidence and Security-Building Measures (CSBMs), was a major break-through for arms control after the end of the Cold War. These pan-European measures are now being implemented, including also at the subregional level. Within subregional groups, CSBMs are beginning to be extended to the non-military security field. There is also some discussion of whether and how CSBMs might be developed subregionally in the military security field. The limits and possibilities in this field are now being explored within the OSCE. NATO's Partnership for Peace (PfP) and the Euro-Atlantic Partnership Council (EAPC) also have important subregional dimensions.

By virtue of the fact that they include both small and large states, as well as members and non-members of the EU, the Western European Union (WEU), NATO and the Commonwealth of Independent States (CIS), subregional structures have important potential in the area of confidence-building. Meetings of subregional groups are often a very useful platform for informal, confidence-building political dialogues which have considerable value in terms of security. On occasion, such dialogues can even contribute directly to the settlement of conflicts or disputes.

5. Overcoming the continent's old dividing and confrontation lines is today the greatest task we face in constructing the new European security order. Integration plays a basic role in this respect. The various regional and subregional integration processes all face this challenge. The European Union grew out of the idea of healing scars and leaving behind the injustices of the past. Similarly, subregional cooperation can contribute to removing old perceptions. We all have our responsibility to do away with old thinking both within and between states. Subregional cooperation can also, in various ways, play a role in facilitating broader European integration through specific support programmes. In the EU context, subregional groups can help candidate countries to prepare for free trade and facilitate the various approximation processes necessary for eventual EU membership.

In terms of security, we should not underestimate the significance of the fact that NATO countries, countries that have applied for membership of NATO, countries that do not participate in military alliances and other non-applicants all cooperate on concrete projects within non-military subregional groups. As NATO and EU enlargement move ahead, with their associated risks of new 'dividing lines', subregional groups can play a significant part in bridging the gap between the 'haves' and the 'have-nots'.

THE LIMITATIONS OF SUBREGIONAL SECURITY AND COOPERATION

Having outlined the potential 'comparative advantages' of subregional structures and the specific contributions they can make to security, one should not neglect their limitations and disadvantages. Some of these limitations are, however, practical – rather than fundamental – problems, which can at least partially be resolved. Lack of resources is one such constraint with relevance, for example, for large subregional infrastructure projects. Other limitations could be addressed through the subregional cooperation processes themselves and thus, over time, gradually removed. Different legislative and administrative systems can be cited as examples here.

There is one important area, however, where subregional structures do not have the capacity to play a role – the area of strategic military security. In my view, by an intrinsic logic, military strategic issues should be excluded from the subregional agenda. Thus, matters relating to 'hard security' – disarmament and especially military defence guarantees – should, in particular, be excluded from consideration in whatever agreements may be concluded within subregional frameworks. Military strategy by definition concerns a number of states outside a subregion. Military imbalances, in particular if there is only one nuclear power in a subregion, cannot sensibly be addressed in a subregional framework. Moreover, the differing security choices of states – membership and non-membership of military alliances – involved in subregional groups constitute a very tangible obstacle to agreements on matters of military strategic importance. Bringing such matters into subregional frameworks, even if only for purposes of discussion, might even have detrimental effects on other aspects of subregional cooperation. (All this being said, military issues, more or less explicitly strategic, might in certain cases have to be included as part of a comprehensive peace agreement at a subregional level and/or as a temporary arrangement in exceptional cases).

The exclusion of strategic military issues, however, should not prevent states from investigating other possible areas of military cooperation at the subregional level – for example, in the fields of CSBMs, developing peace-keeping/peace support capabilities and coordination with non-military security instituions (in such areas as safety at sea, rescue operations and the control of land and sea borders). This kind of cooperation could (and sometimes should) also be extended to states outside the subregion.

It should be underlined that for some countries – not least those that have recently (re-)gained their independence and/or become entirely sovereign states – subregional arrangements are not only, as indicated above, inappropriate for providing military security but also provide too little of political 'warmth' and support for their needs. In other words, the security contribution of subregional structures will in many cases also depend on the openness and inclusiveness of the larger and 'harder' European structures. Membership of subregional groups should not (and cannot) be seen as an alternative to membership of larger organizations.

Naturally, subregional formats have other important constraints and limitations. They are evidently too small to be appropriate frameworks for decision-making on major global issues (although not for the implementation of global agreements at the subregional level, in areas such as the environmental 'Agenda 21'). The comparatively small size of subregional frameworks also makes them unsuitable for a normative role of any great significance.

European Security: The Subregional Contribution 15

For these reasons, and others, it is important to develop appropriate relations and cooperation arrangements between subregional groups and the 'major' European structures and organizations (in particular the EU and the OSCE), covering such matters as observerships, exchanges of information and experiences, reporting on certain agreed matters and implementation of norms. There should be scope for a division of labour between the two levels in areas such as conflict prevention, democracy and human/minority rights monitoring and specific economic projects. The regional organizations should be able to give their political and, where appropriate, practical support to the subregional organizations. The OSCE, as the primary pan-European security organization, has a special responsibility in this regard. This responsibility was stated clearly for the first time at the OSCE's December 1996 Lisbon Summit. It was developed further with a special OSCE seminar on the subject in summer 1997 within the framework of the OSCE's work on a 'Common and Comprehensive Security Model for Europe for the Twenty-First Century'.

WAYS AHEAD

The process of transforming old security institutions and constructing new ones is still at an early stage. As in previous post-war periods, this will be a long-term process. Indeed, in the post-Cold War era, this process is particularly complex and likely to be of longer duration than other similar processes in this century. This judgement certainly applies also to subregional arrangments and not least their security dimensions. Thus, there are great opportunities (and realistic hopes) for increasing the contribution of subregional arrangements to European security. The webs of cooperation across the old dividing lines, after all, are still relatively thin.

I would like to briefly suggest six areas of possible action for the future strengthening of the not yet fully exploited security dimension of subregional frameworks. This sketchy 'programme' may also be seen as a cautiously optimistic prediction about the likely future contribution of subregional arrangements to European security. First, there is great room for 'more of the same' in terms of developing subregional cooperation in relation to economics, the environment, democracy and people-to-people contacts and thereby indirectly enhancing security. Second, the currently, mainly bilateral cooperation between non-military security institutions – such as police, customs forces, border and coast guards and civil defence and immigration authorities – could be developed more subregionally (as well as regionally) and expanded to include new cooperative projects.

Third, even if there are definite limits to the prospects for military cooperation within subregional frameworks, I could envisage cooperation in areas such as special subregional CSBMs, mine-clearance, sea-rescue and developing peacekeeping capabilities. Such cooperation might also include subregional training, joint exercises and even joint operations. The open – and important – question here is within which subregional or wider institutional framework such cooperation should take place. Possibilities include OSCE subregional 'tables', NATO's 'enhanced PfP', the EAPC, or specific subregional groups (for example, a CBSS special group in the Baltic case). The choice will depend, inter alia, on the kind of measures foreseen, including their 'hardness' and 'territorial reach'. I see potential in this area, but military security guarantees, common territorial defence arrangements and arms control agreements would be inappropriate issues to address at the subregional level – and efforts in this direction might even be counter-productive.

Fourth, the links between the subregional organizations and the larger regional security institutions such as the OSCE, EU, the Western European Union (WEU), PfP and the EAPC are still very weak. Further institutional integration is needed. Exchanges of information, material support, operations 'in the spirit of', mutual observerships and so on could in many cases be strengthened. Again, the OSCE has a special role and potential in this area.

It is worth noting here that the links and relationships between subregional groups with no explicit security agenda and the larger security institutions and instruments with strategic security tasks have not been much explored. Nor have they been a matter of much policy analysis (even less policy-making) to date – although discussion of this issue has been initiated within the EAPC/'enhanced PFP' framework, as well as in the OSCE. The absence of dicussion of this issue is somewhat surprising considering the new, post-Cold War security challenges and the drastically diminished relevance of the strategic (military) balance. Possible explanations for this uncharted territory may be: the inherent strength of existing military institutions; the situation in and uncertainties related to Russia; NATO's adaptation, including enlargement; the need to develop new institutions and instruments themselves before shaping links between them; and, finally, the complexity of the matter itself. In my view, links between institutions at different levels will have to be carefully crafted and balanced, but could be based inter alia on the principles of the indivisibility of security, mutual reinforcement, subsidiarity and an integrated and broad concept of security.

Fifth, there is also a need to strengthen the subregional institutions organizationally. Strengthening the organizational capacity of subregional groups and the development of new mechanisms are not simply questions of administrative neatness and effectiveness – they will also increase the ability of subregional organizations to contribute to security. Secretariats, regional councils, consultation mechanisms and so on could play a significant role in this area.

Finally, subregional arrangements can also provide useful fora for political dialogue, often on an informal basis. The potential is there – if not always ripe today and not in all situations – for subregional groups to act as 'facilitators' or provide 'good offices' (or even mediation) in situations of tension or disputes between members. Mandates and agendas might have to be amended. However, the institutional frameworks for such roles could be strengthened without necessarily being too formal, legal or bureaucratic. Experiences from the cooperative tools of the OSCE could be used and further developed in a subregional context, based on the political commitments and norms agreed upon within the OSCE.

FUTURE INSTITUTIONAL ARRANGEMENTS

A number of important institutional elements can help to promote common security at a subregional level. The many, different bilateral (and trilateral) cooperation networks can be seen as cornerstones of a policy to promote subregional cooperation. An important role can be played by cross-border institutions. In this area, cooperation programmes could include broad-ranging support in the fields of economics, environment, judicial/legal systems and culture (in a broad sense). In this context, bilateral assistance and cooperation aimed at building up security functions which are normal for every sovereign state are of particular interest. Cooperation could cover, for instance, areas such as police forces, customs, border and coast guards, authorities undertaking mine clearance, peacekeeping and reforming military conscription and training systems.

In the absence of developed institutional and administrative frameworks, subregional cooperation will depend on political support. In providing this political support while preserving the flexibility of subregional cooperation, high-level political meetings are particularly significant. In addition, institutional frameworks might be strengthened in order to improve the implementation of decisions, coordination (at all levels), the provision of information and the preparation of joint meetings. Such subregional structures could also, when required, serve as channels for communication with, for example, the European Commission.

The enlargement of the European Union may be seen as the single most important step towards political stability, economic prosperity and security in a broad sense in each respective subregion. The aim must be to stretch the borders of the EU's broad integration process, so that it includes the candidate countries in any subregion and they become part of what might be called a system of 'mutual, political security guarantees'. The European Commission has launched a number of programmes (often with significant subregional dimensions) designed to help the Central and Eastern European and former Soviet countries and thereby contribute to wider European integration. Projects assisting the Central and Eastern European candidate countries with the task of approximation with the EU's 'acquis communautaire' are particularly important at this stage. In order to ensure equality of opportunity for all applicant countries, promote reform processes and avoid creating (or exacerbating) divisions within and between subregions, a simultaneous opening of negotiations with all candidates, followed by a process of differentiation, will be extremely important. (The candidate countries, however, must show that they are willing and able to continue the processes of reform in their societies. If the coherence of the Union were diluted by enlargement, we would run the risk of loosing much of the EU's great potential for contributing to security in Central and Eastern Europe, including at the subregional level).

The enhancement and deepening of activities within the Partnership for Peace and the Euro-Atlantic Partnership Council frameworks has the potential to contribute to security at the subregional level. PfP and the EAPC have an important role to play in promoting subregional cooperation in areas such as strengthening peacekeeping capacities, the promotion of openness and democratic control over armed forces and the development of crisis management capacities. This cooperation should permit broad participation, including states beyond the particular subregion concerned.

The Russian Federation is part of most of the 'new' subregional groups, as well as a member of larger European structures. Considering the past history of East-West animosity and the importance of Russia to European security, the participation of Russia is of special relevance to efforts to build subregional security and cooperation in Europe. Ties with Russia are thus an important element of any policy for subregional cooperation. For security and stability in Europe, we need to facilitate and strengthen Russia's integration into a wide variety of structures designed to promote cooperation and dialogue. There is also a need to enhance cross-border and border control cooperation between Russia and its neighbours, in order to build confidence and stabilize their relations. While supporting Russia's integration into European structures and recognizing that it is an important power, we also expect it to act in accordance with pan-European norms in its behaviour towards its neighbours.

Subregional security and cooperation should also have a broad European and transatlantic dimension, not least given that subregional security often has strategic importance. As stability and cooperation in any subregion is of importance for European security as a whole, continued US involvement in subregional cooperation is necessary for the development of a pan-European security order.

Finally, the OSCE with its inclusive, pan-European membership, its broad definition of security, its focus on prevention and its cooperative approach has an important role to play in the various subregions of the OSCE area as a whole. As suggested above, the OSCE should strengthen its links with the cooperative arrangements in its various subregions.

PROSPECTS FOR THE FUTURE

I am convinced that the subregional 'children of the post-Cold War era' will grow in strength, provided that no major new tensions or conflicts emerge at a 'bloc' level or between the larger European states. A transition to a 'cold peace' would obviously have adverse effects on subregional cooperation. A number of possible scenarios might push developments in this negative direction and thereby undermine subregional cooperation. In my view, however, most of these scenarios are not probable, at least in their worst variants. These scenarios include: an isolated, aggressive and nationalistic Russia; an inward looking and narrowly self-interested EU; the collapse of democracy and emergence of renewed instability in Central and Eastern Europe; wider war in the Balkans/South-Eastern Europe; a global economic downturn, perhaps including a major energy crisis; wars and collapsing states on the periphery of Europe with major consequences for Europe itself.

My optimism – which is thus not unreserved – is founded on the fact that subregional cooperation is increasingly seen by governments in all the countries involved as a vital political and security interest. No one, either inside or outside the subregions, finds subregional structures threatening. They are generally seen as a complement to wider forms of regional cooperation, capable of making unique contributions of their own to security and cooperation. The broad commitment of the actors engaged in subregional cooperation at all levels (including non-state and sub-state actors) suggests that subregional cooperation has a promising future. There is a great, pent-up popular longing for the 'fruits of peace' in the 'new' subregions of post-Cold War Europe. There is also great economic and energy potential which has been untapped for many decades. The EU's recognition of the importance of and increasing involvement in subregional structures is another 'guarantor' of the future expansion of subregional cooperation.

In many subregions within the OSCE area, however, organized subregional cooperation is non-existent. For various reasons – recent or on-going armed conflict, serious mistrust between states, a lack of political will, insufficient resources, the absence of previous experience of such cooperation – these subregions do not benefit from the fruits of subregional cooperation. Without underestimating the extent of the obstacles to subregional cooperation in some of these areas, there is scope for exchanging information at inter-governmental and non-governmental levels as to how existing models of subregional cooperation may be relevant to other 'problematic' subregions. The challenge is to properly demonstrate the great mutual advantages that can be gained from such cooperation, as well as to find the proper cooperative structures.

Subregional cooperation provides an important framework for strengthening European security and thereby contributes to wider, pan-European security. The main task now is to fill the new subregional frameworks with resources and innovative ideas and to develop the tools that we need in order to implement subregional cooperation. This is a task that we should accept for the benefit of us all.

Part II
Subregional Cooperation: From the Barents to the Black Sea

3 The Barents Euro-Arctic Council

Pertti Joenniemi

There was more dividing than uniting Europe's High North during the post-war years. The borderlines and territorial delineations remained quite strict leaving little, if any, room for subregional entities to challenge the prevailing order. However, with end of the Cold War, the door was opened for much more flexible arrangements.

This chapter examines the unfolding of subregionality in northernmost Europe as exemplified by the Barents Euro-Arctic Council (BEAC). It provides information on the facts pertaining to the founding of the Council, its organization, the actors involved, the scope of its activities and analyses the images employed in the process. One of the issues examined is whether the Barents cooperation relates to conflict resolution, the growth of confidence and stability in the area or whether it alternatively contributes, as has sometimes been claimed, to the emergence of strains and tensions. The overall aim is to provide insight into the more variegated landscape that emerges as the trend of subregion-building comes to the northernmost reaches of Europe.

A DIFFERENT GRAMMAR

The European Arctic was for decades locked into the position of an object in the constellations brought about by the Cold War. The unfolding of political space reflected the general necessities imposed by the East-West conflict. This brought about a landscape identified by clearcut hierarchies and statist configurations organized primarily into two opposing politico-military blocs. The construction of order was based on strict classifications of 'them' and 'us'. There was hardly any space for alternative, more pluralist thinking. New ideas were interpreted as constituting the spread of ambiguity, dissidence and anarchy. These were to be held in check for reasons of security. Nor was there much room for local concerns, and this despite the fact that the conflict was, in substance, almost totally detached from anything local.[1]

However, these interpretative horizons have now, with the disappearance of the Cold War overlay, become rather dim. They have lost much of their power to influence the unfolding of political space and it has become possible, as evidenced by the Barents initiative, to defy the previous lines of demarcation. The 'iron curtain' is no longer what it used to be. As high politics has changed its tune, there is less concern about security, and issues relating to centrality and distance, participation, identity and signification have taken the front seat. The transcending of previous barriers is seen as presenting options and resources necessary for the improvement of one's own relative weight in the contest between centrality and marginality in the new integrative Europe.

The initiation of the Barents subregion took place in order to make use of this 'window of opportunity'. It was stimulated by the initiation of a number of subregional projects transcending the previous East-West divide, particularly the establishment of the Council of Baltic Sea States (CBSS).[2] Moreover, the aim was to respond to the openness to reforms, including the willingness to open up vis-à-vis the West, that prevailed among the Russian leadership at the beginning of the 1990s.[3]

The plan was first aired by the Norwegian Minister of Foreign Affairs, Thorvald Stoltenberg, in a speech delivered in April 1992. As a first step, agreements on cooperation were signed between a number of Norwegian and Russian local administrative regions, later to be joined by (Finnish) Lapland and (Swedish) Norrbotten. In spring 1992, Finland, Russia and Norway agreed to hold a meeting of the Foreign Ministers of the relevant countries to discuss the framework for subregional cooperation. In January 1993, the Foreign Ministers of Russia and the five Nordic countries and a representative of the European Commission met, together with observers from thirteen other countries, in the Norwegian town of Kirkenes. As a result, a Declaration on Cooperation in the Barents Euro-Arctic Region was signed.

According to this document, the cooperation initiated is open to countries interested in playing an active role. Membership has been limited to the Nordic countries, Russia and the Commission of the European Union (EU), but a number of significant external actors have found it important to link up with the Barents subregion. The United Kingdom, France, Germany, Poland, the United States, Canada and Japan were all present in Kirkenes and were granted the status of observers in the new BEAC. The Netherlands and Italy were later given the same status.

The text of the Declaration reflected a fairly high level of ambition, setting the task of creating a framework for handling the practical side of post-Cold War realities in the European Arctic. The subregional arrangement launched was, in a number of ways, seen as a complement to the Baltic Sea cooperation, although the organs established by the Declaration were expected to play a more direct role in the financing and management of subregional development projects.[4] The Declaration provided the project with clear foreign policy aims by positioning it as an essential part of European cooperation and integration; the aim was more particularly one of strengthening stability and fortifying the links between the northern and continental parts of Europe. In essence, cooperation spans a broad variety of fields: economy, trade, science and technology, tourism, environment, infrastructure, educational and cultural exchange, as well as improvements in the situation of the indigenous peoples in the north, with priority given to environmental and economic matters.[5]

THE INSTITUTIONAL SET-UP

The institutional structures created around the Barents subregion are characterized by a duality between central and regional (provincial/local) authorities. The overall arrangement is clearly multi-layered and rather complex, as the previous, more vertical structures of power and influence that prevailed in the region have been complemented by more horizontal ones. This latter feature is significantly stronger in the case of the Barents project than in European subregional arrangements in general.

Originally, the Barents subregion covered a geographical area of 1.23 million square kilometres (an area twice the size of France). There are no major unifying centres in the subregion and the population is unevenly distributed with most of the barely 4.4 million inhabitants living in the Russian territories. The area is extremely well endowed with natural resources in the form of oil, gas, fish, timber and minerals and has, therefore, the nature of a resource subregion. Its cultural diversity is reflected in the nine different languages spoken by the inhabitants of the subregion. These main languages – leaving aside the minority languages – are divided into the Scandinavian languages (Danish, Swedish and Norwegian); the Finno-Ugric languages spoken in Finland, some parts of Karelia, northern Norway and northern Sweden; and Russian. The linguistic diversity is, in many cases, a hindrance to cooperation, and most of the work of the Council has to take place with the help of interpreters. There is no official common working language, and the meetings of the Barents Council are conducted in its working language, English, although it has become customary that the meetings of the Regional Council are held in Scandinavian languages and a Russian translation is provided. Apart from the Finns, all participants use their native tongues.

The sessions of the Barents Council, which constitutes the central level institution, are held once a year at Foreign Ministerial level. To date, ministers of environment, transport, economics, culture and education, and health have convened their own meetings, some of them already twice. Cooperation has, in other words, remained at the level of ministers and has not taken the form of regular meetings among heads of state as is now the case with the CBSS. The Barents Council functions as a platform for inter-governmental cooperation in the Barents subregion and is not geared towards the establishment of supranational rules or the creation of any central authority. All the sessions and bodies operate on the basis of consensus. The chairmanship rotates between the four core members having territories within the subregion itself, Finland, Norway, Sweden and Russia, and may, potentially, also include the EU Commission in future. Each presidency hosts a ministerial meeting at the end of its year in office. During the interim period, work is guided by a Committee of Senior Officials (CSO), as well as Working Groups on economic cooperation, the environment and the Northern Sea Route connecting Europe with Asia. The administrative workload is borne by the party holding the annual presidency. There is no permanent secretariat due to a policy of keeping organizational structures light, although lower level secretariats have come to exist in Kirkenes, Lulea, Rovaniemi, Murmansk, Arkhangelsk and Petrozavodsk.

In addition to the Barents Council, there is a significant transnational dimension present in the form of a Regional Council. This body, reflecting a certain subsidiarity or attempt at decentralization and the shifting of influence towards the local level, consists of representatives of provincial authorities and the indigenous peoples (the Sami, who live in all four countries of the subregion, and the Nenets and the Komi of northwestern Russia). This dual way of structuring the Barents cooperation reflects a desire to maintain central political control while leaving day-to-day operations and practical initiatives to substate regions themselves. The Regional Council is comprised of the Arctic and sub-Arctic parts of Europe. Membership involves two Russian oblasts, Murmansk and Arkhangelsk, and the Republic of Karelia; the counties of Finnmark, Troms and Nordland in Norway; the county of Lapland in Finland; and the county of Norrbotten in Sweden. The counties of Vasterbotten in Sweden and Oulu in Finland have been granted the status of observers. Chairmanship in the Regional Council alternates, with two year intervals, among the participating counties. Once a year, the Council convenes an extended meeting with the participation of three additional persons from each county and a group of indigenous peoples. The aim of this procedure is to provide room for sufficient political participation at the local level. The Council has established ten different Working Groups, with the aim of specifying concrete projects and areas of cooperation.

TOP-DOWN OR BOTTOM-UP

Obviously, subregionality reaching across borders has become a major theme influencing the political scenery in northernmost Europe. This is quite a change, considering that the constitutive principles were previously almost exclusively statist and sovereignty-based. The subregion-formation of recent years follows another pattern, in being less administrative, rigid and restrictive. It is not oriented towards the preservation of hierarchies and has, instead, become an innovative and rather flexible tool for inserting new linkages and providing local actors with increased freedom to pursue cooperative policies of their own.

The openness and emphasis on the local embodied in the Barents subregion are essential parts of the new landscape. Olav Stokke and Rune Castberg remark that 'it would be incorrect to portray the current regionalization around the Barents Sea as something created by foreign policy elites'.[6] A publication on the Barents project, prepared under the auspices of the Norwegian Foreign Ministry, stresses that the first initiatives towards reducing the impact of the East-West border were taken at the local level. They occurred primarily in the spheres of culture and sport and had a rather spontaneous character.[7]

No doubt, the Barents project is one of subregionalization, but it also contains elements of subregionalism, that is features of something movement-like. The membership of the European Commission in the BEAC adds considerably to the multi-layered character of the overall construction blurring, to some extent, the division into top-down and bottom-up. There is clearly more diversity and heterogeneity present in Barents cooperation than in many other European subregional arrangements and considerable leeway has been created for the expression of different interests and identities. The structures established seem to encourage the crossing of borders and the transcending of hierarchies to an unusual degree.

More particularly, the EU's membership creates a situation in which a considerable amount of activity occurs between states, but there are also important substate and 'above-the-state', dimensions, thus strengthening the features of an emergent three-level game. As members of the Regional

Council may take part in the work of the Barents Council as observers, there is a link between the substate and the 'above-the-state' levels. If this hybridity is exploited by local actors, for example by establishing direct contacts with Brussels in regard to the allocation of EU funds for regional development purposes, the Barents project will assume features of a 'state by-passing' arrangement. It would thereby be in line with more general European developments, with influence flowing away from states, both upwards and downwards. There are no strong indications that this trend is really happening in the context of the BEAC to date, but structurally the preconditions for it to happen are already present far more clearly than in most other European subregional arrangements.

The growing significance of non-traditional actors does not imply, however, that the project is outside central, state control. Basically, it is policy-driven, with core initiatives coming from the top. The aims of the project have often been viewed as composed of moves originating in the centres in the south of the Barents countries, with the results gradually trickling down to the local level in the north of the countries. The top-down influence seems to have been particularly important during the initial period of the Barents arrangement. Given that the project covers a highly militarized area which still hosts considerable concentrations of nuclear weapons, including the bulk of the Russian strategic nuclear submarine force, this top-heaviness is easy to comprehend. The opening up towards different constitutive principles and calling for subregionality that transcends the previously rather strict lines of demarcation, would hardly have been possible without considerable political dedication on the part of the relevant capitals.

It should be added that the arrangement has been characterized by a certain contest between the top-down and bottom-up aspects. In practice, however, the two are intricately linked. Both are strongly present, with a certain division of labour. The Norwegian foreign policy leadership concluded from the very beginning that the counties of the north had to be included in the institutions of the project and given influence as regards its content and direction. This was thought to be essential if the endeavour was to be convincing and realistic. As the Norwegian counties have traditionally had a strong position in the administrative and political structures of the country (exemplified among other things by their elected, rather than government-appointed, governors), their inclusion was seen as vital in order to assure that there was sufficient local support for the project. The idea was also explicitly one of transferring more responsibility to the local level, with the centre focusing increasingly on the broader European issues.

These moves had rather far-reaching consequences in opening up a foreign policy framework to the influence of local actors. They signalled that Europeanization, in the form of transfrontier subregionalization, implied new opportunities and openings for local level actors. They were offered a kind of European theatre of their own, composed of links with neighbouring areas previously barred from cross-border cooperation. Hence, the initiative clearly underlined that subregionalization had assumed other meanings than simply those pertaining to a customary transfer of resources from the centre to the periphery. This endeavour at providing a parallel space for local actors met with some initial resistance on the Russian side, but was finally accepted as a point of departure at both central and local levels.[8] The Russian counties, in particular, found the arrangement interesting, although the pattern of cross-border cooperation deviates considerably from their previous experiences.[9]

The establishment of the Regional Council as a 'second chamber' of the subregional cooperation originated with the thinking – finally accepted by all the state-parties – that the project had to be internalized locally if it was to survive as a true subregional endeavour. It seems, therefore, that the particular conditions in the north, and the previously strong dominance of statist principles, led to a political innovation in European subregionality. The bottom-up features strengthen the policy-driven nature of the Barents project, but they also provide additional room for various forms of local interaction and market-related forces. Adding in general to the horizontality of the new political structures in northernmost Europe, the existence of the Regional Council gears the Barents project more concretely towards subregional economic development and subregionality in a functionalist sense. It is conducive to networking, embracing, for example, chambers of commerce, local officials, businessmen, organizations dealing with the environment, the universities of the subregion and entities such as the non-state communities of the indigenous peoples – actors previously more or less isolated from each other by the predominance of the nation-states and their demand for unchallenged sovereignty.

In general, the Barents project has turned out to be a fertile mixture of top-down and bottom-up elements. Both are needed for success to be achieved. The dual structures do not seem to have burdened the functioning of the project. If there are conflicts between the views taken by the Barents Council and the Regional Council, the former tends to have the final say. This seems to be evidenced by the handling of the issue of enlargement, with the Regional Council opposing the inclusion of Oulu,

Vasterbotten and some new regions in northernmost Russia, and the Barents Council adopting a much more positive view, paving the way for the membership of the applicants. In some cases, counties have resisted the policies pursued by their own government,[10] although in the end the views of the centre have determined the outcome.

THE POLICIES OF THE RELEVANT ACTORS

Although entering into Barents cooperation was formally rather easy, designing policies and making use of the opportunities opening up has been quite demanding for all the actors involved: the state-parties, the European Union, as well as the local level actors. As observed by Castberg, Stokke and Ostreng, the states of the subregion have been embedded in different spheres of interaction: Norway with its strong desire to avoid dealing with Russia without being backed up by its Western allies and its orientation towards Britain and the United States; Sweden, economically tuned to Germany and politically blending a non-aligned position with a Western orientation; Finland, combining its special relations with the Soviet Union with quite strong ties to the West; and of course, Russia, which until the demise of the Cold War strove to build a competing political and economic frame of interaction within the socialist world.[11] It can be assumed, against this background, that contributing to the Barents subregion has been particularly demanding for Norway and Russia although, to some extent, the new arrangement involves reconsideration by all the actors involved.

Norwegian determination to go ahead and launch an initiative had both an external and an internal basis. The project was regarded, for good reasons, as a major move with far-reaching implications and considerable diplomatic as well as financial resources were spent to advance it. A prime motivational factor seems to have been a fear that developed among the foreign policy elite that Norway might become politically marginalized with the demise of the East-West conflict. It was thought that the previous backbone of their foreign and security policy, consisting of intense transatlantic relations, might lose some of its value. At the same time, the European Union was attracting more attention on the political scene and showed signs of becoming an increasingly influential actor in northern Europe.[12] Another factor was a recognition that subregional formations played an increasingly important role in European development and, while Norway was one of the less central actors in the context of the CBSS, this would not be the case in the context of a complementary Barents configuration. The advancing, then, of subregional relations in the High North would fend off the danger of marginalization in a dual manner: it would open important channels to the EU and simultaneously allow the establishment of closer relations with Russia, the overall pattern boosting the position of the country taking the initiative.

The normalization of relations across the previous divide and the establishment of an additional channel of communication with Moscow constituted a major shift in Norwegian foreign policy, and the Barents concept facilitated the initiation of this effort to build ties with Russia. Building on a multilateral context composed of Nordic-Russian relations and an upgrading of local actors made the step feel less dramatic. More concretely, an invitation was presented to Russia to become part of the new, increasingly subregional Europe. It was thought that the response would be positive as, by joining the scheme, Russia could make use of its strengths (given that considerable natural resources are located in its northwestern areas) and become a key player within the proposed subregional setting.

Similar concerns figured to some extent in Finnish and Swedish thinking, but Norway – being a member of NATO and having invested mainly in transatlantic relations – had a more pressing need for innovative policies. In trying to exploit the openings available, the effort was one of linking the cooperation proposed within a Nordic-Russian framework to Norway's approaching the European Union: 'the more strongly the Norwegian-Russian ties develop, the more important will the Norwegian membership of the EU become'.[13] A subregional scheme, with a turn towards the northeast, formed an integral part of a more Europeanist design in Norwegian policies.

The domestic rationale behind Norway's launching of the Barents initiative pertained to rather practical needs like solving substate regional problems such as pollution and the need to stimulate economic growth, while also attempting to address the massive scepticism regarding Norway's EU membership that prevailed in the northern parts of the country. It was recognized that the Barents project, being closely linked with Europeanization, could hold considerable electoral potential. Providing room for linking up with the neighbouring areas in the north could potentially ease opposition to EU membership and demonstrate, in a concrete fashion, that northernmost Europe could benefit from linking up with the new constellations by gaining more room for manoeuvres of its own.

Many of the reasons underlying the Barents initiative are still relevant, although some revision has taken place since the referendum yielding a 'no' to Norwegian membership of the EU in 1995. With Norway outside the EU, the Barents arrangement serves as one of the inroads to the EU. The emphasis on bilateralism in Norwegian-Russian relations has grown, but there is also a will to add to the broader multilateral framework. Norway, therefore, remains a strong advocate of the Barents cooperation. This is evidenced, among other things, by recent efforts to preserve the momentum of the Barents initiative by drawing upon closer relations with other European subregions and perceiving these as a belt linking Central Europe to other parts of Europe. Such an arrangement might also be of value in softening the various divisions originating with some applicants joining the EU and NATO and others remaining outside. The idea of linking the 'three Bs' (Baltic, Barents and Black Sea cooperation) has so far remained a mere vision, but implementation of such a scheme would contribute to the emergence of a network consisting of the subregional arrangements themselves and add further to a multi-layered Europe. Somewhat similar ideas have figured in the Finnish debate on how to strengthen the EU's northern dimension.

The interest of Finland and Sweden in the Barents project has grown with their membership of the EU, although for both countries the Baltic Sea remains a higher priority. Finland was initially worried that the Barents project could reduce the attractiveness of another diplomatic initiative aimed at structuring northernmost Europe, the so-called Rovaniemi process. The latter focused on environmental issues in the Arctic and has thereby been less political. The Russian-Nordic setting, central to the Barents arrangement, could potentially infringe upon Finland's bilateral relations with Russia. Sweden, where the government has been under less pressure from local actors in the north, initially assumed a somewhat passive attitude, although this too has changed over time. Finland has stressed the importance of concrete economic cooperation[14] and Sweden has emphasized the tackling of environmental hazards (such as transboundary air pollution), nuclear safety and cleaning up the legacy of the military build-up.[15] During its chairmanship of the BEAC in 1997, Sweden pledged to make special efforts to strengthen links between the EU and the Barents cooperation.

Russia's attitude has been rather favourable, as well as practical, all along. As argued by Castberg, Stokke and Ostreng, 'it seems fair to say that the Russians have been the real driving forces for the Barents Initiative'.[16] The clash of cultures that unavoidably followed the opening up of previously rather closed borders has remained less significant than sometimes feared by the cooperation's Western initiators. The trend towards a more decentralized governing of territorial space and the inclusion of various oblasts or republics located in the north-eastern part of the country does not seem to have generated any decisive obstacles for Russia's participation, although the issue remains to some extent controversial in Russian domestic politics (with extreme nationalists opposing such trends).[17] In general, Russia has opted for low-key policies. There has been an emphasis on the technical, de-politicized nature of institutional cooperation, including trade, investments and linkages to the Nordic countries. The relative absence of disruptive political factors has no doubt facilitated involvement in such cooperation. However, the Barents project has also been seen as a way of flexibly approaching the EU.[18] It provides, in addition to the CBSS, a window to European integration. With Russia now aspiring to membership of the EU, as stated by both President Boris Yeltsin and Prime Minister Victor Chernomyrdin, this aspect of participation in the BEAC will grow in importance.

All the countries geographically part of the Barents subregion have tried to use the Barents cooperation to support the national goal of achieving regional/provincial development in their own northern areas. This need has, over recent years, been particularly pronounced in the case of Russia. The interaction across the previous divide helps to keep the wheels of the economy turning and relieves distress in an area plagued by a number of social, economic and environmental problems.[19] It contributes to economic and social stability, thereby reducing social discontent amongst the local population, and alleviates the pressures for outward migration in the northern areas.[20]

The subregional perspectives opening up in northernmost Europe have also forced the EU to develop a more active policy towards the subregion. Prior to Finland and Sweden becoming members, the area was nothing but a blank spot on the mental maps of the EU. The borderline to the north was seen, from the Union's perspective, as being located somewhere between Denmark and Sweden. On the EU's mental map, the options for intense growth and development were depicted as being located to the south, and the north-eastern direction attracted very little attention. This conception has changed over recent years, albeit gradually.

The very participation of the European Union adds to the weight of the BEAC. More concretely, structural policies in the form of the TACIS and Interreg programmes of the Union, are of significance in strengthening the interactionist aspects of the subregion: they contribute to an awareness that the Barents subregion really exists. In practice, the European Commission seems to have pursued somewhat restricted policies. Grand moves have been avoided and instead there has been a favouring of bilateral expressions and a focusing almost exclusively on trade, economic transactions and investments.

The avoidance of any grand gestures is also present in another form. A programme was prepared in June 1996 outlining EU policies towards the Baltic Sea subregion but no similar document exists for the Barents subregion. Obviously, there has been some unwillingness present in the policy pursued by the EU. The slow start might be explained by a deliberate avoidance of getting too deeply entangled with the various environmental problems – some of them quite grave. Involvement might result in considerable costs. The modest profile could also be explained by the diversity of the Barents arrangement. Membership in the BEAC might have turned out to be problematic for the Commission as around the table there are also EU member states: Denmark, Finland and Sweden. However, the unbinding and often declaratory nature of the Council's proceedings has meant that this potential for tension between the Commission and the EU member countries also participating in the BEAC has not become overtly problematic.

Although often practical in appearance, involvement in the Barents Council nevertheless has some more general value for the EU. It is one of the vehicles that facilitates moderation of the centripetal forces in Europe. New channels for participation are opened up for the advancement of integration and coping with the consequences of fragmentation. The Barents arrangement advances diversity and decentralization, as evidenced by the principle of subsidiarity. It is conducive to the stimulation of growth and innovation, the strengthening of local identities and it invites the peripheries to cluster themselves in order to resist marginalization. It lowers, more generally, the barrier between EU members and non-members and opens up important channels towards actors such as Russia in a multilateral context. This is true both in a mental and a literal sense. The Barents context is not burdened – except in a very general strategic sense – by any extra-subregional conflicts or tensions, nor is it to any larger degree influenced by expectations that it may function as a 'pre-accession strategy' for EU membership. In these ways, the Barents subregion provides better prospects for communication and cooperation than many other fora.

It may be expected that the importance of the Barents subregion for the EU will continue to grow once the various territorial and management disputes between Norway and Russia are settled and options pertaining to resource management in the subregion are really opened up. The same is true for the utilization of the Northern Sea Route where the obstacles are more of a technological and financial character.[21] In general, the more the arrangement becomes market-driven, the greater the prospects for EU involvement.

The local, sub-state actors have good reasons to welcome the new subregional formation, although they may also have some reservations. The more general divisions of the post-war period also severed the local actors from one another, each of them focusing on their relations with their respective national centres in the south instead of pooling local strengths. There was no local actor to counterbalance this as the northern subregion has been void of any major centre of its own strong enough to turn the tide and broaden local cooperation. Interaction at the local level, as evidenced, for example, by the lines of communication, has been modest. Transportation still to some extent flows – despite clear improvements over the last few years – mainly in a north-south direction, linking the various parts of the subregion to their respective capitals rather than to each other. This holds true even for the Nordic counties, one of the reasons being that they tend to be too homogeneous for any broader exchange to emerge.[22]

One of the reservations about the Barents initiative is that the counties in the subregion had, prior to the Norwegian proposal, for quite some time manoeuvred to strengthen the North Calotte cooperation among the northernmost counties in Finland, Norway and Sweden. Their aim was to extend this cooperation gradually, making use of the Nordic framework of cooperation and the regions 'Nordicity', to reach across the East-West divide to include oblasts on the Russian side. The provincial actors, however, saw the North Calotte cooperation as a competitor and a formation that stood in the way of extending a framework closer to their hearts. The experiences gained over recent years have alleviated these concerns, although some of them remain. These concerns also coincide with the broader argument that the Barents initiative has contributed to an unwarranted complexity. It is sometimes argued that there are too many arrangements covering one and the same area and competing over a limited number of projects. It is suggested that in order to remedy the situation, the Barents subregion should be allowed to slide into the shadows.

THE RECORD OF THE FORMATIVE YEARS

Considering that the High North has, over a long period, been unusually lacking in transfrontier interaction, the growth of recent years has been impressive. A number of initiatives have been taken at the state level, societal interaction has risen and the European Union is increasingly emerging as an actor contributing to and stimulating activities across borderlines. Many activities have been centred on the Russian parts of the subregion as intra-Nordic cooperation in the area is already quite advanced and is supported by other programmes and institutions, and because funding for cooperative activities, to a large extent, originate from Nordic sources aimed at assisting Central and Eastern European countries. Funding, which has remained relatively modest (the contributions by Finland, Norway and Sweden in the context of the Barents programme amounted, in 1996, to some seven million ECU), is based on the principle of equal contributions from all of the participating countries, although Russia has, on a number of occasions, been allowed to make contributions in the form of manpower, facilities or administrative resources, thus avoiding direct monetary expenditure.[23]

In the sphere of economic interaction, there has been a considerable increase in foreign trade and investments. There exists almost 500 western companies or joint ventures, most of them Nordic in origin, in the Russian part of the subregion. Russian enterprises have activities on the Norwegian, Finnish or Swedish sides of the border.[24] Trade and economic activities are, in some cases, quite essential for local actors such as the county of Finnmark (which imports considerable amounts of fish from Russia), but they are less essential for the subregion as a whole and not so significant for the state members of the subregional arrangement.[25]

It appears that, in many cases, the institutional framework functions as a vehicle for identifying areas and projects particularly suitable for distinctly de-politicized collaboration, but it is rarely involved in the financing or implementation of the projects. A five-year programme with 84 projects was adopted in 1994 by the Regional Council covering the fields of infrastructure, culture, education, indigenous peoples, environment and economic development. The proposals then selected for governmental sponsorship, at the ministerial level, included projects such as modernization of the nickel works, shipbuilding industries, ports and airports in northwestern Russian, and the creation of a railway link between Norway, Finland and Russia. Most of the projects are planned to be implemented – and in some cases also conducted – on Russian territory.[26] The schemes of financing and implementation are often bilateral or trilateral, for example Finnish-Norwegian-Russian, and occur at the fringes of the Barents arrangement. Some of the credit for initiating cross-border interaction goes to the North Calotte cooperation or pertains to EU programmes, in particular, the Barents Interreg-II Programme launched in 1995. The Union's dealings with the subregion, which for a substantial part used to be bilateral in nature, are increasingly multilateralized. As to the overall pattern, the interest in EU-financing, or contributions by such EU-related institutions as the European Bank for Reconstruction and Development (EBRD), add to the strength of the subregional framework of the Barents arrangement and bring the EU into an increasingly central position.

One achievement simply consists of a certain continuity which allows problems to be tackled more systematically and invites a pooling of resources. A certain legitimacy has been achieved during the formative years which is of importance in drawing attention to the previously poorly developed cross-border infrastructure, a variety of environmental problems requiring broad international action and the potential of the Northern Sea Route as a real alternative for international shipping.[27] In the sphere of improving infrastructural conditions, quite a number of results have been achieved. These include: the establishment of bus, air and ferry links; improving telecommunications in the Russian part of the subregion; launching a monthly newspaper in Norwegian, Russian and Finnish; erecting permanent and functioning border-crossings; and the establishment of consulates and trade representations. These projects contribute considerably to the subregional character of the project, although the extra-subregional patterns of interaction are still far more dense than the intra-subregional ones.[28]

On a societal level the features of the network have grown quite considerably. In addition to the companies and joint ventures with cross-border activities, there are now contacts between universities, hospitals, humanitarian organizations, churches, media organizations and chambers of commerce, as well as environmental groups. Traditional 'friendship town' relations have grown into something more than courtesy visits with folk-dance groups, and are viewed as an important – sometimes prime – aspect of local development strategies. The framework applied is increasingly one of reaching across the previous divide, and this is one strong indication that the Barents subregion is 'beginning to show teeth'.[29]

SUBREGION-BUILDING AND SECURITY

During the heyday of the Cold War there was just one concept of security present in Arctic Europe, one equating security with defence and high levels of military preparedness. The predominance of this geopolitical, statist and sovereignty-geared understanding contributed to the subregion becoming one of the most militarized areas in the world with a high level of tension and strict lines of territorial demarcation.

With the demise of the Cold War, a variety of conceptualizations have emerged in the security debate. These are also present in discussions pertaining to the High North. However, the traditional understandings continue to enjoy considerable support in this subregion: the tendency to think in geostrategic terms is more alive in northern parts than elsewhere in Europe and seems to have outlived the East-West conflict.

The strength of traditional thinking is also evidenced by the fact that room has not been provided for subregionalization across the previous divides due to the occurrence of some alternative – or complementary – conceptualization of security. No doubt a discursive shift has occurred, although it is implicit rather than explicit, but there is no change of security-thinking per se, and neither is there any decisive decline in the military arsenals, although some reductions have taken place.[30] The presence of strategic nuclear weaponry and doctrines such as that of deterrence or the preservation of an assured second strike capability are not conducive to subregionalization. These are broad issues detached from anything local. Security is not seen as divisible and therefore alternative configurations of political space can only appear if sufficiently detached from security.[31] There has to be a fundamental disjuncture between the geostrategic outlook and the one underpinning transborder subregionalization.

It is not surprising that against this background there are fewer contacts between the military on either side of the previous divide and fewer signs of a reduction of armaments in northernmost Europe than, for example, in Central Europe or around the Baltic Sea. The resilience of the north seems to be considerable and may prevail, as indicated, for example, by the argument often put forward that due to reductions elsewhere in Europe the relative importance of military might accumulated in the Barents and Arctic areas has grown.[32] This way of thinking colours attitudes towards the future arrangements of conventional forces in Europe (such as under the Conventional Armed Forces in Europe – CFE – Treaty). The High North seems to be both conceptually and in practice detached from general developments in the sphere of security, and if there is a correlation, it must be seen to be negative.

However, attitudes are less alarming than they used to be and security has a less distinct position on the political agenda than previously. One might speak of a certain inflation of the concept and conclude that it has lost some of its ability to dictate the political agenda. The debate on security, in a strict military sense, has not been altered but it has been left aside. Consequently, various civilian-related issues dominate the agenda. This profound discursive shift is particularly marked in the Barents and Arctic arenas as they were previously depicted almost exclusively as spheres of danger, superpower rivalry, bloc confrontation and nuclear competition.

This is also to say that the occurrence of subregionality in the Barents area is not linked, in the first place, to any alternative understanding of security. The aim is not one of out-competing the traditional conceptualizations pertaining to the state and the military sector by introducing some deviant, more 'soft', cooperative and subregionalized approaches. Rather, the new forms of political space are there due to a detachment from the theme of security. It seems that subregionality has grown in subjectivity by being associated with themes such as economic growth, development, connectedness and the assuming of new identities and by being free from narrow concerns about security. As security is no longer at the core, as a common language, of constructing political space, room has been provided for other conceptualizations and concerns to step in and influence the unfolding of the political landscape.

The debate about subregionality in the High North has thus not been about security to any significant degree. It rather appears that this theme has been avoided and instead rather depoliticized – only indirectly security-related themes have been brought to the forefront. The strategy appears to consist of de-securitization rather than endeavouring to create alternative or complementary conceptualizations of security. The Kirkenes Declaration reflects the same approach as security does not figure among the aims outlined for the Barents subregion. The conceptualizations applied have been quite important in allowing the Barents subregion to take off, but the debate has not been preoccupied with the issue of security and instead aims such as normalization, stabilization, creation of confidence, increasing transfrontier contacts and Europeanization have been mentioned.[33] There has been an emphasis on networking which tends to dissolve the distinction between foreign and domestic policy and blur a borderline important for the conventional security debate. The entrance of themes such as networking invites the inclusion of a number of other non-security issues on the international agenda and these developments might, taken together, indirectly have the effect of making traditional security concerns increasingly redundant.

It appears, in general, that subregional cooperation in the High North is searched for only if the traditional understandings of security allow for such moves. The situation thus differs from the one prevailing, for example, around the Baltic rim. There, the endeavours of de-securitization, the use of various 'soft' conceptualizations of security, as well as, in some cases, employment of rather traditional understandings of security are all increasingly conducive to subregionalization. Consequently, there is far more space available around the Baltic rim for subregional arrangements as the various understandings, including those pertaining to security, all point in the same direction.[34]

This does not imply, however, that security has been totally left outside the debate on subregionalization in the High North. It has been one of the concerns demanding attention, and has on occasions appeared in the discussion. For example, the founding fathers of the Barents project thought it proper to guard themselves against the argument that the implementation of transborder subregionalization hampers security. The views put forward by Thorvald Stoltenberg, in initiating the Barents project, seem to lean on the belief that the danger of traditional security-threats has become far less imminent, and instead one has to pay attention to various instabilities originating from larger changes underway. The Barents project is viewed, in this context, as an instrument to check and influence relevant developments, and to accumulate the resources necessary to prevent problems from emerging in the first place. It also offers opportunities, it is argued, to tackle such problems if they do occur, and this without the problems spilling automatically over to the military sphere. A concession is made to those staying with the old agenda by stating that it is good to have the European Union as a member of the BEAC and a number of important Western countries as observers. One may lean on them if the small countries of the subregion need backing against some power attempting political bulling in the context of the new cooperation.[35]

The 'soft' thinking on security has been able to draw upon the opening initiated by Mikhail Gorbachev in his Murmansk speech in 1987, which introduced a clear distinction between military and civilian security. The Barents initiative went a step further by focusing on the latter and providing it with a position of its own. The traditional, military-oriented conceptualizations were still there and both types – both the old and the new – have been regarded as vital. The latter has not been contrasted with the former, but it appears that the military side has simply been left aside in the context of the Barents initiative. This strategy of delinking the various aspects of security – rather than endeavouring to broaden the traditional understanding of security – appears to have yielded results.

It may, however, be observed that the thinking behind the project appears to have changed over time, at least among the Norwegian initiators. Sverre Jervell speaks of going from a first phase to a second, and somewhat different one, in the context of advancing the Barents project.[36] The strategy of de-securitization is becoming more explicit. As the East-West conflict has faded away and the probability of major war has declined radically, concerns are now related more to instability and problems that flow from unpredictability and uncertainty. The project's framework is now centre-periphery focused rather than East-West focused. The handling of these issues has become a core foreign policy concern, and the aim is seen, in general terms, not as one of preventing the instability characterizing the periphery from penetrating the stable centre, but rather of extending the stability of the centre to cover the more peripheral areas. In this context, the Barents project is seen as a kind of European 'Rio Grande' with transborder subregionality needed in order to keep various social and economic trends in check.[37]

The purpose, then, is to tackle issues such as pollution, migration or criminality at their source. The aim is to prevent them from spreading across borders in a way that allows openness to prevail and other, more positive forms of interaction to grow. The talk is about risks rather than threats, so that some concepts central to the traditional discourse on security are being left aside in the vocabularies employed.[38] A variety of problematic issues are addressed in the context of the normal, civilian agenda. There is no hiding the fact that some of these issues are difficult to resolve, but efforts to address them can take place without reverting to a framework pertaining to military preparedness, strict territorial delineations or the understanding that the underlying issue consists of averting the danger of war between the states concerned.

Furthermore, keeping 'hard' security outside the Barents framework allows a more balanced situation to emerge between Russia, as a major power, and the three small Nordic countries. The Nordic countries, while being inferior to Russia (according to prevailing views) in military terms, have significant political, economic, technological and cultural resources. On a broader scale, the Barents arrangement, in offering full partnership for Russia, pre-empts charges of exclusion and reduces security-related fears of 'encirclement'.

CONCLUSION

An essential aspect of the Barents initiative is that it employs vocabularies different from the previous debates that have influenced the unfolding of the political landscape in northernmost Europe. It does so by downplaying the canonical threats associated with the Cold War and by tackling indirectly some present ones. Security is hence no longer an absolutely central, overarching theme and it seems that issues of economic growth, cooperation, integration and interdependence have occupied the foreground. The subregion has gained significant bridging functions. It is viewed as something unifying, instead of being depicted in terms of a scene of conflict between major actors in international relations. Calls for homogeneity and standardization are toned down and the emphasis is increasingly on heterogeneity and the importance of the local.

Moreover, the Barents cooperation tends to alter the images of the High North as being mainly characterized by peripherality, in calling for transboundary solutions, both governmental and non-governmental, at various levels. It paves the way – with the utilization and pooling of various local-specific strengths by overlapping forms of governance – for an improvement of the subregion's relative weight in the constellations of an integrative Europe. Instead of being doomed to the position of a hinterland, the area may become more central. It can, due to an increasing permeability of borders, become part of a continuous economic, social and cultural landscape. A system of closer interaction among the participating entities has been called for, with the option of creating integrated spaces that diminish the hindrances caused by distance. It may well be expected that European developments continue to spur such policies.

The demise of the previous rigidity has released a considerable amount of human energy. Rules have changed in the sense that the crossing of borders and the transcending of hierarchies is now encouraged rather than penalized. Many fresh ideas have emerged, and a network of political, economic, cultural and environmental contacts has been established. Essential borderlines break down, including the binary division into 'us' and 'them'. What used to be depicted as the outside, and thereby the sphere of danger, becomes part of the inside – with attendant connotations of prosperity, good life and peace. The previous otherness turns into something interesting to explore as a category between far-reaching similarity and profound otherness.

In the course of this process, the political agendas have been transformed in the capitals as well as at the level of societies: the core issues pertain increasingly to authority and influence, centre/periphery issues within the new European economic geography, marginality and a struggle between those who are makers of politics and those relegated to the status of objects of the policies pursued by others. In this context the Barents subregion becomes a political construct identified as particularly suited to deal with these concerns in northernmost Europe.

With the upgrading of subregionality much of the old has been pushed to the sidelines and room has been created for new and less restrictive constellations. This is in line with the more general developments that add to the subjectivity of subregionality in European affairs. But the specificity of the Barents project seems to indicate that there is much left of the old and the new is still in the making. The old and new do not clash in any radical manner and instead they seem to coincide without one having to surrender to the other.

The incomplete, insufficient, open, manifold and in some ways light nature of the Barents arrangements might be taken to mean that it is low on political subjectivity. This is certainly true if judged on the basis of classical standards, particularly as there has been an emphasis on processes rather than structures. It should be taken into account, however, that the forms of new subregionality tend, in general, to be light, innovative, spontaneous, in no way self-evident and perhaps at times even opportunistic. The reading might be that these qualities are assets rather than liabilities. Subregion-building attracts interest because subregions have a strong conceptual and visionary side; they are incomplete and still in the making. The conceptual break-throughs, transforming them into joint platforms of communication, are important as such. Different actors are invited to meet across a broad set of issues. They may struggle for control and dominance, as is the case also, to some extent, in the context of the Barents arrangement, but there are good chances that in a larger perspective everybody participating stands to win. The subregion does not, in the first place, stand for something administrative, closed and regulatory as the power tends, in the final analysis, to be located in the networks. This is why conventional analysis based on classical, statist criteria often has difficulties in grasping the meaning of formations such as the Barents subregion and in evaluating their endurance and importance.

It may be observed that the introduction of new conceptual departures and the transforming of these into a concrete project has taken place in a relatively harmonious manner. There have been worries that the introduction of subregionality in the High North might spur local conflicts or invite dissidence and that the acceptance of diversity could lead to uncontrolled developments in a subregion of great importance for the functioning of the mechanisms of 'hard' security. However, the experiences accumulated during the early years of the Barents subregion do not confirm this view. Some tensions have undoubtedly been present, such as those originating with the elevated position of the indigenous peoples of the subregion, but they have, without exception, been unproblematic if seen in a larger perspective, and perhaps even fruitful in drawing attention to previously hidden problems and helping to find resources for the remedies needed.

In general, the effects of subregionality and the establishment of the Barents subregion seem favourable. The project has been conducive to security in a more general sense of assuring particular arrangements into the future, thereby providing meaning as well as the visions and horizons needed for change. As subregionality tends towards inclusion rather than exclusion, there is the promise that the changes introduced – despite their inherently radical nature and some contrary elements – remain basically peaceful. Subregionality seems mostly to contribute to the devaluation of historical and territorial quarrels, and functions constructively in appeasing and creating an outlet for discontent. Instead of polarizing too far, it also draws – in forms such as the Barents arrangement – attention to common experiences, real or imaged, thereby contributing to the communicative capacities of the actors in question. Multiple identities are strengthened: local, subregional, national and European, which counteracts the formation of distinct, narrow and uniform identities, conducive to the drawing of tight, impenetrable boundaries as well as processes of bifurcation and thereby conflict on a larger scale.

Moreover, there is a tendency for 'high politics' to become domesticated if exposed to subregionalism, and this also seems to be case with the Barents subregion. As 'Europe' becomes linked up with something local, it also tends to become more familiar and easier to accept – this being particularly important along Norway's northern coastlines and in northwestern Russia. This inclusive and rather open way of conceiving 'Europe' is not built on moves of exclusion, claiming Europe for some distinct category of Europeans. It is not seen as a given, ready-made and crystallized politico-geographic entity with clear geographic, political and cultural borders; a sphere which can be either joined or kept at a distance. Instead, it tends towards the extending of previous borders and lowering them, thus preparing the ground for configurations such as a 'Europe of the neighbourhoods'.

It appears that the Barents subregion, in cutting across the previous East-West divide, functions very much along these lines. It provides access to the 'European', thereby also influencing the contours of the whole configuration. This is important for Finland and Sweden as new members of the EU, as well as for the Union itself. However, the arrangement is of particular significance for Norway, given the 'negative' result of its 1995 referendum on EU membership, and for Russia, with bleak prospects for achieving membership of the EU or NATO in the short run. With the option offered by subregionality, one may become 'European' without first having to change into some exclusive category of European-ness. The potential of the Barents arrangement thus reaches far beyond the formative years and its immediate beginning.

4 The Council of Baltic Sea States

Carl-Einar Stalvant

The end of the Cold War has transformed Europe's political environment. The complex interaction of domestic, international and transnational change in post-Cold War Europe has been conducive both to the re-emergence of older mental maps of Europe and to new ideas of how to realize and organize the continent's political communities. This has allowed new transnational subregional processes to take root. Fuelled by the drive for increased autonomy within the European Union, various tendencies coalesced in the call for a 'Europe of the regions'.

As a historically meaningful formation, the Baltic Sea subregion was re-established within the space of a few years, providing a frequently used frame of reference for joint actions among governments, sub-state actors, cities and municipalities, businesses and non-governmental organizations. Actors of different statuses and sizes pooled their resources in new endeavours within the Baltic subregion. Subregional ties at new levels below and above the nation-state were articulated and established, spanning the boundaries between and within states and societies. This was a remarkable revival for a part of Europe where the Cold War divide had barred regular contacts and prevented close cooperation for two generations. No longer a barrier, the sea 'highway' brought the two shores of the Baltic together. Baltic subregional cooperation took strength from the synergistic effects of numerous decentralized initiatives, collaborating institutions and network-building processes. Political relations developed as the countries in the subregion drew closer and inter-governmental cooperation began to flourish in many functional fields. Individual governments developed policies designed to address the new subregional conditions and promote subregional cooperation. Moreover, the drive for subregionalism reduced the pre-eminence of the state-centric order in European society. Thus, a wider understanding of 'international politics' is necessary to understand the new dynamics of the Baltic Sea space. In order to address and manage the need for intensified cooperation and coordination among the Baltic Sea states, a new political body, the Council of Baltic Sea States (CBSS), was established – the character of which was left rather open.

THE BIRTH OF A SUBREGIONAL 'UNDERTAKING'

The idea to create a Baltic inter-governmental forum had been aired in many quarters before the Danish Foreign Minister Uffe Ellemann-Jensen and his German counterpart Hans-Dietrich Genscher launched the initiative during bilateral discussions in Rostock in autumn 1991. The representatives of the nine Baltic Sea littoral states (Denmark, Estonia, Finland, Germany, Latvia, Lithuania, Poland, Russia and Sweden) plus Norway and the Commission of the then European Community met in March 1992, establishing the Council of the Baltic Sea States.[1] In 1996, the circle of partner states was enlarged to include Iceland.

With the June 1997 CBSS Foreign Ministers meeting in Riga, the new Council – or subregional 'undertaking' to paraphrase its founding document – celebrated its sixth year of activity. An extraordinary and unprecedented summit of Heads of States and Government of the eleven CBSS members was held in Visby, Sweden, on 3-4 May 1996. The Visby summit lent further weight to the Baltic Sea subregional cooperation by including the highest political level in the web of unfolding relations. The Visby summit also represented a watershed in the history of CBSS in other respects. Until then, the CBSS had been an almost invisible undertaking in the midst of larger domestic and international transformations. The summit inspired the framing of a new and different subregional agenda. A comprehensive work programme was adopted shortly afterwards by the CBSS Foreign Ministers. The concept of 'civic security' was endorsed politically as a joint interest and a means of promoting stability. Moreover, these deliberations coincided with decisive stages in two larger issues on the wider European agenda – the separate but parallel processes of the enlargement of the European Union (EU) and the North Atlantic Treaty Organization (NATO). The Visby summit, therefore, draws a line – even if somewhat arbitrarily – between two phases in the story of Baltic Sea subregionalism and the CBSS. Indeed, perhaps one can even talk of a second quinquennat and the beginnings of a post-transition agenda.

This chapter describes these developments and the role of the CBSS in more detail. It examines the Council, its specific activities, its working methods and its achievements to date. It seeks to answer a number of specific questions. Why and how was CBSS established in the first place and how is it organized? What were the primary objectives behind the establishment of the Council? How has it adapted to various challenging international processes and events, changes in national policies and to developments in subregional relations? What are its main achievements and problems? What contribution has the CBSS and the subregional dimension it embodies made to European security and cooperation? These questions are fundamental, yet not easily answered. Before addressing them, it is necessary to recall the main events and driving forces which have reshaped the Baltic political landscape in the early years of post-Cold War period in order to understand the characteristics and parameters of subregional affairs in the Baltic Sea space. An appraisal of the role of the CBSS has to recognize both the Council's unique subregional foundation and its position within a system of organizational pluralism.

POLITICAL CHANGES IN THE BALTIC SEA SUBREGION

The positive sense of self-identification reviving the contours and content of a Baltic Sea subregion in the early 1990s was shaped by many forces. Europe-wide changes interacted with subregional processes, resulting in a rethinking of policies and theoretical discourses. To a very great extent, events were shaped by the extraordinary opening of normal and direct contacts between peoples, organizations and institutions. This 'bottom-up' perspective explains many of the driving forces of Baltic Sea subregionalism. At the same time, external influences provided the main pillars of the institutional architecture, opening up new possibilities for the Nordic and Baltic countries to join or develop relations with the dominant European institutions (especially the EU and NATO), prompting reappraisals of bilateral relations, but also raising possible new dangers.

The unification of Germany and the break-up of the Soviet Union radically altered the geopolitical situation in the Baltic subregion. Russia's direct presence on the Baltic coastline contracted to the exclave of Kaliningrad and the Leningrad oblast. The three Baltic states – Estonia, Latvia and Lithuania – were reborn. The number of Baltic littoral states grew from seven to nine, with Norway an adjoining country guarding the distant mouth of the Baltic straits. As a result, the number of bilateral diplomatic relations within the subregion rose from 21 to 45. While most relationships benefited from the new spirit, some were tinged with mutual suspicion and unresolved issues which might impinge on the subregion as a whole.

In northwestern Europe and the countries bordering the Baltic Sea, the fall of the Berlin wall had particular symbolic import. The end of the Cold War unlocked the political order in the subregion, creating new possibilities for cooperation. In the economic field, the dismantling of ideological obstacles (and accompanying administrative barriers) to trade was likely to feed new impulses into social interactions and to boost growth and restructuring. The location of a reborn metropolis on the subregion's southern perimeter, however, led to obvious conclusions about likely economic developments within the subregion and the re-emergence of suppressed political apprehensions among Germany's neighbours. As a result, both fears and expectations fuelled the subregion-building process, founded on divergent historical experiences and frameworks for interpreting the dynamics of change.

One influential strand of opinion maintained that recurrent historical patterns were discernible in the midst of turbulence: Germany on the rise; an unpredictable and erratic Russian heartland; and fears of ambiguous grey zones, a reborn glacis or a power vacuum in-between these two major powers.[2] Geopolitical reasoning suggested a shift in political gravity from Moscow to Brussels and Berlin. Some observers maintained that perennial dilemmas in the relations between small states and their large neighbours were once again exposed. Baltic Europe has had negative experiences of historical shifts in the balance of power between the major powers, as Polish history illustrates. The Tilsit syndrome describes a convergence of interests between the leading power in the east and the leading power on the continent at the expense of smaller nations, as with the secret protocol on spheres of influence added to the Soviet pact with Nazi Germany. Having achieved independence, the driving force behind the three Baltic states' security policies has been the desire to eliminate such a possibility through full integration with Western security structures. The relatively small Nordic states also have similar geostrategic concerns: oscillations between tension and detente during the Cold War, for example, restrained the freedom of action of Finland and Sweden.[3] Once the concentration on a single hegemonic threat waned, an enlarged menu of choice emerged for all actors.

However, it would be erroneous to base thinking only on historical analogies, ignoring the many unprecedented, new elements in the overall Baltic constellation. Russian-German reconciliation was undoubtedly a beneficial factor for subregional relations. The small countries in the Baltic subregion could also take comfort from the unbroken German policy of integration into NATO and the EU. German Chancellor Helmut Kohl specifically sought to assuage Nordic concerns in an address to the Nordic Council in March 1992. In dealings with the Baltic states, a cautious and restrained German attitude prevailed. Progress in East-West arms control (even though Finland, Sweden and the Baltic states were not parties to the Conventional Armed Forces in Europe – CFE – Treaty)[4], membership of the inclusive, pan-European Organization for Security and Cooperation in Europe (OSCE) and the presence of the EU and NATO in the subregion were further stabilizing factors.[5] Last but not least, the dismantling of mutual enemy images and threat perceptions enabled the countries of the Baltic subregion to overcome the traditional security dilemmas of an anarchic world and broaden their conception of security.

The opening up of hierarchically organized and closed societies to transfrontier cooperation and the pursuit of distinct local and sub-state interests also helped to equalize and facilitate relations between parties of different sizes and strengths (although these processes also created new local tensions and security problems). In tune with calls for a 'Europe of the regions', national legislation and administrative structures were changed to cope with the new trends and to further social communications and transnational cooperation. While no novelty in German federalism, these were innovative practices for other countries. The Finnish-Russian Friendship Treaty of 1992 encourages the promotion of relations between elected assemblies and between central, regional and local authorities. Poland acceded to international instruments dealing with transfrontier cooperation and in 1993 enacted regulations that facilitated and legitimized such cooperation.[6] A 1993 change in the Swedish municipal government law removed certain restraints on local authorities in this area.

The various Baltic Sea states responded to these developments differently, reflecting their differing geostrategic situations, histories and politics. The Central and Eastern European states - Poland and the three Baltic states – sought to 'return to Europe' through integration with the EU and NATO. Poland was able to normalize its bilateral relations with its neighbours and by the mid-1990s had established itself as a primary candidate for NATO and EU membership. Poland also sought to promote multilateral Baltic Sea cooperation, for example co-sponsoring with Sweden a conference on marine environmental problems held in Ronneby, Sweden, in September 1990 (- the conference also provided a framework for the three Baltic states to participate as independent actors).[7]

The three Baltic states, having regained their independence and won international recognition only in August-September 1991, dissociated themselves rapidly from the collapsing Soviet centre and embarked on a course of securing their position. The three countries sought to integrate themselves with the EU and NATO, but also – as part of this process – to develop close relations with their Nordic neighbours. Their Soviet heritage and proximity to Russia, however, made their integration with the West slower than that of Poland. Disputes over the withdrawal of Russian troops, the rights of Russian minorities and economic and border issues also made their relations with Russia difficult. Association Agreements were concluded with the EU in 1995 and the Baltic states participated actively in NATO's Partnership for Peace (PfP). Although in summer 1997 Estonia was included amongst the group of Central and Eastern European states with which the European Commission recommended the opening of EU membership negotiations, exactly when and in what circumstances the Baltic states might join the EU and NATO remained unclear. Against this background, Baltic-Nordic relations expanded and intensified, manifested by the introduction of the 'five-plus-three' cooperation framework (the five Nordic states and the three Baltic states), as well as close bilateral ties. Such cooperation was seen as a way of facilitating the Baltic states integration with the EU and NATO.

Russia's size, great power status and geography make it a case apart in the Baltic subregion (as in Europe as a whole). Russia's perspective and interests differ significantly from those of the other Baltic states.[8] Nevertheless, Russia has sought to develop a role in the Baltic subregion and the other Baltic states have recognized the need to develop cooperative relations with Russia. The EU and NATO have sought to develop special, cooperative relationships with Russia commensurate with its weight. Elements of these, such as the 1995 EU-Russia Partnership and Cooperation Agreement and Russia's involvement in NATO's PfP, may have practical relevance for cooperation in the Baltic subregion. The specific geographic and military situation in northern Europe, however, has important implications for Russia's role in the Baltic subregion. Russia's only direct land borders with Western Europe and the EU run through the Baltic Sea subregion. While the Russian military presence has been removed from Central Europe, substantial Russian forces remain in the vicinity of Finland and Norway in the Leningrad military district. From a military point of view the northwestern theatre remains crucial. The autumn 1996 adaptation of the CFE Treaty, further, permits considerable reinforcement of Russian forces in northern Europe. Russia maintains a direct presence on the Baltic coast via the Kaliningrad military exclave.[9] Russia also retains substantial submarine-based strategic nuclear forces based in the Barents subregion, giving the northern dimension of European security significance beyond the immediate Barents or Baltic subregions. In addition, descriptions of the Baltic states 'as a source of threat to Russia'[10] and Russian opposition to the possible NATO membership of the Baltic states[11] have become issues of concern. While the other Baltic Sea states remain wary of Russia's military potential and great power ambitions, Russia's weaknesses rather than its strength have posed greater immediate security problems. Thus, uncertainties about the future direction of Russian foreign policy, potential conflicts within Russia and between Russia and its former Soviet neighbours (including the three Baltic states) and issues such as refugee flows, arms and nuclear material smuggling and environmental degradation have become significant security concerns.

The Nordic states' security situation and policies have also changed significantly. The end of the Cold War allowed Finland to re-interpret its 1948 Treaty of Friendship, Cooperation and Mutual Assistance with the Soviet Union and then to conclude a new treaty with Russia which no longer includes commitments to joint defence activities and consultation in case of security of threats. Norway has remained strongly committed to NATO, but has also sought to develop cooperation with Russia and draw the EU into the Barents region through the Barents Euro-Arctic Council. Denmark has benefited particularly from the disappearance of East Germany and the Warsaw Pact, while also taking a leading role in promoting security cooperation with the Baltic states in 'the spirit of PfP'. The end of the Cold War, the growing integration of the EU and fears of marginalization from Europe's political-economic core also made the EU increasingly important for the Nordic states and the Baltic subregion as a whole. Thus, Finland and Sweden joined the EU in January 1995 and have subsequently sought to increase the EU's engagement in the Baltic subregion. Norway and Iceland, being more Atlantic in their identification and endowed with less vulnerable economies, opted to stay out of the EU, creating something of a split in the Nordic area.

Despite this 'split' and some fears that centrifugal forces might undermine the Cold War 'Nordic system of stability'[12], the Nordic states retained much in common and also found a shared interest in supporting stability in and developing new contacts with the Baltic states, Poland and Russia. Channels for transmitting Nordic technical assistance to the countries in transition were quickly established both bilaterally and multilaterally. The various cooperation and assistance schemes are likely to disseminate Nordic experience and values and the notion of cooperation with neighbouring areas has quickly penetrated working programmes and institutional arrangements. The Nordic countries, which previously refrained from any explicit security cooperation, have also increasingly developed common security policies towards the Baltic rim – their contribution to the setting up of a Baltic peacekeeping battalion being the most conspicuous example. Denmark and Sweden have given concrete assistance by including contingents from the Baltic states and Poland in their peacekeeping battalions in Croatia. The Nordic states have also helped the Baltic states to develop their border control capabilities in order to forestall illegal migration and 'people smuggling'. Although the priorities of the five Nordic countries differ somewhat, the combined effect of their national policies and joint action programmes is to target large parts of northwestern Europe. A division of labour is also discernible, whereby Norway concentrates on the Barents subregion and the Kola Peninsula, Finland on Karelia and the vicinity of the Gulf of Finland, Sweden on the three Baltic states (although relations with Estonia and Latvia are more intense) and Denmark on Lithuania and northern Poland.

Nor, further, did Nordic cooperation itself end. Rather, it moved in two directions. It was elevated to the highest level by the institutionalization of meetings between Prime Ministers and by inserting reports from Foreign and Defence Ministers onto the Nordic Council agenda. Despite an established record of non-interference with national foreign and defence policies, the Nordic Council also embarked on a post-Cold War pursuit of collective foreign relations. This was a bold reversal of policy, which quickly won wide acclaim and profoundly restructured both thinking about and the traditional organization of Nordic cooperation. In 1994, the Nordic Council changed its previous committee structure, splitting into three major areas of attention: two committees deal with external affairs (relations to adjacent areas and relations with the EU and the European Economic Area) and only the third deals with the traditional heritage of culture and 'Nordism'.[13] The Nordic Council has also developed a special role in relations with the three Baltic states. After a period of discussion of and vacillation over whether, and under what conditions, the Baltic states should be included in the work of its committees and plenary sessions, the Nordic Council settled for a policy of encouraging the renewal of separate but homologous cooperation with the three Baltic states. The re-establishment of the Baltic Council by Estonia, Latvia and Lithuania in 1992 facilitated a continuous dialogue. In contrast to the restraint previously displayed by the Nordic Council in security matters, the Foreign Ministers and Heads of Governments of the three Baltic states decided to address high political issues directly (for example, pressing for their countries membership of NATO and the EU). Institutional links between the Nordic and Baltic Councils were established in 1992, have grown in intensity and scope since and now comprise regular meetings in almost every field of governance (including meetings of Foreign and Defence Ministers and joint meetings and seminars on common issues).

Parallel to changes resulting from the break-up of the Soviet bloc and shifts within the Nordic countries foreign policies, the European Union emerged as a key but multifaceted factor in subregional development. In a way, this is a new and unprecedented development, as the Nordic countries (bar Denmark) previously remained aloof from legally based integration and committing themselves to political finalities which required a transfer of sovereignty. The accession of Sweden and Finland to the EU and the membership applications of Estonia, Latvia, Lithuania and Poland raises the prospect of a transformed foundation for subregional relations in the future. The European Commission's membership of the CBSS; the Union's bilateral Association/Cooperation Agreements with the three Baltic states, Poland and Russia; and its provision of various forms of technical and economic aid to these states have drawn the EU into the Baltic arena as a significant actor.

At the same time, the process of EU enlargement is also likely to create some new tensions within the Baltic subregion. The Commission's summer 1997 opinion on the membership applications from twelve Central and Eastern European countries argued that Estonia and Poland (but not Latvia and Lithuania) are among the five candidates which have made most progress in meeting the Union's membership requirements and should be included in its first wave of eastern enlargement. Such a selective strategy went against the Swedish and Danish position that all applicants should start on the same line. The stance was, however, supported by Germany and Finland who maintained that differentiation without discrimination was possible and desirable. Moreover, it was argued by some that by singling out Estonia the prevailing notion of a Baltic geopolitical entity composed of the three Baltic states was doomed to marginalization. Thus, while the EU's role in the Baltic seems likely to grow as it enlarges, the process of enlargement is also likely to complicate relations in the Baltic subregion, particularly with those states excluded from membership of the Union, whether initially (as seems likely with Latvia and Lithuania) or in the longer term also (as with the Russian Federation).

In combination, these various developments created a complex web of international relations, transnational relations and multiple institutions in the Baltic Sea subregion. The number of state actors increased and sub-state relations proliferated. A number of historical legacies re-emerged, some driving Baltic Sea subregionalism, others restraining it. The new constellation gave substantial scope for the Nordic states, Poland and the Baltic states to further their interests and influence the subregion building process. With regard to 'high' political security, the prevailing perception was that the core issue was no longer the 'German question' but rather the 'Russian question'. In many respects, however, traditional diplomatic 'games' were replaced by a broader concept of security, focused on promoting stability in the 'transitional' post-communist states and combating low level threats and unrest.

In many ways, the Baltic Sea is a microcosm of wider European society. It transcends the core of the former politico-military divide. The territories surrounding the Baltic Sea include large and small states; established democracies/market economies and new democracies/countries in transition; and big discrepancies between rich and poor states and between certain regions and areas within individual states.[14] In terms of international affiliations, there is a plethora of institutions and relations: involving both inclusive institutions, such as the CBSS and the OSCE, and exclusive ones, such as the Nordic Council, the EU and NATO. Four countries are members of the EU, while four have applied for membership and three have opted for other relationships. Four states are long-standing members of NATO, while Poland was included in the first three Central and Eastern European countries invited to join the Alliance in July 1997. The three Baltic states have applied for NATO membership, but the Alliance has politely postponed their request while reaffirming a policy of keeping the door open. Russia's special position and right to be consulted was expressed in the NATO-Russia Founding Act in May 1997. All the countries of the subregion, moreover, are engaged in NATO's PfP. The two neutral states, Sweden and Finland, have upgraded their engagement with NATO/PfP both politically and militarily.

THE ORIGINS OF THE CBSS

A variety of forces and ideas propelled the re-emergence of a Baltic Sea configuration. Geography, selective readings of ancient history and culture, and genuine concern for the environmental status of a common sea basin provided the ideé-force for a vague but appealing notion. The contentious issue of an identity-based project emerged as the cultural and spiritual appeal of notions such as Ostseeraum, a new Hansa and a Nordic-Baltic space won public recognition in the discourses and seminars of intellectuals.[15] However, as time went by, other arguments were advanced to underpin the subregional concept. The case was made for a political, institutional unity to support economic development and functional cooperation in areas such as the environment, transport and physical planning.

One of the first politicians to argue the case for subregionalization and the establishment of a Baltic Council was the then Head of Government of the German lander Schleswig-Holstein, Minister-President Bjorn Engholm. Engholm's interventions were noticeable both because of the arguments he forwarded and for the positive response they received. He claimed that:

> the common background among Northern European countries covers a wide spectrum and runs deep. What we need now is a joint effort or rather common strategy for the future.

A number of common social and mental attitudes, he suggested, united the peoples of the Baltic. One tangible motive for cooperation was the prospect of economic spoils. Northern Europe, it was said, must meet the competition from other faster growing parts of Europe and unite in order to safeguard its economic interests and renewal. Accordingly, European integration would lead to a shift in Schleswig- Holstein's self-perception 'from a peripheral area of Europe to Norden's South'.

The exact nature of the proposed Council was long undefined. The early proposals were inspired by the new Hansa concept of a non-statist body where actors representing different territories and units bordering the Baltic Sea could meet, rather than by a more traditional design.[16] German Foreign Minister Hans-Dietrich Genscher is said to have sent a letter to Engholm complaining that such plans infringed on the prerogatives of the Bund. The plausibility of this interpretation is strengthened by the lukewarm response given to a similar early proposal put forward by the then Swedish Minister of Trade Mats Hellstrom. There were also other impediments. Moscow was included in soundings during autumn 1991[17], but it was only after the dissolution of the Soviet Union that the proposals matured.

The acceptance of the idea of a Baltic Council nevertheless represented a departure from past polices, not least from a Nordic perspective. Given the preponderant size of the Soviet Union, there was always much hesitation about involving that country in Nordic cooperation. The then Swedish Foreign Minister Sven Andersson fended off overtures to that end from Moscow in a decisive manner in 1974. Nordic reservations were also grounded in the observation that the Soviet Union had long opposed subregional cooperation in which it was not involved. Nor, further, did Soviet President Mikhail Gorbachev's 1987 Murmansk speech on the 'Northern floor in the common European home' elicit a positive response. Despite Gorbachev's 'new thinking' in foreign policy, disagreements over the intricacies of a Baltic nuclear weapon free zone involving parts of Soviet territory dragged on. After the break-up of the Soviet Union, however, a Baltic Sea framework with the participation of all independent states, including an open and democratic Russia, was more reassuring for the Nordic states.

Faced with rapidly unfolding developments, it appeared that the Baltic governments would be the last actors to jump on the bandwagon. A Council of a 'traditional intergovernmental nature', in the hands of Foreign Ministries and with almost no budget and staff, was under the circumstances not a very bold move. The Council's characteristics were described in very restrained, negative rather than affirmative, terms: 'this new Council should not be seen as a new formalized institutional framework with a permanent secretariat'. The official purpose was rather broadly defined: 'to serve as a forum for guidance and overall co-ordination among the participating states'. There may have been concern on the part of Foreign Ministries at a possible loss of control, since the substance of cooperation consisted of issues that fell within the confines of other ministries and cooperation was already being established through unofficial channels, involving many other actors.

The terms of reference of the CBSS list the following subjects:
- Assistance to new democratic institutions;
- Economic and technological assistance and cooperation;
- Humanitarian matters and human health;
- Protection of the environment and energy cooperation;
- Cooperation in the field of culture, education, tourism and information;
- Transport and communication.

The CBSS was seen as a means of recapturing lost ground in terms of subregional cooperation. Danish Foreign Minister Uffe Ellemann-Jensen, the first chair of the CBSS, described 'the purpose of the Council as (to act as) the driving political force ...which gives an impetus to the cooperation already underway'. A similar ambition was expressed by the succeeding chairman, the Finnish Foreign Minister Vayrynen who underlined the need for a "useful and efficient coordinator...collecting different cooperation activities under its umbrella'.[18] A less explicit function of the Council might be the pre-emption of as yet undefined but sensitive demands by circumscribing in advance the proper scope for cooperation. Security was thus not included in the Council's areas of competence, although there is no formal obstacle to its taking up 'other matters or possible subjects for cooperation' should the members so decide.

THE CBSS: ACTIVITIES AND PERFORMANCE

The Council kept a rather low profile during its first years of existence. This modest role may have been due to the tensions which prevailed in relations between the Russian Federation and the Baltic states. Another factor may have been the preoccupation of the Nordic states with EU membership. The most simple explanation is that the forum, once it had been established, was valued more as a symbol than as a motor. It was only one of many meeting points between the governments within a wider web of relations and competing demands for operational action. In one of the hallmarks of Baltic Sea cooperation, the Comprehensive Environmental Action Programme launched at the Ronneby meeting in 1990, the CBSS was relegated to the sidelines. The Comprehensive Environmental Action Programme functioned also as a vehicle for transmitting support to countries in transition. Its weight in subregional cooperation reflected prevailing priorities, as the environmental dimension is more central in assistance programmes and financial credits in the Baltic subregion than in other European schemes for subregional cooperation.[19] No less than 138 Baltic environmental 'hot spots' were identified, becoming targets for investments and joint assistance from international partners. This process was already firmly in the control of national environmental ministries and the Helsinki Commission (HELCOM – set up within the framework of the 1974 Convention on the Protection of the Marine Environment in the Baltic Sea). Thus, as plans in this area were drawn up before the CBSS was established, the Ronneby conference and the body established for implementing the Action Programme set precedents for the organization and nature of Baltic subregional projects. Participants included the European Commission, international banks, research organizations and transnational, subregional, non-governmental organizations, plus adjacent countries like Norway and the Czech and Slovak Republics. Such a mixed actor constellation was an innovative means of developing policy, setting a precedent for other subregional institutions and arrangements.[20]

Another factor restraining the development of the Council was the expansion of intergovernmental contacts outside the CBSS framework, through bilateral encounters and in contexts bringing together the majority of but not always all CBSS members. In cases when all or the majority of CBSS members were represented, there was little inclination to hold such meetings under the auspices of CBSS (despite the fact that Council's terms of reference include the possibility of expanding its agenda).[21]

In 1994 the Council established a special Commissioner on Democratic

Institutions and Human Rights, Including the Rights of Persons Belonging to Minorities. This innovation was partly inspired by what was seen as the useful and supportive role played by the OSCE High Commissioner on National Minorities in addressing the situation of the Russian speaking minorities in Estonia and Latvia. It was made clear in the carefully worded mandate that the CBSS Commissioner could take his/her own initiative but should scrutinize all countries and that individual appeals could be made to the Commissioner. The Commissioner has conducted several surveys of democratic practices, legislation and specific situations and forwarded his criticisms and recommendations to governments. Moreover, extensive yearly reports have been presented to sessions of the Baltic Sea parliamentary conferences and the CBSS itself. The Commissioner's mandate was extended in 1997 and the incumbent, Professor Ole Espersen of Denmark, was reappointed as Commissioner.

The Council stepped up the level and visibility of its activities from 1994. Perhaps one can say that for a certain period the Council appeared to be shopping around among different ideas and initiatives rather than acting as an overall coordinator. Twelve seminars were held under the auspices of the Council or its working groups from 1993 to early 1996.[22] While being valuable in themselves and for the inputs they provided in addressing various functional issues, these seminars lacked a clear focus and did not provide the underlying principles or a longer term foundation for the CBSS. With the Visby summit in May 1996 and the adoption of three Action Programmes at the CBSS Foreign Ministers meetings in Kalmar in June 1996, however, the Council determined a number of priorities and the prospects for its fulfilling a role commensurate with its mandate improved. Moreover, new working methods adopted at the same time will make it easier for the CBSS to follow up high-level decisions. The three Action Programmes agreed in June 1996 were:[23]

- *Participation and Stable Political Development:* this programme consists of seven elements aiming at promoting democratic practices and participation, facilitation of people-to-people contacts, support for independent civil organizations, combating crime, support for education and student exchanges and promotion of cultural contacts.
- *Economic Integration and Prosperity:* this programme has the ambitious goal of developing the Baltic Sea subregion into an integrated, competitive and dynamic area of sustained growth through the creation of a subregional market for trade investment and cooperation. The programme has five components: supporting trade liberalization and improving the business climate; supporting the

integration of the three Baltic states and Poland into the EU; transport; spatial planning; and energy.
- *Sustainable Development and Environmental Protection:* this programme is based on the Comprehensive Environmental Action Programme and has been translated into a subregional version of the UN's environmental 'Agenda 21' – the first subregional 'Agenda 21' of its kind. The programme is based on a long term analysis of the Baltic environment, with national governments/ministries cooperating with various non-governmental organizations and observers to develop proposals and criteria for future policies.

The CBSS has also held discussions and developed contacts with various other trans-Baltic organizations and groups with regard to converging fields of cooperation. The Council's terms of reference include provisions for encouraging subregional cooperation by the 'invitation of special participants' to its meetings and by giving attention to the representatives of other Baltic groupings, sub-state regions and international organizations. To fulfil the Council's mission as a forum for discussion of Baltic Sea issues, various dialogues are maintained with actors from within and beyond the Baltic Sea subregion. General endorsements of proposals or projects by the Council have also been an asset when discussing projects and ideas with funding organizations and banks. A pattern has crystallized whereby representatives of the main Baltic Sea organizations enjoy regular access to the Council's sessions. Representatives of the umbrella organization for sub-state regions (the Baltic Sea States Subregional Conference), the Islands of the Baltic (B-7) group and the Union of the Baltic Cities are noteworthy in this respect. The Council has stressed that 'cooperation with and among the sub(-state) regions around the Baltic Sea (is) an indispensable basis for a growing regional identity'.[24] This development is a small scale reflection of the rise of 'Euro-regions' within the EU context, where an international body encourages and legitimizes transnational organizations and facilitates their institutionalization and positioning within a larger framework. Beyond this set of actors, the CBSS has developed relations with the main financial institutions operating in the subregion. The Council has also been involved in providing ideas, political impulses and solutions to the many infrastructural problems in areas such as transport, telecommunications and energy.

THE CBSS'S ORGANIZATIONAL STRUCTURE

The CBSS was established with the intention that it would be supported organizationally by the country holding the chair each year. The same practical principle of one country acting as chair and providing organizational support was also adopted for the Council's working groups. Over time and as the load of the working groups has increased, it has been necessary to enlist more secretarial support and to address the issue of sustaining activities and maintaining consistency as the chair rotates between succeeding member states. The introduction of a troika mechanism (with the previous and next chairs working with the current chair) has given longer preparation time to the incoming Foreign Minister and Ministry.

The absence of a secretariat has not been an obstacle to building up smaller support structures nationally. Despite the original intention of avoiding any permanent institutional structure, the issue was raised during Sweden's tenure of the chair in 1995-96. Although German Chancellor Helmut Kohl rejected a proposal to create a CBSS common structure or secretariat at the Visby summit, he nevertheless accepted a Swedish offer to establish a support group within Sweden providing services to the state chairing the CBSS. During 1997, a majority of ministers expressed themselves in favour of a small secretariat and the issue was under consideration by senior officials. At the 1997 CBSS Foreign Ministers meeting, only Sweden expressed interest in hosting such a secretariat.

Besides the troika mechanism assisting the current chair, the maintenance of CBSS affairs between the meetings of Foreign Ministers lies in the hands of a Committee of Senior Officials (CSO). It appears that this is the central locus in the overall operation of the CBSS, as the CSO meets relatively frequently (for example, meeting nine times during 1995-96).

In order to undertake its operational work, the Council has also established three working groups on:
- Assistance to democratic institutions;
- Economic cooperation;
- Nuclear and radiation safety.

THE CBSS AND SECURITY

When discussing subregional security matters one might expect that the CBSS would be a rather marginal actor. There is no consensus on subregional security and stability, although this is the declared purpose of most individual national policies. At the same time, the problem of managing subregional security and stability under conditions of political change and transition cannot be separated from the general European issues of military strategic stability, cooperative security and the contributions of the various larger, interlocking institutions.

The security dialogue in the Baltic subregion is increasingly divided between two tendencies. Public declarations on the part of all the governments in the subregion indicate this dichotomy. A quotation from the commander of Latvia's armed forces typifies such reasoning:

> the military threat is only one and probably not the most immediate danger. Security depends on defence against political, economic and criminal threats as well as a number of specific causes for concern such as illegal migration, and the illegal activities of anti-government groups, foreign intelligence services and certain retired military officers...

But if these threats could not be properly addressed by peaceful means, economic growth and international cooperation, concluded the commander, then a military threat could become a danger that should not be ignored:

> Thus, Latvia's security posture must also include a military deterrent and defence elements and... a serious military threat would require the assistance of Western security organizations.

Latvia is not alone in adopting such an approach. The Russian Federation has similarly adopted an overall security strategy which combines different instruments, a peculiar mixture of two strategic concepts emphasizing traditional power politics on the one hand and cooperative interaction with the external environment on the other. The latter substrategy calls for cooperative security and underlines the importance of non-military aspects of security and of organizational bulwarks against fragmentation and civil instabilities. The twenty-seven members, associate members, partners and observers of the Western European Union (WEU) have also agreed that 'a comprehensive approach should underlie the concept of security and that cooperative mechanisms should be applied in order to promote security and stability in the whole of the continent'.

So, traditional, intergovernmental security concerns remain, focused on issues such as armaments, force deployments, security guarantees, offensive versus defensive intentions and the capabilities of identifiable, rational actors. These 'hard security' concerns, however, are supplemented by new phenomena rooted in problems such as social and ethnic tensions, neglect of human rights, discontented minorities and uncontrolled violence spilling over national borders. Such challenges and trends call for cooperative security and the development of a new range of policy instruments. Hence, a second agenda of 'soft security' has added new features to the overall understanding of security in the Baltic subregion. This concept is rich and elastic. It comprises support for feeble democratic institutions and administrative structures, the propping up of virgin sovereignty claims and the safeguarding of secure and controlled borders. A wide gap between the temptations of quick profit and the likelihood of punishment, further, has exacerbated instability by encouraging transnational organized crime (for example, 'people smuggling', the trafficking of nuclear materials and 'black market' trading).

Two aspects prevail in the promotion of soft security within the Baltic subregion. One is straightforward and hardly contentious: there is a widely recognized need for transnational cooperation on 'civic security' as a goal in itself. The second aspect acknowledges the potential security implications of civic vulnerabilities: if they are not properly handled, such problems may escalate, endangering traditional security. Hence, one can discern an implicit theory among many national decision-makers, couched in terms of calls for stability: under certain conditions, should pre-emptive actions and conflict prevention not succeed, a 'chain of events' could be set in motion and dismal alternatives might follow. At this point, consensus on how to define and where to locate the threshold between 'hard' and 'soft' security ends. Hence, there is much scope for institutional innovation and measures that could forestall crises and minimize the disruptive consequences of instability.

Against this background, how can the contribution of the CBSS to Baltic security be assessed? First, one can note that a direct attempt to introduce security issues onto the CBSS's agenda was made when Poland forwarded a proposal in 1994 to discuss security within the CBSS. The three Baltic states have also pressed for the direct inclusion of security issues within the CBSS, but changed their minds in 1996-97, fearing that such a step might detract from their efforts to integrate themselves with NATO and obtain security assurances from the Western powers. The idea that 'hard' aspects of security should be discussed in the Council has not received widespread support. The Nordic countries and Germany have preferred to push such contentious issues to the side-lines, arguing that discussions on other, practical matters might be impeded by trying to address 'hard' security issues. Addressing security in terms of direct state interests might also accentuate the different positions of the Nordic countries with regard to security guarantees (both as beneficiaries of such guarantees and as possible providers of guarantees to others) and thereby undermine their willingness to undertake joint commitments with regard to subregional cooperation. The Baltic Sea states have also maintained this position within the OSCE, opposing discussions on and proposals for subregional Confidence- and Security-Building Measures within that framework. The conclusion appears to be that the CBSS members favour subregional cooperation but not the subregionalization of security.

One can note, however, traces of the subregionalization of security in channels and contexts outside of the CBSS. Norwegian, Danish and (from 1997) Swedish proposals to hold joint military exercises or at least sea rescue operations with Russia are a concrete manifestation of the often declared policy that cooperation should be built with Russia and not against it. NATO – on the initiative of the United States – has invited all Baltic riparian countries to participate in annual, joint naval exercises (entitled BALTOP) to improve sea rescue competence. Such exercises have precedents, but the new context links the transatlantic dimension of security to subregional naval cooperation. Swedish pledges not only to participate in but also to lead PfP exercises bear witness to that country's ambition to play a leading role in the Baltic subregion but also confirm that NATO's new instruments are something different from collective defence obligations. Thus, through the backdoor of PfP and through actions 'in the spirit of PfP' a platform for military cooperation between Baltic Sea countries has been established.

Within the CBSS, in contrast, efforts have been made to circumvent direct security questions by focusing on indirect, non-traditional security issues and by introducing related measures onto the subregional agenda. The omission of certain sensitive subjects from the Council's competence by defining them as falling outside its remit did not prevent the Council from noting and even evaluating certain security relevant subregional events in the statements from the annual Foreign Ministers meetings. As a rule, however, interventions by ministers have respected the confines of the Council's mandate. Russian criticism of the Baltic states desire to join NATO, for example, has been forwarded at press conferences and outside of the discussions proper.

Given the ambiguous nature of the various security issues in the Baltic subregion and the difficulty of separating different issues in the transition processes, these developments are not astonishing. The concept of security in the Baltic subregion has turned out to be quite elastic. Gradually, a practice has evolved where so-called 'soft' security issues are dealt with by the CBSS. The frontier, however, is constantly moving. In 1996, the concept of 'civic security' was introduced, endorsed and explored in the deliberations of the Council. With the purpose of furthering cooperation in such areas, the term 'civic security' denotes, inter alia, issues such as immigration, asylum, border control and combating organized crime. The most concrete expression of this attempt to address 'soft' or 'civic' security is the establishment of a task force on organized crime (chaired by Sweden in 1996-97). The origins of this effort go back to the Visby summit, where the issue was taken up by Chancellor Kohl. Kohl's initiative was supported by other Baltic Sea leaders and the meeting immediately endorsed a proposal to create a pragmatic and instant channel for dealing with a growing problem. The task force is composed of personal representatives of the Prime Ministers, but is associated with the structure of the Council itself.

THE EU DIMENSION

As was noted earlier, the EU has emerged as an important actor in the Baltic Sea subregion in the post-Cold War era. The EU's growing engagement in the Baltic has included an important and direct role in the CBSS. As a founder member, the European Commission has been actively involved in the Council since its inception. The Commission is also involved in other aspects of subregional cooperation, acting on the behalf of the EU member states in convention-based functional institutions. In 1997, for example, representatives of the Commission held the chair in the Helsinki Commission for Protection of the Marine Environment and in the Gdansk Commission for the Management of Fisheries.

The bedrock of the EU's presence, however, is made up of its series of bilateral relations with individual Baltic Sea states. This imposes certain constraints on the Union's relations with and involvement in the Baltic, partly working against a subregion-wide approach. This problem – and the need for greater engagement in the Baltic – was recognized by the Union and the Commission, which then moved to frame a more subregionally oriented approach. The Commission's Baltic Sea Initiative, presented to the Visby summit in 1996, in particular acknowledged the need for measures targeted at subregional conditions at large. The initiative outlined proposals for intensifying subregional coordination and for a more concerted use of the EU's main structural programmes (Intereg, PHARE and TACIS). Borders in the Baltic Sea subregion, however, often consist of lines in the water between countries belonging to different EU target categories. This problem prompted an adaptation of the EU's policies and efforts to identify and remove Union/Commission bureaucratic hurdles to transfrontier cooperation. In a more general sense, however, the Union/Commission and specific programmes such as Intereg, PHARE and TACIS are important programmatic instruments supporting the transition process and strengthening stability and democracy in the Baltic Sea subregion.

Hence, the Union is a centre of gravity in many walks of subregional life. The representative of the Commission occupies a 'king pin' position between the actions of the CBSS and the Union's institutions in Brussels. Security through integration – the basic philosophy underlying the origins of the Union – is much supported by Nordic states as a long range policy likely to bring many benefits and to prevent potential threats.

CONCLUSION: APPRAISING A SUBREGION

The birth of the CBSS and the intensification of normal interactions between the societies of the Baltic Sea rim represent an institutionalization of a political space which almost nobody forecast a decade ago. Baltic Sea subregionalism is thus not only a potent factor in policy-making, it is also a challenge for analysis and understanding. Perhaps one can say that Baltic Sea subregionalism was not initially driven by security concerns *per se*. Other motives prevailed. For this reason, a short assessment of the nature of subregion-building around the Baltic will improve our evaluation of the role of security in that wider context.

A non state project? The notion of a Baltic Sea subregion was initially an idea competing with many traditional national problems and state instruments because it delineated a terrain and concerns that did not coincide with established states, nations and interests. One point of departure is the coastal connection. Such a criterion cuts through Russian, German and sometimes also Polish territories by confining eligibility to certain parts of the national territories (that is to say, coastal regions and their hinterlands). Much cooperation within the Baltic subregion is based on non-state ideas, where the foundation for action and organization is a community of interests between sub-state regions, municipalities and islands. The intergovernmental aspect, however, is also secured through the CBSS. Compared to other subregions in Europe, the Baltic Sea area has within a short period of time developed a rich and distinct transnational infrastructure conducive to community building and stability.

The Baltic Sea is a subregion of variable contours and hence part of a Europe of overlapping circles of cooperation. The boundaries of the Baltic formation are not fixed but display variable contours, depending on the criteria or functional need underpinning them. One may discern a core area where loosely bounded, although not irreversibly fixed, territorial references overlap. Subregions are not static: they are subject to contentious disputes, changes and modification.

Underpinning the intergovernmental, state project of the CBSS is a political authority at odds with a conventional view of Baltic Sea realities. The composite area of the CBSS stretches (theoretically) from Thule/Nuuk/Reykjavik to Vladivostock. There is no restriction on the spatial domain inserted into the Council's terms of reference. Only the accompanying declaration of the founding meeting brings out the context, defining the Council's role as to serve 'as a regional forum to focus on needs for intensified cooperation and coordination among the Baltic Sea states'.[25] Thus, the issue of which states are eligible to join has not been fully settled. Iceland was accepted after Nordic lobbying and against German inclinations. Belarus has made overtures to become an observer and its possible membership is supported by certain CBSS members.

At the same time, discussions on sectoral/functional issues appear to proceed pragmatically, based upon a consensual but variable understanding of the subregion. Shifting boundaries are evident from a series of cooperative undertakings. Ministers of physical planning include the Kola Peninsula and northern Norway within their discussions. Cooperation on migration questions includes Belarus. The basis for cooperation on environmental protection includes a functional and widely accepted definition of the Baltic Sea drainage area encompassing 14 different national territories, including Norway, the Czech Republic, Slovakia and Belarus alongside the Baltic riparian states. Only the three Baltic states are entirely within the CBSS's boundaries. In all the other countries involved, subregional management needs and territorial authority patterns do not coincide.

The balance in the subregion has changed. This conclusion is quite clear. The prospects opened up by Estonia and Poland's likely accession to the EU in the first round of that organization's eastern enlargement and Polish entry into NATO within a few years implies that more states in the Baltic subregion will be drawn into closer relations with these two core structures. EU enlargement harbours many benefits, but it could create new cleavages and divisions in the subregion, and especially in relations with Latvia, Lithuania and Russia. It will also bring Estonia closer to the Nordic mould. NATO expansion which does not embrace the three Baltic states is on the one hand likely to result in intensified Nordic-Baltic 'five-plus-three' relations, but will also put an extra burden on Finland and Sweden's non-aligned postures and call for a reassuring American engagement short of formal security guarantees. Under these conditions, heavy responsibilities will fall upon all members of the CBSS to manage a divided economic area and a distinct although not entirely separate strategic home in northwestern Europe.

5 The Visegrad Group and Beyond: Security Cooperation in Central Europe

Andrew Cottey

Since the Soviet bloc collapsed in 1989, the strategic priority of the countries of Central and Eastern Europe has been their integration with the West, in particularly joining the North Atlantic Treaty Organization (NATO) and the European Union (EU). The established democracies and market economies of Western Europe and North America represent the model to which the countries of Central and Eastern Europe aspire. They see NATO and the EU as the only bodies capable of providing them with credible security guarantees and economic security. For them, membership of NATO and the EU will both symbolize their full integration with the West and underpin the democratization and reform of their societies and economies. In short, the countries of Central and Eastern Europe are seeking to return to the democratic Europe from which they were separated by forty years of Soviet domination. At the same time, they have sought to normalize and re-build relations with each other and with their Western and former Soviet neighbours. For the most part, this has taken place in the context of bilateral relationships: through the negotiation of state treaties guaranteeing existing borders and minority rights and committing states to develop cooperative relations; and through various more practical forms of bilateral political, economic and military cooperation.

Within this strategic context of integration with the West and the normalization and re-building of bilateral ties, however, the countries of Central and Eastern Europe have also engaged in the various subregional groups which this book examines. One of the more prominent of these, particularly in the early 1990s, was the Central European 'Visegrad group' – established by Poland, Czechoslovakia and Hungary to support their integration with the West. During 1991-92, the Visegrad group emerged as an important feature of Central and Eastern Europe's post-communist landscape. It helped to define the three Central European states as a distinct group and the primary candidates for integration with Western institutions. It also facilitated bilateral political, economic and military cooperation amongst these states and gave birth to the Central European

Free Trade Agreement (CEFTA). The Visegrad group, however, differed significantly from the larger subregional groups which emerged at this time. Unlike the Barents Euro-Arctic Council, the Council of Baltic Sea States and the Black Sea Economic Cooperation, it included neither major Western states nor Russia. Instead, it was characterised by its small size, by the Central European states' relative homogeneity, by their shared sense of historic and geo-strategic vulnerability resulting from their location between Germany/the West and the (former) Soviet Union, and by their common goal of integration with the West. As a result, the central role of the Visegrad group and its offspring CEFTA was to promote their members integration with the West.

After the break-up of Czechoslovakia at the end of 1992, however, cooperation within the Visegrad group framework declined. By 1996-97, the group had largely disappeared from the diplomatic map. The end of the Visegrad group was symbolically confirmed in July 1997 when NATO invited Poland, the Czech Republic and Hungary – but not Slovakia – to join the Alliance. This chapter examines the Visegrad group, exploring its rise and decline, its relationship with the EU and NATO and possible lessons for similar efforts to build security cooperation amongst small, homogenous groups of states elsewhere in post-communist Europe. The chapter also examines the prospects for post-Visegrad security cooperation in Central and Eastern Europe, arguing that a new and more complex 'variable geometry' of security cooperation is emerging in the area.

THE EMERGENCE AND EVOLUTION OF THE VISEGRAD GROUP

The first high level proposals for post-Cold War cooperation amongst the then three Central European states came from Czechoslovak President Vaclav Havel in January 1990. Speaking to the Polish Sejm and Senate, Havel called for the 'coordination of policies' and 'synchronization of steps' on the road to Europe, inviting representatives of the Polish and Hungarian governments to Bratislava to discuss what 'institutional forms' cooperation might take. Poland, Czechoslovakia and Hungary, Havel argued, 'should not mutually compete' to join West European institutions, but should rather 'fill with something meaningful the great political vacuum that arose in Central Europe after the break-up of the Habsburg Empire'.[1] Havel and Czechoslovak Foreign Minister Jiri Dienstbier, however, made clear that they were not interested in establishing a Central European grouping separate from the West, but rather wanted to cooperate in joining West European institutions.[2] Accepting Havel's proposal, the

Presidents, Prime Ministers and senior officials from the three countries met in Bratislava in April 1990. The meeting, however, was marred by serious differences over what could be expected from cooperation, the implications of German unification and the rights of the Hungarian minority in Slovakia. The Poles and Hungarians were unable to accept a Czechoslovak proposed trilateral declaration. President Havel later conceded that the summit had been characterized by 'improvization', 'speedy preparation' and 'inexperience'.[3]

The failure of the Bratislava meeting also reflected more substantive differences between the three states. At the time, Poland, Czechoslovakia and Hungary were at different stages in their domestic and foreign policy transitions. In Poland, although Solidarity was the dominant force domestically, the Communist Party retained control of the Presidency and the Defence and Interior Ministries. Poland's primary security concern was German unification (particularly the need to secure a permanent German commitment to the Oder-Neisse border) – leading it to support (at least temporarily) a continued alliance with the Soviet Union. In Czechoslovakia, the 'Velvet Revolution' had led to the rapid removal of communists from the highest levels of government. Czechoslovak security policy was now focused on developing the Conference on Security and Cooperation in Europe (CSCE) into a pan-European collective security body. The Hungarian delegation of the still-ruling Communist Party had been fundamentally weakened by its overwhelming defeat in the election the day prior to the Bratislava meeting. While Hungary's communists maintained cautious support for the Warsaw Pact, the victorious Hungarian Democratic Forum (MDF) opposition sought a rapid Hungarian withdrawal from the alliance. In short, there was no strong basis for cooperation at the time of the Bratislava meeting.

In the second half of 1990, however, the three countries domestic transitions and foreign policies began to converge. The victory of the MDF in the Hungarian elections, the victory of Civic Forum and Public Against Violence in the June 1990 Czechoslovak elections and the election of Solidarity leader Lech Walesa as Polish President in December 1990 meant that all three countries now had fully democratically elected governments. Walesa and Hungarian Prime Minister Joszef Antall both supported Havel's earlier call for cooperation between their countries.[4] The Central European states' security policies also converged. With German recognition of the Oder-Neisse border (confirmed in the September 1990 'two-plus-four' treaty and an October 1990 Polish-German border treaty), Polish concerns over German unification receded and Poland began to re-orient itself towards the West. As it became clear that the CSCE would not rapidly develop into a pan-European collective security body, Czechoslovakia sought more rapid integration with the West. Hungary's new MDF government signalled that its priority was integration with the West.

At the same time, the West - particularly the European Community (EC) – began to treat the three Central European states as a group. In September 1990, the EC's Council of Ministers authorized the negotiation of Association Agreements with Poland, Czechoslovakia and Hungary – based on a European Commission assessment that only these states had made sufficient progress in political and economic reforms to warrant the opening of such negotiations. The special status of Poland, Czechoslovakia and Hungary was confirmed when they became the first Central and Eastern European states to join the Council of Europe in 1990 and 1991.

Perhaps the most important catalyst for the emergence of the Visegrad group, however, was the situation in the Soviet Union. From mid-1990, conservative forces within the Soviet Union, advocating a continued Soviet sphere of influence in Central and Eastern Europe, gained increasing power. The Soviet Union refused to reform or dissolve the Warsaw Pact and warned that it might use Central and Eastern Europe's dependence on Soviet oil and gas to assert its influence.[5] Discussions within the Warsaw Pact 'brought the three states together in a negotiating environment that enabled them to clarify the commonalties in their security needs and juxtapose these needs to those of Moscow'.[6]

Against this background, the Central European states gradually began to cooperate on security issues. In September 1990, the three countries' civilian Deputy Defence Ministers met in Poland to discuss the de-politicization of their armed forces, agreeing to exchange information on the social and human aspects of military reform. This was the first meeting of defence officials from Warsaw Pact countries to which the Soviet Union was not invited.[7] In October 1990, the three countries' Deputy Foreign Ministers met in Warsaw, agreeing to create a consultative committee at deputy foreign ministerial level to 'facilitate the solution of common problems in the region' and establishing working groups to implement regular meetings and prepare a trilateral declaration.[8] At the Paris CSCE summit in November 1990, Havel, Antall and Polish Prime Minister Tadeusz Mazowiecki met, agreeing to intensify cooperation.[9] After a further meeting of Deputy Foreign Ministers in December it was announced that a summit would be held in January in Visegrad near Budapest.[10]

The emerging cooperation was given a further boost by the January 1991 Soviet military crack-down in the Baltic republics. The Central European states suggested that their countries might jointly withdraw from the Warsaw Pact.[11] Czechoslovakia and Hungary, having already secured agreements on the withdrawal of Soviet forces from their territory, appeared to support this position. Poland, facing difficult negotiations with the Soviet Union on the withdrawal of its forces from Polish territory, opposed withdrawing from the Pact.[12] Meeting in Budapest in January, the three countries' Foreign Ministers reached a compromise, agreeing that the Pact's military structures should be abolished by 1 July 1991 and the organization dissolved within a year, supporting the independence aspirations of the Baltic republics and condemning the Soviet intervention. Implicitly, they threatened to withdraw from the Pact if the Soviet Union refused to dismantle it. Hungarian Foreign Minister Geza Jeszenszky warned that 'if this should fail, we shall step on the path of independent action'. The three Foreign Ministers also expressed their support for the Western-led coalition against Iraq in the Gulf war, clearly indicating that they intended to pursue pro-Western policies.[13] Faced with a *de facto* ultimatum, Soviet President Mikhail Gorbachev wrote to the three countries' leaders, agreeing to dismantle the Pact's military structures by 1 April.[14]

Havel, Walesa and Antall met in February 1991 at Visegrad. The declaration from the summit stated that:

> The similarity of the situation which arose in the course of the last decades compels the three countries to work towards the achievement of essentially identical goals:
> The restoration in full of each state's independence, democracy and freedom.
> ...The total integration into the European political, economic, security, and legislative order.
> As both their goals and the routes towards the realization of these goals are largely the same, the three neighbouring states are confronted by similar tasks in a wide range of fields. The coordination of their efforts – bearing in mind their distinct national characteristics – increases the chance of achieving the desired results and brings closer the realization of their goals.[15]

The three leaders expressed their 'common determination to ...harmonize their efforts to foster cooperation and close relations with European institutions' and agreed to 'consult on questions concerning security'.[16]

Thus, the Visegrad group was born. The Central European states moved quickly to develop more substantive cooperation. Consultative meetings were held at ministerial, deputy ministerial and working group level to develop coordinated policies toward the Soviet Union, NATO, the EC, the Council of Europe, the then-Hexagonale group (which later became the Central European Initiative), the crisis in Yugoslavia and military reform issues.[17]

With the demise of the Warsaw Pact, the Soviet Union began to press the Central and Eastern European states to sign new bilateral treaties with 'security clauses' which would restrict their foreign policy independence and commit them to close relations with the Soviet Union. Although Romania signed such a treaty in April 1991, the three Central European states coordinated their opposition to the Soviet demands, successfully resisting Soviet pressure. The three countries also coordinated their response to the August 1991 Soviet coup. A meeting of Deputy Foreign Ministers in Warsaw drew up a joint assessment of the situation; established a deputy ministerial standing committee to coordinate policies, particularly on security issues; resolved to coordinate policies on bilateral treaties with the Soviet Union and securing supplies of raw materials from the Soviet Union; and set up a working group on migration to assess the dangers of an influx of refugees.[18]

The Visegrad states also began to develop a joint approach towards the West. By early 1991 all three states were pursuing the same policies toward the EC and NATO: functional integration in the short-to-medium term, membership in the longer term. When the Visegrad group Deputy Foreign Ministers met during the August 1991 Soviet coup, they agreed to coordinate policies on association negotiations with the EC and agreed the key points of letters to be sent to Western governments by Havel, Walesa and Antall pressing for faster negotiation of the Association Agreements.[19] After the Soviet coup, the three countries increased their diplomatic pressure for more rapid integration with the West, coordinating their approaches to the EC and NATO. The parallel negotiation of Association Agreements with the EC gave the three countries greater leverage, especially in pressing the EC to remove some of the more protectionist elements of the agreements.

There can be little doubt that the Visegrad states' concerted pressure forced the West to address their concerns more directly. By June 1991 NATO Foreign Ministers were declaring that the Alliance's security was 'inseparably linked to that of all other states in Europe' and that their 'freedom from any form of coercion or intimidation' was a 'direct and material concern' of the Alliance.[20] NATO Secretary-General Manfred Woerner warned that any Soviet interference in Central and Eastern Europe would have 'grave consequences'.[21] During the Soviet coup, NATO leaders re-iterated their conviction that the Alliance's security was 'inseparably linked to that of all other states in Europe, particularly to that of the emerging democracies', stated that they expected the Soviet Union 'to respect the integrity and security of all states in Europe' and committed themselves to 'further strengthening' ties with the new democracies.[22] EC Foreign Ministers also agreed to accelerate the negotiation of the Association Agreements.[23]

Cooperation also developed in relation to defence reforms. The Polish, Czechoslovak and Hungarian Defence Ministers met in August 1991, agreeing on a system of regular consultation at all levels of the military and examining possibilities for closer cooperation in military technology, production and procurement. During the Soviet coup later in August 1991, the Polish, Czechoslovak and Hungarian militaries maintained constant liaison and defence officials were involved in the trilateral crisis meeting in Warsaw. Further discussions were held at Deputy Defence Minister level in November 1991. Bilateral military cooperation agreements were also concluded between the three states in the spring of 1991, committing them to consult on defence reforms. The Central European governments stressed, however, that these were cooperation agreements, not military alliances.[24]

Thus, in the six months after the Visegrad summit, substantial cooperation had developed. By the autumn of 1991, President Walesa was stating that 'today ...Warsaw does not do anything without Prague or Budapest ...we are progressing on the same wagon in politics, so we should place greater emphasis on economic and military cooperation'.[25] The growing cooperation between the three states was confirmed in October when Havel, Walesa and Antall met for a second time in Cracow. The declaration from the summit described their cooperation as 'an essential contribution in shaping a new democratic international order in the region'; emphasized the need to fill the 'strategic vacuum' left by the collapse of the Warsaw Pact; and confirmed the three countries' determination to 'participate in Europe's political, economic, and institutional systems as well as in its system of security'. The leaders called for the 'institutionalization' of ties with NATO, the 'extension' of ties with the Western European Union (WEU) and their integration with the EC's foreign policy decision-making process. Committing themselves to a new level of cooperation, they agreed to 'accord their position' in association negotiations with the EC and undertake a 'common policy' toward the Soviet Union. The three countries' Foreign Ministers also released a statement at the Cracow summit demanding the 'upgrading of contacts between their countries and NATO', including their 'direct involvement ...in the activities of NATO'. [26]

Cooperation continued after the Cracow summit. The Visegrad states' ambassadors to Germany joined forces to argue that their countries should be more quickly integrated into the EC and appealed for closer links with NATO and the WEU. In January 1992, Czechoslovak Foreign Minister Jiri Dientsbier announced that the three countries had drawn up a joint plan which would involve Western purchases of their products as aid to the Soviet Union. In March 1992 Visegrad group Defence Ministers met in Budapest, discussing military cooperation, coordination of defence industries, plans for a joint air defence system and a common approach to NATO. Later that month, the three countries' ambassadors to NATO met in Brussels, calling for a 'privileged' relationship between their three countries and the Alliance. The three countries also chose to recognise the independence of Bosnia-Herzegovina together in April 1992.[27]

The Visegrad cooperation was confirmed when the Central European leaders met for a third time in Prague in May 1992. The statement from the summit defined the three countries' cooperation as 'a new pattern of relations in Central Europe ...a stabilizing factor'; reaffirmed the three states' desire to cooperate in establishing a new European security system; stated their desire to establish political dialogue with the EC and cooperate with the EU on its future common foreign and security policy; confirmed their desire to establish institutionalised relations with and eventually become members of the WEU; stressed the need to develop 'qualitatively new' relations with and become full members of NATO; confirmed their support for the CSCE and proposed establishing CSCE peacekeeping forces; and, stated that they wished to be involved in aid to former Soviet states and pressed the former Soviet states to accept the Conventional Armed Forces in Europe (CFE) Treaty and prevent nuclear proliferation. By this point, however, foreign and security policy cooperation was relatively well established and the Prague statement noted the need for 'special attention' to economic cooperation, the creation of a free trade zone, transfrontier cooperation and contacts between citizens. The Visegrad leaders also issued a separate message to EC leaders, confirming their countries' desire to join the future EU. The three countries' Foreign Ministers issued a further statement endorsing transfrontier cooperation between their countries and agreeing to establish a working group on the issue. Havel, Walesa and Antall declared the Prague summit their most successful to date.[28]

Cooperation continued to intensify after the Prague summit. In the autumn of 1992, there were meetings of the Visegrad states defence ministry and military officials, discussing various practical aspects of cooperation.[29] The extension of cooperation into the economic sphere was confirmed in December 1992, when, after difficult negotiations, the CEFTA agreement was signed.[30] The West also continued to treat the three countries as a distinct group, with Central European Prime Ministers meeting as a group with EC leaders for the first time in October 1992.[31] In short, by the second half of 1992, the Visegrad group had become a significant feature of the new international environment in Central and Eastern Europe.

THE END OF THE VISEGRAD GROUP

The break-up of Czechoslovakia at the end of 1992, however, had major implications for the Visegrad group. Czech Prime Minister Vaclav Klaus was an opponent of the Visegrad group, viewing it as 'an artificial process created by the West'.[32] Klaus believed that the Czech Republic was more advanced than its neighbours in establishing democracy and a market economy and would be ready to join the EC before them. While accepting CEFTA, he opposed a common approach to the EC, fearing that close Visegrad group cooperation might delay the Czech Republic's integration with the West.[33] Slovakia's independence and Slovak Prime Minister Vladimir Meciar's populist, authoritarian and nationalist rhetoric raised fears about the prospects for democratization, market economic reforms and continued support for integration with the West in that country. Slovakia's independence and Meciar's nationalism also exacerbated tensions with Hungary over the Gabcikovo-Nagymaros border region hydro-electric project and the situation of the Hungarian minority in Slovakia. In both Hungary and the Czech Republic there were also fears that political instability and economic problems in Poland might prolong, or even prevent, that country's integration with the EC and that being associated with Poland might delay or prevent their own entry into the EC.[34]

Cooperation within the Visegrad group, however, did not break down immediately. The Polish, Hungarian and Slovak governments indicated their desire for continued cooperation, including a coordinated approach to the West.[35] Despite Klaus's rhetoric, the Czech government proved to some extent willing to continue cooperation in practice. In June 1993 the four states jointly appealed to the EC to 'set the date and define conditions for full membership in the Community'.[36] The four countries' Deputy Defence Ministers and Chiefs of General Staffs met in September 1993, agreeing to develop a programme for supplying each other with arms and spare parts.[37] Bilateral military cooperation also continued, with Poland, the Czech Republic and Hungary concluding new military cooperation agreements with Slovakia. The West also continued to treat the now four Central European states as a group, signalling implicit support for the Visegrad process. At its June 1993 Copenhagen summit the EU referred to the Visegrad states as a group, supporting their cooperation.[38]

Serious divisions within the Visegrad group emerged, however, when NATO introduced its Partnership for Peace (PfP) programme in 1994. The United States organized a summit with the four states in January 1994 in Prague to signal its support for them. With Poland, Hungary and Slovakia advocating a coordinated approach to NATO, Czech Defence Minister Antonin Baudys refused to attend a meeting with his Visegrad counterparts to discuss such an approach. Czech Foreign Minister Josef Zieleniec stated that 'we don't believe in organising lobbies or pressure groups to knock on doors'.[39] The Czech government argued that while it supported free trade and economic integration within the Visegrad group, it wanted to maintain autonomy in its dealings with the West.[40] Although the four countries' Heads of State did meet as a group with US President Bill Clinton, this reflected the fact that the Czech government had little alternative but to accept the US proposed meeting. Indicating the growing divisions within the group, a public walkabout by Presidents Clinton and Havel led Poland to accuse the Czechs of hijacking the summit.[41] The public Czech rejection of a coordinated approach to NATO signalled a major break-down in cooperation within the Visegrad group. This was confirmed in March 1994 when Klaus again rejected calls for closer Visegrad cooperation, arguing that the Czech Republic was 'far ahead of all other countries in the region'.[42] In April 1994 Poland and Hungary formally applied for EU membership and the Czech Republic refused to join a common application.[43]

The break-up of Czechoslovakia also resulted in intensified Hungarian-Slovak tensions. From mid-1992, tensions grew over the rights of Slovakia's Hungarian minority (one tenth of the country's population, located largely in region's bordering Hungary), negotiations over a new bilateral treaty (with the Hungarian MDF government linking recognition of the current border to guarantees of minority rights) and the joint Gabcikovo-Nagymaros hydro-electric project (with differences over the need for and environmental consequences of the project). Although the

Gabcikovo-Nagymaros dispute was (at least temporarily) resolved by EC mediation in the autumn of 1992, differences over Hungarian minority rights escalated after Slovakia gained independence. In the summer of 1993, Hungary opposed Slovakia's bid to join the Council of Europe, arguing that Slovakia's treatment of its Hungarian minority violated Council of Europe norms and broader democratic standards. This was a significant set-back for cooperation: for the first time since 1989 one Visegrad state was actively opposing another's membership of a major Western institution. Hungary was subsequently persuaded to abstain from opposing Slovakia's membership of the Council of Europe. The Socialist government which came to power in Hungary in 1994 abandoned its predecessors' policy of opposing Slovakia and Romania's membership of Western institutions and a Hungarian-Slovak state treaty was signed in 1995. Nevertheless, tensions continue between the two states (particularly over minority rights).

Slovakia's independence also had larger consequences for the Visegrad group. The authoritarian and nationalist rhetoric and policies of Prime Minister Meciar, including attempts to constrain the independence and freedom of the media, pressure against political opponents, reported corruption in the privatization process and attempts to weaken the position of the Slovak President Michal Kovac and undermine the independence of the constitutional court, seriously undermined Slovakia's progress in democratization. As a consequence, Slovakia received a series of official demarches from the EU, the European Parliament and the US.[44] The Slovak government continued to state its support for joining the EU and NATO. However, Slovakia's close ties with Russia, cooperation with Romania (echoing the inter-war 'Little Entente' against Hungary) and unwillingness to implement reforms likely to be needed for EU and NATO membership raised serious questions about Meciar and his allies commitment to integration with the West. The extent to which Slovakia had fallen behind its Visegrad partners was made clear in the summer of 1997 when it was excluded from the first wave of countries invited to join NATO and from the first group of countries which the European Commission recommended should be invited to join the EU. Slovakia, further, was the only country excluded from the Commission's recommended group because it did not met the democratic standards necessary. Slovakia's exclusion from the first wave of countries invited to join NATO also provoked tensions with the Czech Republic. Thus, by the mid-1990s, it was increasingly clear that Slovakia was 'falling behind' its Central European neighbours, thereby undermining the basis for quadrilateral cooperation.

The decline of the Visegrad group was also influenced by the break-up of the Soviet Union, which radically changed the geo-strategic situation in Central Europe. The Baltic states, Belarus and Ukraine now lay between Central Europe and Russia, greatly reducing the region's vulnerability to Russian pressure and effectively removing one of the main external rationales for the Visegrad group. The Central European states also now faced significantly different situations on their eastern borders. Poland bordered Russia (along the Kaliningrad region), Lithuania, Belarus and Ukraine. Slovakia and Hungary bordered only Ukraine. The Czech Republic (since the break-up of Czechoslovakia) now bordered no former Soviet state. Given this situation – and the wider decline of the Visegrad group – it was hardly surprising that the Visegrad states ceased co-ordinating policies towards their former Soviet neighbours.

The break-down of cooperation within the Visegrad group also coincided with and was influenced by broader shifts in the dynamics of Central and Eastern European cooperation and integration with the West. Bulgaria and Romania's conclusion of Association Agreements with the EU in the spring of 1993 ended the Visegrad states' special status. This was confirmed in October 1994 when EU Foreign Ministers agreed that the ministers of the six Central and Eastern European associate states should join meetings of EU ministers, including annual meetings of Heads of States and six monthly meetings of Foreign Ministers, in preparation for eventual membership. At the same time, it became clear that both NATO and the EU would make their enlargement decisions on the basis of assessments of the individual merits of each Central and Eastern European country.[45] The accession of Slovenia and Romania to CEFTA in 1995 and 1997 also indicated that that group would expand beyond the four Visegrad states. In combination, these developments – but in particular Slovakia's falling behind the other Central European states in terms of democratization and prospects for NATO and EU membership – contributed to the end of the Visegrad group. As a consequence, by 1996-97, almost all cooperative activities between the four states as a single group had ceased.

THE VISEGRAD GROUP AND CENTRAL EUROPEAN SECURITY

Against the background of the evolution of the Visegrad group traced above, it is worth exploring what contribution the Visegrad group made to the security of the Central European states, how it related to NATO and the EU and what implications it had for other neighbouring states. Above all, cooperation within the Visegrad group strengthened the Central European states in their relations with their more powerful neighbours, the Soviet Union and the West (particularly the EC/EU and NATO). As was seen above, concerted pressure from the Visegrad group in 1991 effectively forced the Soviet leadership to accept the end of the Warsaw Pact and helped the Central European states resist Soviet demands for restrictive 'security clauses' in new bilateral treaties. More generally, the sense of a 'common cause' and mutual support reflected in and facilitated by the Visegrad group helped the Central European states to dismantle the broader structures of Soviet hegemony and communist rule in the immediate post-1989 years.

The Central European states also gained diplomatic influence vis-à-vis the West by coordinating their policies. From 1991 onwards, consistent pressure from the Central European states, including a number of joint Visegrad group statements, put the issues of EU and NATO enlargement firmly on the political agenda. The Central European states' consistent demands for the expansion and institutionalization of their ties with NATO put pressure on the Alliance to address their concerns. Coordination of policies enabled the Visegrad states to extract additional concessions during the negotiation of their Association Agreement with the EC.[46] Cooperation in the Visegrad group also demonstrated to the West that the Central European states were behaving 'responsibly' by cooperating with one another, thereby improving their prospects for integration. As Vaclav Havel observed in 1992:

> coordination has, above all, considerably helped all three countries in their entry into democratic European structures. The democratic world to a certain extent measures our trustworthiness by our ability to reach agreement. They consider us a troika.[47]

The Visegrad group's relations with NATO and the EU were, however, also characterized by a certain contradictions. For the Visegrad states, their mutual cooperation improved their prospects for integration with the West. At the same time, as expressed most strongly by Prime Minister Klaus but also by others in Central Europe, there was a perception that the Visegrad cooperation was to some extent imposed on the countries involved by the West. Within Central Europe, there were fears that the Visegrad group might be seen (at least in the West) as an alternative to NATO/EU membership and that involvement in the group might mean that its members had too wait until the 'slowest' among them was ready before they could join NATO or the EU. The West also sent a somewhat 'mixed message' by stating its support for such cooperation, to some extent treating the Visegrad states as a group, but also treating the Central and Eastern European states individually in terms of their relationships with and prospects for membership of NATO and the EU. As a consequence, the Visegrad groups' relations with NATO and the EU created both incentives and disincentives for subregional cooperation. By the second half of the 1990s, these contradictions were beginning to resolve themselves, as it became clear that NATO and the EU would make enlargement decisions on the basis of individual Central and Eastern European states readiness for NATO/EU membership and not their involvement in or membership of any particular subregional group: Nevertheless, if the EU and NATO wish to encourage subregional cooperation, the experience of the Visegrad-NATO/EU relationship does suggest one significant conclusion. Namely, that the EU and NATO need to make unambiguously clear that – while decisions on membership (and also on 'bilateral' relations NATO/EU and individual Central and Eastern European states) will be made on the basis of individual states behaviour – they strongly support subregional cooperation and see no contradiction between such cooperation and the earliest integration of Central and Eastern European states into NATO and the EU.

The Visegrad group also helped to promote political, economic and military cooperation and confidence-building in Central Europe. Given Central Europe's history, the emergence of the Visegrad group was in itself a signal that the three countries wished to put past disputes behind them, resolve their differences peacefully and support each others' integration with the West. The establishment of CEFTA was an important indication that cooperation would extend to the economic sphere. The substantive content of tri/quadrilateral cooperation was, however, more limited, with key issues often addressed bilaterally.[48] As was seen above, when Hungarian-Slovak tensions emerged they were managed through a combination of bilateral relations and pressure from the EU and NATO.

Similarly, most substantive military cooperation between the Central European states has taken place at the bilateral level (despite a quite large number of tri/quadrilateral meetings and a number of general commitments to cooperate in areas such as training, maintenance, procurement and joint air space control). The bilateral military cooperation agreements signed between the Visegrad states in the spring of 1991 committed Defence Ministers to consult on military doctrines, training and education, possible cooperation in weapons production, the de-politicization of their armed forces, maintaining their Soviet equipment and the possible use of training facilities in the partner country. The Polish-Czechoslovak and Czechoslovak-Hungarian treaties also included transparency provisions, including prior notification of troop movements into or within border regions.[49] A Hungarian-Slovak military cooperation agreement signed in 1993 included commitments to exchange information on large-scale troop movements, exchanges of military observers and co-ordinated air defence in border areas.

At a more fundamental level, the Visegrad group, CEFTA and the various forms of bilateral cooperation between the Central European states are helping to create a 'security community' in the area. At the same time, they are also facilitating the Central European states' functional and institutional integration with the wider Western 'security community'. In this sense, a 'security community' may be understood as an area where political, economic and military cooperation and integration have developed to the extent that war between the states of that region is inconceivable and all differences are resolved by peaceful means.[50] Such a security community, or 'zone of peace', has emerged in Western Europe since 1945. While the roots of security communities are a matter of debate, it appears that the combination of democratic politics, relative prosperity, free trade and institutionalized international cooperation facilitated the development of the Western security community after 1945. Since 1989, Central Europe has experienced a similar combination of trends resulting in the dual process of the emergence of a security community in Central Europe and the subregion's integration with the wider Western security community.[51] This process of security community building, however, is not yet complete - as the setbacks in democratization in Slovakia and continuing tensions between Hungary and Slovakia suggest.

The emergence of the Visegrad group also had implications for the Central European states' relations with their immediate neighbours. The declaration from the Visegrad summit stated that the three countries' 'cooperation in no way disrupts or limits their existing relations with other states, nor is it in any way directed against the interests of any other state'.[52] The Central European states consistently stressed that their cooperation was not a military alliance and was not directed against any other state. Nevertheless, the Visegrad group was, by its very nature, an exclusive grouping, defined by its members' desire to dismantle their Soviet bloc ties and integrate with the EU and NATO. Thus, the Soviet Union regarded the group with suspicion, seeing it as an anti-Soviet bloc. Romania and Bulgaria, in contrast, were wary of the group because it implicitly excluded them as primary candidates for integration with the West – particularly after Romania overtures to join the group were rebuffed.[53] Post-Soviet Ukraine, however, viewed the Visegrad group positively, seeing ties with its Visegrad neighbours as a means of consolidating its independence and facilitating its integration with the West. Some Ukrainian politicians suggested that their country might even join the Visegrad group.[54] Thus, the experience of the Visegrad group highlights two dilemmas of cooperation between small, relatively homogenous groups of states. First, such cooperation risks being seen – rightly or wrongly – as directed against those states not involved. Second, it risks being seen as delaying or excluding other neighbours from wider integration processes – particularly EU and NATO membership. With the decline of the Visegrad group, such issues have become less salient. Nevertheless, as discussed in the next chapter, other Central and Eastern European states have sought to join CEFTA in significant part because it is seen as a symbol of preparedness for integration with the West.

SUBREGIONAL COOPERATION IN CENTRAL AND EASTERN EUROPE: PROSPECTS FOR THE FUTURE?

The demise of the Visegrad group could be interpreted as a major – and somewhat worrying – break-down in subregional cooperation in Central and Eastern Europe – particularly as it was paralleled by NATO's July 1997 decision to invite only Poland, the Czech Republic and Hungary to join the Alliance in the 'first wave' and the European Commission's recommendation that EU accession negotiations be opened with only these countries and Slovenia and Estonia in the first place. Indeed, it remained possible that the first Central and Eastern European members of NATO and the EU might turn away from their neighbours, resulting in a new 'dividing line' and a break-down in cooperation in the region as a whole. As of 1997, however, such a development seemed unlikely. Those countries invited to join NATO (and likely to be invited to join the EU) appeared to be aware that such a break-down in cooperation was not in their interests, that they had a duty to intensify cooperation to ensure that new 'dividing lines' did not emerge and were making significant efforts towards these ends.[55] What appeared to be emerging in Central and Eastern Europe in the late 1990s was a new and more complex 'variable geometry' of subregional cooperation, composed of bilateral ties, various triangular cooperation efforts, residual ties from the Visegrad group, an enlarging CEFTA, the larger subregional groups (the Council of Baltic Sea States, the Central European Initiative and the Black Sea Economic

Cooperation), and various efforts to establish subregional cooperation in South-Eastern Europe. While the overlap of these mainly uncoordinated processes was creating a somewhat 'messy' picture and tensions continued between some states, the overall direction was one of improving relations and intensifying cooperation.

Bilaterally, there was substantial progress in improving relations within Central and Eastern Europe by 1997. Outside the former Yugoslavia, the majority of Central and Eastern European states have concluded bilateral state treaties with their neighbours. These treaties recognize existing borders, commit states to cooperation and often include general guarantees of minority rights. Many Central and Eastern European states have also concluded bilateral free trade agreements – which form the basis for CEFTA. Various bilateral military cooperation and confidence-building agreements have been concluded. Hungary, for example, has made particular efforts to ensure that tensions with its neighbours over Hungarian minority rights do not escalate by concluding military confidence-building measures (including a unique 'Open Skies' agreement with Romania and a neutral airspace border corridor with the rump Yugoslavia). Poland has similarly sought to overcome historic tensions with Ukraine and Lithuania through intensive military cooperation, including the development of bilateral peacekeeping battalions with both countries. Transfrontier cooperation arrangements have also been established between neighbouring regions of Central and Eastern European states.

While the Visegrad group has effectively ceased to act as a quadrilateral grouping, various residual ties continue between its members. The four states maintain close bilateral political, economic and military relations. Personal contacts between officials, established within the Visegrad framework, continue. The Visegrad states also continue to consult one another in relation to issues such as the OSCE and revision of the CFE Treaty. The worsening situation in Slovakia, however, undermined this residual cooperation and led Poland, the Czech Republic and Hungary to cooperate with one another without Slovakia. By 1996-97, bilateral and trilateral discussions between Poland, the Czech Republic and Hungary had been initiated on NATO enlargement, reforms of their armed forces and the procurement of Western military equipment (particularly new fighter aircraft – the major arms procurement decision they faced).[56] By early 1997, Polish President Aleksander Kwasniewski was arguing that 'Poland, Hungary and the Czech Republic are likely to create a consolidated group of partners' in relation to NATO and the EU and would 'jointly constitute the Union's Central European region!'.[57] NATO's decision to invite only these three countries to join the Alliance in the 'first wave' seemed likely to consolidate this emerging trilateral cooperation. There appeared to be little interest in Central Europe, however, in (re-)establishing anything akin to the Visegrad group. Nevertheless, during negotiations with NATO and the EU and once inside these organizations, the three Central European states (and whichever other Central and Eastern European states joined them) were likely to have certain common interests – suggesting that various forms of informal cooperation would continue. In the medium term, therefore, the Central (and Eastern) European states seemed likely to form informal caucasuses within NATO and the EU, similar to those of the existing Mediterranean and Nordic NATO and EU members.

Alongside bilateral and residual Visegrad ties, a number of other forms of trilateral cooperation were also emerging in Central and Eastern Europe: the Polish-German-French 'Weimar triangle'; political, defence and economic cooperation amongst the three Baltic states; Polish-Lithuanian-Ukrainian cooperation (particularly in terms of expressing these three countries concerns over the increasingly authoritarian turn of developments in Belarus); and Hungarian-Italian-Slovenian cooperation (particularly in relation to defence issues). While it is beyond the scope of this chapter to examine these initiatives, it may be noted that they were (in varying ways) helping to build cooperation in Central and Eastern Europe and to facilitate the Central and Eastern European states integration with NATO and the EU.

Aside from more informal Central European cooperation, CEFTA also remained in place. CEFTA's narrow focus on free trade meant that it was not disrupted by the break-up of Czechoslovakia in the same way that the Visegrad group had been. By 1997, further, CEFTA had expanded to include Slovenia and Romania and seemed likely to expand further to include other Central and Eastern European states – making it far less exclusive than the Visegrad group had been. In the context of NATO and EU enlargement, therefore, CEFTA had the potential to acting as a useful cooperative framework, bringing together those states which had been invited to join NATO and the EU with their neighbours which had not yet been so invited. The challenges facing CEFTA in playing such a role are explored in the next chapter.

Despite the decline of the Visegrad group, therefore, there remained a growing network of cooperation in Central and Eastern Europe. While the prospects for future cooperation seemed reasonably good, continued cooperation could not be guaranteed. The process of building a security community – a true 'zone of peace' – was only partially completed.

Changes in domestic politics might bring to power more nationalist governments, less sympathetic to cooperation with their neighbours. NATO and EU enlargement might trigger backlashes in those countries 'rejected'. Some states – Belarus, Serbia, Slovakia – were increasingly isolating themselves as a consequence of their domestic and foreign policy choices. In this context, therefore, it remained vital for all Central and Eastern European countries – but especially those invited to join NATO and the EU in the 'first wave' – to sustain the momentum of cooperation.

CONCLUSION

The experience of the Visegrad group highlights both the value and the limitations of subregional cooperation amongst small, relatively homogenous groups of states located between larger powers. The Visegrad group helped its members to dismantle their old Soviet bloc ties, helped to put the issues of NATO and EU enlargement on the political agenda and promoted the development of cooperative ties between the Central European states. In this sense, it can be argued that the Visegrad group played an important role in facilitating the parallel development of a security community in Central Europe and the integration of the Central European states with the wider Western security community.

The demise of the Visegrad group, however, also illustrates the limitations of such cooperation. For the Visegrad states, their cooperation – while valued in itself – was always a means to the larger end of integration with the West. Within the Visegrad group, there was always a certain tension between subregional cooperation and the larger goal of integration with the West. To the extent that subregional cooperation could improve the Central European states prospects for integration – for example, by strengthening their collective diplomatic voice or by illustrating their ability to behave responsibly and their preparedness for integration – it was viewed positively. To the extent that subregional cooperation might delay integration – for example, if it became 'too' successful and was seen as an alternative to NATO/EU membership or if states were treated as a group in relation to NATO/EU member and therefore had to wait for their 'slowest' partner – it was viewed negatively. Thus, when Prime Minister Klaus believed that the Czech Republic might join the EU before its Visegrad neighbours, it was hardly surprising that he prioritized EU membership over subregional cooperation. Similarly, when Slovakia fell behind its neighbours in terms of democratization and prospects for NATO and EU membership, the other three Visegrad states had obvious disincentives to continuing defining themselves as a group with Slovakia.

The experience of the Visegrad group also suggests that a minimum of common values and goals, the absence of serious conflicts and significant external incentives to cooperate are important for such cooperation. The Visegrad group emerged when Poland, Czechoslovakia and Hungary shared similar domestic situations and foreign policy goals and were seriously concerned by the direction of developments in the Soviet Union and their own strategic vulnerability. When the strategic situation changed – with the break-up of the Soviet Union – and Slovakia appeared to be turning away from the goals of democratization and Western integration shared by the other three states, the Visegrad group became moribund. Similarly, when serious disputes emerged between two of its members – Hungary and Slovakia – the Visegrad group was unable to play a role in resolving them.

These conclusions may have significant implications for other subregions of post-communist Europe where cooperation between reasonably small, relatively homogenous groups of states could be a possibility (for example, the three Baltic states, South-Eastern Europe/the Balkans, the three Caucasian states or the Central Asian states). They suggest that such cooperation can play a significant role in strengthening small/medium states vis-à-vis their larger neighbours, improving their prospects for integration with NATO and the EU and promoting peaceful relations between them. At the same time, these conclusions also suggest that – given the primary importance of integration and/or relations with neighbouring major powers and the existence of serious domestic and foreign policy differences between many states – such cooperation will be difficult to develop and sustain. If the EU and NATO want to promote such cooperation (for example, in South-Eastern Europe), these conclusions also suggest that it will be vital for them to minimize the potential tensions between subregional cooperation and integration. In particular, it will be important for them give their full support to such cooperation, while at the same time making clear that states prospects for integration will not be undermined (and, indeed, may be enhanced) by engagement in subregional cooperation.

For Central and Eastern Europe, the demise of the Visegrad group signals not a break-down in cooperation *per se*, but rather the break-down of a particular form of cooperation which reflected a particular set of political and geo-strategic circumstances. As was suggested above, what appears to be emerging in Central and Eastern Europe in the second half of the 1990s is a 'variable geometry' of overlapping forms of cooperation (bilateral, trilateral, CEFTA, the CEI, as well as the larger cooperative outreach programmes of NATO, the EU and the WEU). The challenge, as NATO and the EU enlarge, will be to ensure that new 'dividing lines' are avoided, opportunities for cooperation are maximized and no state is unnecessarily isolated.

6 The Central European Free Trade Agreement: Problems, Experiences, Prospects

Andrzej Kupich

On 21 December 1992, in Cracow, the Visegrad group countries concluded the Central European Free Trade Agreement (CEFTA). The multilateral agreement regulating the organization of free trade between Poland, the Czech Republic, Slovakia and Hungary entered into force on 1 March 1993. Slovenia joined CEFTA at the beginning of 1996 and Romania followed suit in the summer of 1997. The preamble to the agreement states that the signatories will create a free trade area in accordance with General Agreementon Trade and Tariffs (now World Trade Organization) provisions. The objectives defined in the agreement include 'supporting, through expansion of trade, harmonious development of economic relations between the parties and the advancement thereby of economic development, improvement of living and working conditions, growth of productivity and financial mobilization'.

The principal aim of the CEFTA member states is membership of the European Union (EU). This was emphasized in the agreement signed in Cracow. Intensification of cooperation within the framework of CEFTA was intended to help to prepare the Central and Eastern European countries for integration with the EU. Thus, CEFTA should not be understood as an end in itself, but rather as a means to the strategic goal of European integration. The aim is not to create a new integrative group *per se* but to accelerate integration with the EU. CEFTA was a logical consequence of the agreements concluded by the Central and Eastern European countries with the EU and the first step towards the revitalization of trade between them following the collapse of COMECON. At the same time, CEFTA is not a closed block: it is open to other states pursuing the goal of European integration and willing to move towards free trade – as the accession of Slovenia and Romania shows.

The assumption underpining CEFTA is that accelerating the process of adjustment to integration with the single European market will depend in no small measure on the level and nature of subregional economic cooperation. The organization and stimulation of economic cooperation in

Central and Eastern Europe, particularly in the CEFTA framework, is important for the countries concerned for a number of reasons. First, to the extent that the CEFTA countries are able to increase their trade with one another, this will promote their general propserity and support their transitions to market based economies, thereby also facilitating their integration with the EU. Second, the EU countries hope that as the CEFTA members integrate with the European market they will be able to act as a bridge encouraging the expansion of economic relations between the EU and the rest of Central and Eastern Europe's transforming nations. Third, the course of the CEFTA countries' adaptation to the rules and standards of the single market will in part depend on the level, and stability, of relations with economic areas outside the EU. Fourth, the deepening of subregional cooperation within the CEFTA framework could be an important factor in framing a common adaptation strategy within the whole group and thereby strengthening its members' bargaining power in entry negotiations with the EU. Fifth, given the varying pace of change in each CEFTA country and other internal differences, deepening subregional cooperation will necessitate harmonization and create new requirements in the field of, primarily, long-term economic policy. Accelerating and deepening the process of CEFTA cooperation can make it easier to halt economic decline and encourage the adaptation/modernization of industries. Sixth, deepening cooperation can prevent irrational competition within the group for capital and investment from advanced Western countries, especially Germany, and open the way to collaboration on a parternship basis in this field. More generally, the establishment of CEFTA reflects a willingness on the part of its members to cooperate with each other economically, rather than pursuing the protectionist economic policies which characterized the inter-war years. This chapter examines CEFTA, exploring the spurs and barriers to economic cooperation in Central and Eastern Europe, the evolution of CEFTA to date and its future prospects (especially in the dual context of likely phased enlargement of the EU and further expansion of CEFTA itself).

SPURS AND BARRIERS TO ECONOMIC COOPERATION IN CENTRAL AND EASTERN EUROPE

Economic links between the CEFTA countries are not being created from scratch. Such ties existed earlier under COMECON. Then, however, 'multilateral' economic relations took a specific shape, furthering the development of links amongst the Central and Eastern European states only to a small extent. The bulk of intra-COMECON trade comprised bilateral exchanges with the Soviet Union and its intensiveness was high. As a result, trade between the Central and Eastern European countries themselves was limited.[1] Such a pattern of trade was not conducive to the formation of complementary economic structures, while the absence of market mechanisms undermined efficiency. The command system took account of and reconciled the interests of 'the high contracting parties' but did not involve the actual producers and exporters in the interplay of interests. Attempts at reform failed to produce results, invariably going no further than declarations and quasi-action. Nevertheless, these built-in shortcomings and defects notwithstanding, a certain network of specialization/participation and trade links did take shape in Central and Eastern Europe. It ensured continuity of production, a market for products (regardless of their poor quality) and payment in the form of surplus raw materials.

This specific kind of 'economic security' ended in 1989. The introduction of market economic, convertible-currency settlements and world prices and the break-up of COMECON resulted in a collapse in trade, the end of collaboration and a search for new trading partners, primarily in Western Europe. The sharp decline in trade – over fifty per cent – was, of course, largely caused by the general crisis in the Soviet Union and Central and Eastern Europe. A dramatic slump in investment had crucial repercussions for the structure of trade: the steepest drops were in machinery, equipment and consumer goods. It should be noted, however, that trade between Czechoslovakia, Poland and Hungary was less severely affected in 1990-91 than in the case of other countries in the area: the fall in their trade was almost fifty per cent smaller than that of the former Soviet countries. This was partly due to the fact that the size of this trade was smaller than turnover with the Soviet Union. It can also be concluded, however, that the links between the countries which now form the CEFTA group proved, despite all their flaws, more durable and better (which is not to say well) suited to market requirements than those of their former Soviet neighbours.

There are many factors creating the conditions and foundations for economic cooperation between the Central and Eastern European countries. But there are also many barriers to and constraints on such cooperation. The principal factors working in favour of closer economic relations between the Central and Eastern European countries include territorial proximity, a similarity of historical and contemporary economic experiences, an affinity of economic systems and an in-place network of communications, transport and trade links. All of this means that the degree of mutual understanding of economic issues and potential for economic cooperation is and can be quite large amongst the Central and Eastern European countries. A number of other factors also support cooperation. First, the fact that the Central and Eastern European countries are following broadly similar directions in terms of economic reform and the implementation of market economics (in terms of both objectives and problems) creates significant potential for the development of mutual trade and projects in the sphere of intra-industry collaboration and specialization and joint investments. Although there are also obviously differences amongst the Central and Eastern European states – for example, in the pace of their economic transitions – the points in common are unmistakable.

Second, the Central and Eastern European countries share the goal of integration with the European Union. Their period of association with the Union can therefore also be a process of intensification of Central and Eastern European cooperation, which would be a good testimonial to the area's ability to integrate with the EU. The chances of this have been increasing of late thanks to a growth of subregional 'integration consciousness'. Third, certain untapped opportunities for expanding cooperation lie in the potential complementarity of economic structures. Inter-industry, this potential is relatively limited. Intra-industry, however, it is larger (though largely dormant). In the past, such cooperation formed the basis for co-production arrangements which were not very widespread but have now almost entirely disappeared. It is, however, worth noting that similarity of technologies and directions in the restructuring of industry creates the conditions for the development of cooperation in this field. Fourth, the forging of new economic links will be encouraged by economic recovery in the CEFTA countries. The growth of internal demand will boost interest in trade in capital goods and joint projects in this area. This will be made all the more necessary by the fact that capital goods production could come under severe threat from the highly industrialized EU countries and in such a situation collaboration would be desirable. An additional spur to subregional economic cooperation could come from agreement among political elites on the necessity and advisability of undertaking joint action and making the most of the potential for cooperation.

There are, however, also many serious barriers to and constraints on the development of economic cooperation in Central and Eastern Europe. One handicap is the legacy of the recent past – what may be defined as a 'COMECON syndrome'. The experience of this organization casts a shadow over present mutual economic relations. The links between the former socialist countries were characterized by centralism, the prevalence of political over economic motives, an inefficient economic mechanism, a lack of mutual trust, and the one-sidedness of relations (biased towards the Soviet Union) in a purportedly multilateral system. In the altered circumstances of today, there is still a lingering distrust of neighbours and partners tend to be sought in more distant countries. Another major obstacle to the development of economic cooperation is the frail condition of the Central and Eastern European economies and the progressive deterioration of capital equipment. In all the countries concerned, investment had already ground to a halt by the late-1980s. The rate of investment is still low. This state of affairs is beginning to change and a gradual improvement is setting in. Demand for plant and machinery (but only of the highest world standards) will increase. However, the less than complete economic recovery in the area and the related shortage of capital means that neither domestic production nor CEFTA partners will be able to meet this demand. Central and Eastern European firms will direct their import orders to the West. In the longer run, the requirements of restructuring and modernization of industry could become a spur to the development of collaborative arrangements in Central and Eastern Europe. The lack of intra-industry links, however, is a sizeable obstacle to cooperation. Disparate levels of economic development (reflected, for instance, in differing degrees of competitiveness of goods and services) further undermines the prospects for economic cooperation and trade expansion.

A further serious barrier to the expansion of trade is a general shortage of surplus foreign exchange balances among firms in the CEFTA countries, which makes provision of export credits impossible. This hits exports of capital goods particularly hard since in world trade practice these are usually credit transactions. In addition, relatively high prices and mediocre quality of goods mean that the competitiveness of Central and Eastern European countries is low. This situation will change gradually, as export promotion funds are created. Plans announced in Poland and Hungary indicate that these will be of significant assistance to exporters. At present, firms trading within the CEFTA framework also enjoy none of the preferences available in other areas. There are, therefore, no incentives to do business in the CEFTA area, especially as it is also subject to non-tariff restrictions. Barriers of this kind have not been removed by recent modifications to the CEFTA Treaty.

Trade and economic cooperation between the CEFTA countries also suffer from inertia and the continuing influence of old structures and forms of action. The big trading organizations which still account for a large proportion of turnover are unable (and probably see no need) to undertake marketing and other activities for the purpose of establishing and maintaining footholds in the markets of other CEFTA states. This is doubtless due to an ingrained belief that such efforts are unnecessary in these markets. Yet the fact is that the former COMECON area is precisely one in which marketing tailored to its specific conditions and taking account of, for example, the still considerable influence of the state on foreign trade is essential. Recent theoretical and conceptual studies of the economic climate and marketing in Central and Eastern Europe could be of some help in choosing the right kind of action and an aid in developing a new corps of trade managers in the CEFTA countries.

Another feature of the Central and Eastern European states is natural competition in movement towards the EU. Structural parallelisms in their economies and conflicts of certain, especially short-term, national interests have led the Central and Eastern European countries to compete in their economic relations with the West. The consequent distrust of partners was aggravated by the bad experiences of the past (– the 'COMECON syndrome' refered to above). This was particularly strong in the early days of subregional cooperation, but still exists. One can agree with the view that it would be wrong to eliminate this element of competition since, like all such economic phenomena, it has a positive side and can speed up the adaptation process. That said, in the short term the absence of at least a minimum of coordination of relations with the EU does not facilitate cooperation. However, a number of recent joint moves in the EU forum are evidence of a change for the better in this field, even if they were prompted by external factors.

The CEFTA countries also have no common or orchestrated external economic policy and compete with one another in third markets, including in an area as vital as the Commonwealth of Independent States (CIS). Harmonization of action in this market would bring greater benefits to each country and, in the first place, be a quick stimulus to intra-regional cooperation and trade. Similar competition is also to be found in the sphere of access to foreign capital and various sources of aid. Competition in place of cooperation does not increase the inflow of foreign investment and makes for less effective use of the credits supplied by international funds set up to assist in the stabilization and restructuring of the economies of Central and Eastern Europe.

The conclusion to be drawn from a survey of the factors promoting and hindering economic cooperation in Central and Eastern Europe is that such cooperation is possible and will be realized, but that it will be achieved only slowly and at varying speeds amongst differing Central and Eastern European states. Such cooperation will become more dynamic once the participants see that, far from being an obstacle to integration with the EU, links within the CEFTA framework will actually be of assistance in integrating the whole group with the EU.

No one any longer questions that the EU is now the centre of economic gravity in Europe. It is equally beyond dispute that the road to the Union does not run through destruction of the natural economic links in the Central and Eastern parts of the continent. Accordingly, giving a new impetus to subregional cooperation can help to shorten the route to the EU. In the present circumstances, at least two tasks have come to the fore as preconditions for galvanizing subregional relations. The first is the convergence of the economic systems of the countries concerned. The second is the effective elimination of the barriers to international cooperation left behind by the malformation of both internal and external structures of economic growth.

The first of these preconditions is probably the most important since comparability of systems is essential to the employment of similar tools, instruments and methods of generating trade and cooperation. These cannot acquire the desired momentum as long as different economic systems coexist. That stage now belongs to the past. The Central and Eastern European countries have made their choice in terms of strategic development: namely, the thorough-going construction of a market economy, which will make possible full and equal membership of the EU. Association with the EU in itself set the seal on the transition formula. That being so, there is no need to look for a 'third way'. For these reasons, the Central and Eastern European states most engaged in the expansion of subregional economic links are primarily those which have set themselves similar goals, are following the same kind of transition policies and have, moreover, reached a similar level of socio-economic reform. From this point of view, it was hardly surprising that the Visegrad countries, which had already committed themselves to deepening mutual cooperation and combining efforts in their common movement towards an integrating Europe, took centre-stage in (re-)establishing economic cooperation in Central and Eastern Europe.

The Central and Eastern European countries might benefit in a number of ways from economic cooperation with one another. First, such cooperation might strengthen their joint bargaining power in the process of association with the EU and the negotiation of the best possible terms for rapid entry into the Union. The lesson to be learned from the evolution of relations within the EU is that acting on a subregional basis carries much more weight in the negotiating process than acting as individual countries.

Second, the revitalization of economic cooperation can help the Central and Eastern European states to utilize the productive capacities which were cut back as a result of the systemic changes introduced in the early 1990s. As noted earlier, the degree of complementarity of the Central and Eastern European economies is relatively small. In these circumstances, the only prospect for expanding trade lies in deepening intra-industry specialization and widening inter-industry technical and economic cooperation.

Only a part of the plant employed in Central and Eastern Europe fulfills the requirements of advanced European and world markets. The rest needs to be intensively converted to new uses and adapted to meet the new challenges. This is, however, a lengthy and extremely capital-intensive process. That being so, a large proportion of productive capacities ought to be either scrapped or found, for an interim period, less demanding markets. That means both the internal markets of the individual Central and Eastern European states and the external markets which these countries provide for each other. It would, therefore, be a major error if economic policy in the Central and Eastern European countries were to be oriented solely to the West. The process of adaptation to the requirements of the European Union's market can act as a catalyst for subregional economic cooperation in Central and Eastern Europe if that process allows for the possibility of simultaneous expansion into eastern markets.

Third, subregional economic cooperation can also help in harmonizing the systemic economic reforms bringing the Central and Eastern European countries into line with EU standards, rules and requirements. Choice of economic transition policies is, of course, a sovereign decision for each nation. In each country there are certain specific features which prevent the exact duplication or imitation of policies across Central and Eastern Europe as a whole. However, there are a number of systemic measures which, by their nature, require harmonization if new barriers and obstacles to cooperation are not to arise. This applies in particular to such detailed aspects of reform as price-fixing policy (which determines the shape of price relationships), the formation of capital markets and the related question of the requisite financial and banking system, tax and tariff policies, and joint business enterprises. This whole sphere requires the application of common, compatible rules. Divergent patterns of development in these areas could undermine the prospects for attaining comparable systems. Because the ultimate objectives of the Central and

Eastern European countries in undertaking systemic economic reforms are the same and because the problems they face are almost identical, they would be well advised to find a common denominator for their economic reform policies.This, of course, does not mean establishing joint decision-making in tackling the problems in question, still less adopting binding rules in these areas.

Overall, subregional trade cooperation within a framework such as CEFTA has the potential to facilitate and speed up the economic adaptation process in Central and Eastern Europe, counteract discriminatory trade practices and expedite the passage of EU legislation and the implementation of EU standards. Combined economic efforts can also reduce marketing costs and enhance competitive power. Simulation analyses carried out at the Foreign Trade Research Institute in Warsaw indicated, for example, that:
- the removal of barriers to market access in Central and Eastern Europe would contribute to the intensiveness of mutual trade, especially in goods which cannot at present be absorbed by Western markets;
- exporters' revenues would be increased as a result of the reduction of import charges;
- indirect benefits arising from the reduction of the costs of imports would result in a lowering of production costs and prices across the whole economy;
- the direct and indirect benefits of liberalization would probably offset any losses in budget revenues resulting from tariff reductions.

THE EMERGENCE AND EVOLUTION OF CEFTA

Recognition of the need for and potential benefits of subregional free trade led the Central European leaders to establish CEFTA. At their Visegrad summit at the beginning of 1991, the leaders of Czechoslovakia, Poland and Hungary declared that 'in order to promote free movement of capital and labour they will develop market-based economic cooperation and mutually profitable trade in goods and services and will also seek to create favourable conditions for direct cooperation between enterprises and for foreign capital investment that furthers enhancement of economic efficiency'.[2] The declaration of the October 1991 Cracow summit of the leaders of the Visegrad countries stated that there was 'a strong need to accelerate work on the elimination of barriers in mutual trade' and affirmed the 'will to conclude agreements on mutual liberalization of trade as soon as possible'. The aim of these agreements was to 'ensure a degree of

CEFTA: Problems, Experiences, Prospects 99

liberalization of trade comparable to that provided in agreements with the European Communities and EFTA'.[3] On this basis, the Visegrad leaders decided to establish what was to become CEFTA.

In November 1991 the Visegrad countries' Trade Ministers met in Warsaw, signing a memorandum on the 'gradual elimination of all barriers to trade'. It was decided that a free trade area would be put in place over a period of five-to-ten years and encompass all groups of industrial and agricultural products. The Ministers also decided on the phasing-out of tariffs, quotas, fiscal or export charges and internal taxes discriminating against trade. The text of the proposed agreement was to be based on the provisions of agreements already or about to be concluded by the Visegrad countries with the European Free Trade Area (EFTA). A Central European Cooperation Commission with a rotating presidency and secretariat was set up at ministerial level to coordinate work connected with implementation of the Association Agreements with the then European Community (EC) and represent agreed interests in dealings with the EC. Provision was also made for consultations between the Visegrad countries on cooperation in the fields of financial services, investment, transport, telecommunications, diversification of energy sources, and environmental protection.

In the course of 1992, intensive work by groups of experts resulted in the drafting of the text of the CEFTA agreement together with the appropriate annexes. Certain delays in the agreed timetable were due primarily to difficulties over some of the clauses of the agreement and even bigger problems in the negotiation of concessions, especially for agricultural products. Another highly controversial issue was rules of origin. In order to expedite the negotiation of tariff concessions, a methodology similar to that employed in the Association negotiations with the EC was adopted. Three lists of goods were drawn up: schedule A covered goods subject to zero tariffs on the agreement's entry into force; schedule B covered goods on which tariffs would be phased out according to an agreed timetable; and schedule C covered 'sensitive' products excluded from the liberalization process and requiring separate negotiations. As was noted at the beginning of this chapter, the resulting CEFTA agreement was signed in December 1992 and came into force in March 1993.

Under the original plans, implementation of CEFTA was to take eight years. There appeared, however, to be possibilities for shortening this period, which would mean a more rapid liberalization of trade within CEFTA than of its members' trade with the EU. As well as the CEFTA agreement itself, a declaration on speeding up the liberalization of trade was also adopted at the Cracow summit. Negotiations between CEFTA government experts then began in May 1993 and several months later agreement was reached on the measures needed to expedite liberalization. These were set out in an additional protocol to the agreement signed by Trade Ministers at an extraordinary session of the CEFTA Joint Committee in April 1994. Under this protocol, greater liberalization of trade in agricultural products consisted mainly in the addition of further goods to the CEFTA agreement, another reduction in tariffs and an increase in preferential quotas for goods already enjoying this concession. It should be noted, however, that despite the multilateral character of CEFTA, the scope of some of these decisions varied in the specific bilateral relations between the various CEFTA members. For example, for Poland, the degree of liberalization of agricultural trade with Hungary was much wider than with the Czech Republic and Slovakia.

The April 1994 additional protocol called for an increase in the number of goods with a zero tariff rating as from 1 July 1994, which meant bringing forward the abolition of duties by three years. The goods affected were primarily ones which had been found not to require tariff protection or were not yet being traded. It was decided that some goods would, however, be protected by tariffs until 1 January 2001 or 2002, that is to the end of the originally planned period for implementation of the agreement. These included mainly cars and metallurgical products. The remaining modifications concerned only tariff rates, but it was clear that tariff restrictions would continue to be a barrier to mutual trade. Despite efforts (particularly on the Polish side), it proved impossible to eliminate the various kinds of taxes and charges in force in mutual trade. Provision was made for on-going supervision of the implementation of the agreement and the modifications set out in the additional protocol. Any problems that arose were to be dealt with by the Joint Committee in permanent session.

The trade figures for the first year of CEFTA revealed that though the desired intensification of trade had not yet taken place, the downward trend had at least been halted. Intra-CEFTA trade remained small. For Poland, trade with the Czech Republic, Slovakia, and Hungary decreased as a per centage of total foreign trade: from 5.1 per cent in 1992 to 4.8 per cent in 1993 for exports, and from 4.1 per cent to 3.6 per cent for imports. Various barriers to the expansion of trade in goods and services were still in place. The absence of a satisfactory payments system also created problems. Polish enterprises trading with CEFTA countries complained, in particular, about the inefficiency of financial and banking services and the non-harmonization of rules governing international transactions.

Gradually, however, CEFTA began to produce benefits. The April 1994 additional protocol initiated a faster liberalization of trade in industrial goods and a widening of mutual concessions for agricultural products. A declaration adopted in Poznan in November 1994 by CEFTA Prime Ministers called for the further acceleration of trade liberalization and the expansion of the scope of the agreement. This meant that, as from 1997, customs duties would be levied on only a few tariff items. CEFTA thus overtook the tariff reductions timetable of its members' Association Agreements with the EU (which mandate the liberalization of trade between the EU and each individual Associate). The November 1994 Poznan declaration included two other important decisions. First, agreement on enlarging the scope of CEFTA by including provisions (similar to those included in the Association Agreements with the EU) concerning freer movement not only of goods, but also of services and capital. There was no consensus, however, on free movement of labour. Second, agreement on the opening of CEFTA membership to other countries which belong to the World Trade Organization, have concluded Association Agreements with the EU and have bilateral free trade agreements with all CEFTA countries. This was a major step, since it implied that CEFTA was in principle open to all the Central and Eastern European Associates of the EU – opening the way for a potentially quite large expansion of CEFTA (but also placing implicit limits on such expansion). On this basis, accession negotiations were begun with Slovenia and that country joined CEFTA on 1 January 1996.

In August 1995, at a meeting of the CEFTA Committee of Trade Ministers in Warsaw, a further additional protocol was signed, under which zero tariff rates are to apply to goods of average sensitivity and duties on the most sensitive products are to be halved. The new protocol also called for the application of zero rates to all industrial trade from 1 January 1997. For the next four years customs duties would be levied only in exceptional cases, the list of which is not long (though still too large).

On 11 September 1995, at a meeting of CEFTA Heads of Government in Brno, it was decided to conduct studies on the free movement of services and capital. Poland was made coordinator of studies on capital movement and cooperation in the banking sector. Agreement was also reached on acelerating the work of experts on mutual recognition of certificates, which should improve the flow of goods. Present at the meeting in Brno as observers were delegations from other countries associated with the EU and interested in joining CEFTA: Bulgaria, Romania, Lithuania and Slovenia. The Brno CEFTA meeting clearly illustrated the interest of other

Central and Eastern European states in joining the agreement, suggesting that the group is likely to expand further in future. On this basis, Romania became the sixth CEFTA member in the summer of 1997.

PROGRESS IN TRADE LIBERALIZATION?

At present, economic cooperation between the CEFTA countries is in effect limited to trade, but in this field, too, it is being pursued chiefly by traditional means unreinforced by modern market methods. Both Western observers and local analysts emphasize that while trade with the West has been clearly liberalized, intra-CEFTA trade is still beset by traditional restrictions, a lack of flexibility, reliance on directives and disregard of partners.

A range of factors inhibit the expansion of trade within Central and Eastern Europe. The biggest hurdle for intra-CEFTA trade is the lack of liquidity and export credit facilities. A feature of Czech commercial practice, for example, is the discrediting of importers making purchases in former COMECON countries. It has been noted that in trade negotiations with former 'eastern' partners, in conjunction with the introduction of convertible currency settlements, all states concerned displayed very little flexibility in fixing prices. As a rule, the prices proposed in dealings between them are higher in fact than those offered to firms in Western Europe. Additionally, intra-CEFTA trade still suffers from considerable inertia. For example, Czech and Slovak partners from the former state foreign trade companies are so used to neighbours clamouring for their goods that they show no interest in courting buyers. This situation is changing, but only very slowly. The sluggishness of marketing activities still to be found in intra-CEFTA trade may also be due to the fact that very many of the firms which obtained the right to trade abroad lost at the same time the services of staff with experience of this field. Lacking the necessary manpower, their selling efforts make little impact. This phenomenon was also observed in the former Czechoslovakia. Recent years have also revealed that very often intra-CEFTA trade is transacted via third parties. This is evidence of a lack of enterprise on the part of traders, and of course, also pushes up prices. Among the areas affected are trade in new technologies and capital goods – in other words, production factors, which increases manufacturing costs.

There is a definite paucity of capital links amongst the CEFTA countries. The joint ventures hitherto established in CEFTA countries by investors from the area are chiefly involved in retailing. A few joint ventures have been set up in construction, but there are virtually none in manufacturing industry, although conditions for such enterprise already exist. The Polish Commercial Counsellor's Office in Budapest has, for example, drawn attention to the power and food industries as areas in which effective cooperation could be developed. Certain opportunities for joint investment have been opened up by the privatization taking place in the CEFTA countries. All that is needed is the proper legal and economic framework. The agreements concluded on protection of investment and intellectual and industrial property could be of assistance in this respect. Experts believe that there could be good prospects for joint ventures in the field of ecological installations and infrastructure. Cooperation between banks and other financial institutions (for example, stock exchanges) is also considered very necessary.

Despite these problems, since 1992-93 there has been an expansion of trade between the CEFTA members. In 1994, Poland's trade with CEFTA countries came to over $1.7 billion and increased by 21 per cent compared with 1993. Exports increased by 19 per cent and imports by as much as 35 per cent, which was due to the demand created by fast growing production. This resulted in a trade deficit for Poland with its CEFTA neighbours, though in 1993 and 1992 there had been a surplus. Analysis of the dynamics of the flow of goods within CEFTA shows that the largest increase (50 per cent) was between Slovakia and Hungary and between the Czech Republic and Poland. A lower growth rate was recorded between Poland and Hungary, with Polish imports rising much faster (by 34 per cent) than exports. Detailed analyses (by, for example, the Polish Commercial Counsellor's Offices in Budapest and Prague) have shown that the 1994 increase in Polish exports to Hungary and the Czech Republic was driven largely by supplies of goods exempt from customs duties. In 1994, almost half of the trade between Poland and the Czech Republic had zero tariff rates, and a large percentage of goods was covered by the system of mutual concessions. This contributed to the growth of trade. Concessions were also applied to agricultural products. The value of these exports from Poland to the Czech Republic was almost 100 per cent higher in 1994 than in the preceding year.

The structure of intra-CEFTA trade does not differ much from the structure of the CEFTA countries' trade with other areas (such as the EU). The only noticeable differences are a higher share of industrial goods and a lower share of mineral fuels, machinery and transportation equipment. Intra-CEFTA trade (except between the Czech Republic and Slovakia) is, however, per capita lower than the CEFTA states' trade with their Western neighbours.

Despite the progress in trade liberalization, the transition processes and problems connected with modernization of industry have created a need/demand for special protection of domestic production. In such cases, administrative and non tariff measures are employed. For example, in 1994, Poland applied countervailing duties to imports of some agricultural products, restored tariffs on some types of telecommunications equipment and banned imports of used combine harvesters and utility vehicles. Hungary raised customs duties on agricultural products before the establishment of the WTO. Slovakia introduced similar protective measures.

In terms of trade liberalization within Central and Eastern Europe as a whole, it is worth noting that CEFTA does not restrict the right of its signatories to conclude bilateral free trade agreements with other countries. Thus, the original four CEFTA members signed bilateral free trade agreements with Slovenia and Romania before these two states joined CEFTA. Poland has done so with Lithuania and is also holding consultations with Latvia, Bulgaria, Israel and Turkey. New free trade areas and accords may emerge from these and other agreements and consultations.

On the record of CEFTA, it can be said that its signatories are blending well into the regionalization and liberalization trends in world trade. It is already clear that trade increased considerably amongst the CEFTA members in the spheres where liberalizationtion was implemented. At present, some 80 per cent of industrial tariff lines are subject to zero rate and further reductions are expected in 1997.[4] The year 1995 was marked by a significant increase in intra-CEFTA trade. Polish exports to the Czech Republic, Slovakia and Hungary increased by 51 per cent, and imports by as much as 77 per cent – resulting in a deficit of $380 million. Half of this, however, came from trade with the Czech Republic, which is Poland's biggest trade partner among the CEFTA countries, accounting for 56 per cent of all its trade within the group.[5]

The trade of all of the CEFTA countries was characterised by an equally high growth rate, but only Poland had an import surplus. Poland's trade deficit is partly explained by the facts that it is a large and ready market, absorbing a large volume of exports, and that it still has not taken full advantage of the greater liberalization of trade within CEFTA and the opportunities to sell its products on the markets of other CEFTA states. Opportunities certainly exist in this area, as is indicated by a reasonably high degree of complementarity in some sectors (for example, electroengineering and chemicals).

The structure of Poland's trade with CEFTA countries is very diverse. The dominant groups in exports are mineral products (23.5 per cent), non-ferrous metals (23 per cent), electro-engineering (17 per cent) and chemicals (16 per cent). Exports to the Czech Republic have a similar structure, but first place in exports to Hungary is occupied by nonferrous metals, followed by chemical industry, mineral and electro-engineering products. Poland's main imports from CEFTA countries are products of the chemical (28 per cent) and electro-engineering industries (17 per cent), agricultural products (14.5 per cent) and nonferrous metals (14.5 per cent). The same groups predominate in imports from the Czech Republic, with the exception of agricultural products, whose share is smaller than in total imports from CEFTA countries. From Hungary, Poland imports mainly chemical industry products (including pharmaceuticals) and foodstuffs. Such a structure is primarily due to simple exchange, unlinked to industrial collaboration. This is especially true for electro-engineering. Collaborative deals/projects are still far down the road.

The considerable increase in trade within CEFTA which took place in 1995 was mainly due to progress in the liberalization of merchandise flows between the CEFTA countries. The maintenance of this tendency and the planned liberalization of trade in food articles means that there are favourable prospects for the further expansion of intra-CEFTA trade in the future.

However, despite the rapidly developing mutual trade amongst the CEFTA countries, it is worth remembering that this trade is still at a very low level as a share of the total trade of the CEFTA countries. Trade with the other CEFTA states constitutes barely 6 per cent of Polish foreign trade and only 4 per cent in the case of Hungary. Trade with Hungary and Poland is similarly low for the Czech Republic and Slovakia. Trade between the Czech Republic and Slovakia is markedly different because of the two states previous integration as Czechoslovakia. Slovakia's share in Czech foreign trade, for example, is much larger, at 15 per cent, making Slovakia one of the Czech Republic's most important trading partners. Poland, with a share of less than 5 per cent, is in fourth place among exporters to the Czech Republic. In contrast, the other CEFTA countries are not among Poland and Hungary's biggest trading partners. This situation is likely to change only if trade liberalization agreed within the CEFTA framework is implemented consistently and the Central and Eastern European economies become more competitive and develop sufficiently to become much larger markets for one another, which is likely to be a much longer term process.

In summary, CEFTA has helped to facilitate the expansion of trade amongst its members. The acceleration of tariff reductions for industrial goods, the considerable widening of concessions and prospective tariff reductions for agricultural products have created a good platform for growth in intra-CEFTA trade. The decisions and measures adopted have also begun to give some impetus to industrial collaboration, intensification of trade in capital goods and stabilization of the international market in the subregion. The promised liberalization of trade in agricultural products, however, will not bring immediate results: full implementation of what has been agreed in this area will be quite unrealistic without a comprehensive approach to agricultural policy, including subsidies and other financial supports, quality certification, health and sanitary regulations and so on. Specialists point out, further, that the possibility of achieving trade-creation effects in CEFTA is limited. They depend largely on the economic restructuring measures being undertaken in the individual CEFTA countries, which will require a much longer period of time to work themselves through.

THE FUTURE OF CEFTA

The practical problems of economic cooperation in Central and Eastern Europe are acknowledged by experts and politicians within the subregion. Nevertheless, there is an appreciation of the importance of CEFTA. Aside from its contribution to increasing mutual trade amongst its current members, CEFTA could also facilitate the expansion of trade with other Central and Eastern European countries (both by further enlargement to include other states in the area and through the development of ties with states who do not join CEFTA) and enhance the bargaining position of the group in relation to the EU through the elimination of internal competition.

A number of crucial questions have emerged relating to the current functioning and future of CEFTA: the effects of trade liberalization, the need for institutionalization of CEFTA, the expansion of its membership, the possible expansion of CEFTA's scope beyond purely trade and economic issues, and the future of the group after the admission of some or all of its members to the EU.

In the economic literature various methods of deepening economic cooperation have been proposed, including the formation of a customs union, a payments union and a common market.[6] Some of the preconditions for expanding the scope of cooperation already exist (for example, a broadly similar degree of progress in economic transition amongst CEFTA's members and some interest from enterprises in subregional cooperation). It must be stated, however, that the intensification of economic cooperation, especially expansion of the scope of CEFTA's activities, cannot take place without the active participation of the European Union or at least some of its members. The reasons are not technical, but spring primarily from the necessity of attracting the resources and expertise required to assure the success of any proposed ventures.

The expansion of economic cooperation amongst the CEFTA countries, however, will also depend on the definition of certain common interests or projects. The definition of such common interests or projects will require some analysis of the CEFTA members economic situation and priorities. Such a function could be undertaken cooperatively between the appropriate government departments of the CEFTA countries. There seems, therefore, to be a strong case for establishing a modest (in order to avoid needless bureaucratization) but efficient CEFTA institutional infrastructure for the promotion of dialogue and cooperation on economic issues.

As was noted earlier, the influence of intra-CEFTA trade liberalization on the international exchange of the member countries could probably be much bigger than at present. This will depend primarily on the removal of a number of non-tariff barriers and agreement on many detailed questions such as, for instance, mutual recognition of certificates, rules of customs procedure, and so on. The net result of all the steps taken (reduction of import duties and other liberalization measures) should be a growth of both the trade creation and the trade diversion effects. From the point of view of the future, this is the most important matter since so far the value of the intra-CEFTA trade creation effect has tended to be smaller than the value of the trade diverted from third countries, including in the first place ones that are EU members. More generally, empirical studies confirm what many economists have been saying: that the Central and Eastern European countries have a greater inclination towards trade with the EU than with CEFTA countries. In the longer run, the size of the so-called trade effects of mutual trade will depend primarily on an increase in the intensity of the intra-industry division of labour and development of economic infrastructure (especially transport and telecommunications) of the CEFTA countries. Due to this fact, the liberalization of international product exchange will have to take place inside CEFTA. Progress in this area would encourage a significant increase in mutual economic and trade exchange within the framework of CEFTA.

The CEFTA members also need to consider, both individually and collectively within CEFTA, whether and how they may be able to expand economic relations with their eastern neighbours in the CIS.[7] The CEFTA states are likely to retain a relatively high degree of dependence on Russia and other CIS states for the supply of raw materials and energy. In the medium term, there may also be an 'investment awakening' in the CIS, which may boost demand for consumer goods in the CIS. The CEFTA members have the appropriate production abilities and may participate in fulfilling this revival in demand in the CIS. The CIS economies also face the challenge of reconstructing their industries, which will create a demand for investment in this area and for the provision of capital goods. The CEFTA states may also therefore be able to play a role in providing investment capital and modern industrial machinery to Russia and the other former Soviet countries. Within the CIS, the demand for banking and financial services/expertise may also increase. In this area, the CEFTA countries do not have many advantages (compared to Western firms from whom they will face strong competition), although some companies may enter these new eastern markets together with Western partners. In economic terms, the CIS region is also going to be characterized – for the foreseeable future – by a high level of risk. Consequently, financial contacts and payment settlements with eastern partners are going to depend to a large extent on political events. An efficient, international system of financial guarantees is therefore required. Given these circumstances, there is a case for some minimum of coordination amongst the CEFTA members in their economic relations with the CIS states. However, while such cooperation is desirable, it is unrealistic to expect the configuration of a general eastern strategy on the part of CEFTA as a whole.

The CEFTA members also face the question of whether further institutionalization of the group is desirable. Many economists believe that some minimum degree of institutionalization of CEFTA is necessary. There is a case for establishing an official international organ (for instance, a CEFTA secretariat) which would undertake necessary work relating to the coordination of steps aimed at increasing the flow of goods and trade exchange among CEFTA's members. To date, however, this idea has not had many adherents among CEFTA's members. Only Slovakia has consistently argued for the establishment of a CEFTA secretariat.[8] Most of the member countries show little enthusiasm for the institutionalization of CEFTA by establishing a Secretariat or other executive bodies and incline to the view that it is sufficient to form a liaison group composed of the commerical counsellors of the member states in one of the capitals of the group. Needless to say, the present Committee of Ministers responsible for international economic cooperation remains the body which directs tariff policy within CEFTA. One main barrier to establishing a CEFTA secretariat (or similar institution) is the perceptions of politicians who tend to associate the institutionalization of CEFTA with the non-existent and ineffective organs of the COMECON era.

With the admission of Slovenia and Romnania in 1996 and 1997, the principle that CEFTA was an open body, likely to expand to include most Central and Eastern European states was established. As noted above, the November 1994 Poznan meeting of CEFTA Prime Ministers defined the criteria for states wishing to join CEFTA: membership of the World Trade Organization, conclusion of an Association Agreement with the EU and bilateral free trade agreements with all CEFTA countries. The criterion of having concluded an Association Agreement with the EU was most significant because it it implied both that CEFTA was open to the other Central and Eastern European Associates of the EU, but also that states without such Association Agreements could not join CEFTA. Since then, it has been accepted that, in due course, the other Associates of the EU – the three Baltic states and Bulgaria – are likely to join CEFTA. However, some states which are not yet Associates of the EU (in particular, Croatia and Ukraine) have expressed interest in joining CEFTA and it is sometimes suggested that the membership criteria should be treated flexibly to make it possible to admit countries which do not meet all of them. At present, the members' position is that there is no need to change the principles governing the admission of new countries to CEFTA. In terms of expanding trade and also as a symbol of political support, there may be a case for expanding CEFTA to include states which do not have Association Agreements with the EU, in particular Ukraine. Whether Ukraine and other former Soviet and former Yugoslav countries are economically ready for such a step, however, may be open to question. Expanding CEFTA to include countries without Association Agreements with the EU could also create problems in relations with the Union (both politically and economically). It may be the case, therefore, that CEFTA's enlargement will, in part, be limited by how far and how rapidly the EU expands the number of countries with which it has Association Agreements.

As was noted at the beginning of this chapter, the strategic goal of CEFTA's signatories is membership of the EU and CEFTA is seen, in significant part, as a means of achieving this goal. With the likely admission of some CEFTA members into the EU within the next decade and perhaps all CEFTA members in the longer term, the pace and nature of EU enlargement will have major implications for the future of CEFTA. In terms of progress in trade liberalization, three scenarios can be considered. The first scenario implies the continuation of constructing a free trade zone, after CEFTA's members have joined the EU, on the basis of continuing implementation of the existing free trade agreements amongst the CEFTA states. The second scenario – and the one which is effectively being accomplished at the moment – would mean the synchronization of the trade liberalization timetable within CEFTA with the timetables included in the CEFTA members Association Agreements with the EU. This scenario implies that the entrance of the CEFTA countries into the EU will be equivalent with the closure of the functioning of CEFTA. The third scenario involves progress in trade liberalization within CEFTA to a stage significantly in advance of that between the EU and its Central and Eastern European Associates. This scenario might (or perhaps even should) also include the enlargement of cooperation among CEFTA members to include industrial cooperation, the development of common energy, fiscal and monetary policies, as well as expansion into the field of political cooperation. This third scenario appears to be the most rational and might be the most effective scenario for the genuine, authentic integration of Central and Eastern European countries with the EU.

At the same time, however, it appears that such an expansion of subregional cooperation will only take place if the enlargement of CEFTA is limited, which by 1996-97 already seemed unlikely with the admission of Slovenia and Romania and the opening in principle of CEFTA to the other Central and Eastern Europe Associates of the EU. The prospect of EU membership for some but not all members of CEFTA raises another difficult issue for the group. Since the EU has a common external trade policy, Central and Eastern European States who join the Union will almost certainly have to leave CEFTA (since continuing CEFTA membership would imply different and potentially contradictory trade arrangements). Such a development could have potentially negative implications for subregional cooperation. If new members of the Union simply left CEFTA and 'abandoned' other CEFTA members who had not joined the Union, a new economic and political dividing line could emerge between the 'haves' and the 'have nots'. The rump-CEFTA could be seriously weakened. Two steps could help to avoid such a development. First, those states joining the EU could make a commitment to support the membership aspirations of their CEFTA neighbours and to bring the political, economic and security concerns of their neighbours to the attention of the EU. Second, as a way of maintaining a multilateral Central and Eastern European forum for dialogue and as a channel for communication on EU matters, those states joining the Union could maintain some form of special 'observer' status within CEFTA, including continuing to attend its meetings. As all Central and Eastern European states join the EU, however, CEFTA is perhaps likely to disappear. The process of EU enlargement, therefore, is likely to have significant implications for CEFTA. CEFTA in its present form may not have a longer term future. In the final analysis, the will of politicians and, above all, the national interests of the Central and Eastern European countries will determine CEFTA's future.

CONCLUSION

From this analysis of the processes affecting the shape of economic cooperation within CEFTA, a number of conclusions can be drawn, particularly about the process of adaptation in Central and Eastern Europe and these states' integration with the EU. First, for the Central and Eastern European countries, the significance of the CEFTA market is much greater than the group's share of their total trade would suggest. Even appreciable quantitative increases in intra-CEFTA trade (which are now taking place) cannot have any notable impact on the restructuring and level of economies. What can, however, make a very big difference in the adaptation process are the following aspects of intra-CEFTA relations:
- the development, through the process of establishing mutual economic links, of a model tailored to the requirements of a developed market economy;
- the utilization of the strengths accruing from successful expansion of intra-CEFTA links to enhance the CEFTA members' bargaining power and negotiating position in relations with the EU;
- economic ties which encourage trade and cooperation with other Central and Eastern European and former Soviet countries.
- the development of an adequate payments system, linked with the European Monetary System and stimulating the growth of mutual trade.

In the light of these assessments, consistent implementation of the provisions of the CEFTA agreement and its additional protocols should be considered the most crucial component of subregional cooperation within CEFTA. It is also important for CEFTA's members to enter into dialogue as to how they can add momentum to economic programmes convergent with the guiding principles of the EU. Such a dialogue should result in the formulation of an industrial (structural) policy best suited to the CEFTA countries and help to assure them of proper participation in the intra-industry division of labour emerging from the EU's industrial development priorities. The creation of at least a rudimentary CEFTA institutional infrastructure for dialogue, research and the identification of common interests in the process of integration with the EU is also important. Modest institutional arrangements (shorn of any unnecessary red tape) are needed to frame internally consistent programmes and define positions on matters where 'speaking with one voice' is especially advisable. This applies in particular to political and economic issues of the greatest consequence for the building of the new European security system, especially its economic component, and a number of other areas of multilateral economic cooperation.

The process of the complete integration of the Central and Eastern European countries with the European structures (particularly the EU) is likely to be relatively long. CEFTA, therefore, is an important group in the transition period. The functioning of CEFTA does not, necessarily, have to end with the accession of most of its members to the European Union. This matter, however, was only beginning to be discussed by 1996-97. On the basis of the common economic problems facing the Central and Eastern European states and the experiences of other subregional cooperation processes which have continued within the EU (for example, Benelux and Nordic cooperation) it may be argued that there are opportunities for subregional cooperation to continue after the Central and Eastern Europe countries join the EU. The proper exploitation of these opportunities can contribute to securing confidence and harmonious development in the entire European continent.

7 The Central European Initiative[1]

Christopher Cviic

The Central European Initiative (CEI) is a subregional organization made up of 16 member states with a total population of 241 million people and an area of 2,015,137 square kilometres. The member states are: Albania, Austria, Belarus, Bosnia-Herzegovina, Bulgaria, Croatia, the Czech Republic, Hungary, Italy, Macedonia, Moldova, Poland, Romania, Slovakia, Slovenia and Ukraine. Five of these states (Albania, Belarus, Bulgaria, Romania and Ukraine) became full members on 1 June 1996 (previously they had participated in the CEI's Working Groups as Associate Members). Moldova joined on 8 November 1996. The meeting of CEI Foreign Ministers in Vienna on 1 June 1996, noted in its final document that, with the enlargement by five members that had just taken place and with Moldova joining in November 1996, the Initiative had 'approached the limits of its organisational capacity as a regional cooperation'. But not quite.

At the summit meeting of the CEI in Graz on 8-9 November 1996, the Heads of Government authorised the 'Troika' of the CEI, made up of the current (Austria), past (Poland) and future (Bosnia) presidencies, to establish contacts with the rump Yugoslavia (Serbia and Montenegro, officially named Federal Republic of Yugoslavia) with a view to it joining the CEI as a successor state of Yugoslavia. This course was advocated by Italy, supported by Poland, but opposed by Slovenia, Croatia, Bosnia and Macedonia. Italy's view prevailed. At the time of writing, rump Yugoslavia's membership is on hold because of the political turmoil in Belgrade. In the event of rump Yugoslavia being admitted to the CEI as its seventeenth member – as is almost certain, although it may be some time before this actually happens – there will be no more new CEI members.

HISTORY

The CEI grew out of a more modest body – a subregional group called the Alpe-Adria Working Group which was set up in Venice at Italy's initiative in 1978. Its proclaimed aim was to help the frontier regions of Austria, Italy and Yugoslavia. The regions taking part in the Alpe-Adria Working Group were: five Lander (including Vienna) in Austria, three autonomous northern regions in Italy and the two westernmost republics of the then Yugoslavia (Croatia and Slovenia), with Bavaria (a Land of the Federal Republic of Germany) as an observer. In the early 1980s, Hungary's two western regions (Komitats) joined the group.

The main idea behind the project was that, with central governments keeping discreetly in the background, low-key, transfrontier subregional cooperation could more easily develop in politically less sensitive fields like culture, the environment, tourism, transport and others, across what was still a Cold War divide. In northern Italy – especially Trieste – this was a time of growing backlash against the central bureaucracy in faraway Rome, accompanied by a certain amount of nostalgia among the intelligentsia for northern Italy's (once bitterly hated) former rulers, the Habsburgs. An indication of northern Italy's mood at the time was the fact that a best-selling new biography of Emperor Franz Joseph (1830-1916) by the Austrian historian Franz Herre, published in Austria in 1978, soon also became a bestseller in Italy.[2] Professor Claudio Magris (who later achieved fame as the author of a monograph on the cultural history of Central Europe[3]) set up a Department of Central European Studies at the University of Trieste. (This new interest in the Habsburgs and Mitteleuropa had its parallels also in Croatia, Slovenia and Hungary and to a certain extent in Austria). However, not even the open nostalgists for the old Austro-Hungarian Empire, to which all the Alpe-Adria regions (except Bavaria) once belonged, entertained thoughts of resurrecting it in any form. This was repeatedly pointed out by – among others – one of the Alpe-Adria project's main political backers, Gianni de Michelis, a Socialist politician and later Italy's Foreign Minister (who was himself from the Veneto, one of the northern Italian provinces included in the Alpe-Adria group).

Italy, however, did have its own political agenda – the desire to resume, once again, a more prominent role in Central Europe.[4] Under Mussolini, Italy had been influential in Central Europe in the 1930s. In the post-1945 period, however, it has found itself increasingly squeezed out by the resurgent Germany, its old rival from prewar and wartime days. Austria also had some political interest in a group such as the Alpe-Adria which could bolster its separate Central European identity vis-à-vis Germany. To the Croats, Hungarians and Slovenes, membership of the Alpe-Adria group offered a chance of developing ties with Western Europe and of re-entering, by the back door, into Mitteleuropa to which they had belonged, in one form or another, for centuries until the imposition of Communist rule in 1945 forced them to look eastwards.

Interest in the potential economic benefits of membership was a strong common denominator. On the eastern side, membership of the Alpe-Adria had the obvious appeal of a discreet, neighbourhood bridge to the capitalist world for a reforming but still Soviet-bloc, Communist country like Hungary. For Croatia and Slovenia, the two most reform-minded Republics of Yugoslavia and already open to the West, the Alpe-Adria group had another attraction: it offered them friendly backup at a time when the centralist, anti-reform forces in Yugoslavia were steadily gaining ground - notably in Serbia – and making them increasingly uncomfortable. (Additionally, should events turn really nasty in Yugoslavia, for the Croats and the Slovenes, the Alpe-Adria group could be a friendly half-way stage on their later journey westwards into the European Union). On the Austrian and Italian side, the main economic advantage was the possibility that subregional cooperation within the Alpe-Adria group might help to revitalize areas suffering the disadvantage of lying along what was still, essentially a closed, 'dead' border. Within this loose framework, with regions taking turns at the annual chairmanship of the group, some unspectacular, practical cooperation took place in areas such as culture, the environment, tourism, energy and transport. Apart from some critical voices in Belgrade warning against the danger of a Catholic restoration in Mitteleuropa, cooperation within the Alpe-Adria group encountered no visible opposition. And so it might have continued: but history did not stand still.

In November 1989, the month the Berlin Wall came down, a meeting of Deputy Prime Ministers of the Alpe-Adria states, called at Italy's initiative, was held in Budapest. It was decided that Austria, Hungary, Italy and Yugoslavia would set up an association of states, called the Initiative of Four Integration Group or Quadrilaterale, aiming to play a political role in a dramatically changed Europe.[5] The idea was that, under discreet Italian leadership and with Austrian concurrence, the group would ease the entry of Hungary and Yugoslavia into the European political and economic fold. Each country agreed to take responsibility for one area of cooperation: Austria for the environment, Italy for roads and railways, Yugoslavia for communications and the media and Hungary for culture. In May 1990, at a meeting of the Foreign Ministers of Austria, Czechoslovakia, Hungary, Italy and Yugoslavia in Vienna, Czechoslovakia was officially accepted as a member and the group was renamed as the Pentagonale. Participants agreed to hold the first Pentagonale summit in Venice in August 1990.[6] Poland joined in July 1991, whereupon there was another renaming of the group to the Hexagonale. The same meeting agreed that the possibility of operational links with the European Bank for Reconstruction and Development (EBRD) in London should be explored. (The President of the

EBRD subsequently accepted the task of organizing a CEI Secretariat in London).

In 1992, Yugoslavia's membership in the once-again renamed body, now known as the Central European Initiative (CEI), was suspended. This was in response to Yugoslavia's violent break-up in 1991 and the international recognition of Croatia and Slovenia as independent states on 15 January 1992. Croatia, Slovenia and Bosnia-Herzegovina (which proclaimed its independence in April 1992 and obtained immediate diplomatic recognition) became CEI members in July 1992. In January 1993, after Czechoslovakia's dissolution, the Czech Republic and Slovakia became members, followed, in July 1993, by Macedonia.

Extension of CEI membership to other countries was discussed at the summit meeting in Trieste in July 1994. Gyula Horn, the Hungarian Prime Minister, argued that the CEI was not a closed bloc and that the East and South-East European countries, already enjoying the status of associate membership, ought to have the opportunity to reach full membership. This was originally opposed by Croatia and Slovenia who were suspicious of any project that could, as they saw it, drag them back into the Balkans, or even into another Yugoslavian Federation, albeit in a different form. However, under Polish pressure, the principle of extending membership to other countries was eventually accepted (– Poland was particularly in favour of admitting Ukraine). This cleared the way for the admission of Albania, Belarus, Bulgaria, Moldova, Romania and Ukraine into the CEI in 1996.

STRUCTURE AND ACTIVITIES

The Central European Initiative has no fixed, permanent headquarters, no permanent officials and no budget. It operates through a number of regular forums involving senior officials and political leaders. These are:
- Heads of State/Government Meeting (annually, in the autumn);
- Parliamentary Dimension (the CEI Parliamentary Committee which meets in the spring and the CEI Parliamentary Conference which meets in the autumn);
- Foreign Ministers Meeting (annually, in the spring, but Foreign Ministers also attend and take part in the Heads of Government meeting);
- Special Meetings of Sectoral Ministers;
- Meetings of the Committee of National Coordinators (monthly).

The Presidency of the CEI is rotated annually among the Member States. In recent years it has been held by Hungary (1993), Italy (1994),

Poland (1995) and Austria (1996). Bosnia took over in 1997, but faced challenges in discharging its responsibilities in its still extremely straitened postwar circumstances. The working language used at all CEI meetings is English, with translation into other languages provided if and when necessary. The Member State which chairs the CEI provides the secretarial functions. (The lack of a permanent structure is compensated for, to a certain extent, by the work of the CEI Centre for Information and Documentation (CEI-CID) in Trieste). The state holding the annual chairmanship hosts the meetings of the Heads of Government, Ministers of Foreign Affairs, meetings of CEI parliamentarians and meetings of the Committee of National Coordinators. The meetings of National Coordinators and of Working Groups may be convened in other places. The Chairman-in-Office is supported by the former and next Chairmen, who together make up the Troika of the CEI. The National Coordinators, together with the Directors representing Member States in the Board of Directors of the European Bank for Reconstruction and Development, form the Steering Committee of the Secretariat for CEI projects in the EBRD.

At its Heads of Government summit in Warsaw on 6-7 October 1995, guidelines for activities and rules of procedure of the Central European Initiative were adopted. In this document, the CEI defines itself as a 'forum for cooperation in the region' which 'does not replace other, bilateral and multilateral channels of cooperation, neither affects the commitments of the Member States resulting of their respective international agreements'. The document enumerates areas of cooperation within the Initiative as:

- economic and technical cooperation;
- development of infrastructure in transport, energy, telecommunications and agriculture;
- strengthening the democratic institutions and observance of human rights, including the rights of persons belonging to national minorities as humanitarian matters;
- protection of the human environment;
- cooperation in the fields of science and technology, media, culture, education, youth exchange and tourism;
- cross-border and inter-regional cooperation;
- consultations on political matters of mutual interest.

The document states (in paragraph five) that 'participation in the Central European Initiative shall be open to the states of the region as described in the Policy Document of Venice of 1990, that share democratic principles and wish to contribute to the cooperation within the region and harmonise their efforts to achieve the above mentioned objectives'.

One of the CEI's main tools are its Working Groups. Their content is mainly economic, although some are largely political in character. In November 1996 the Working Groups covered the following subjects: agriculture; civil defence; culture; energy; environment; information and media; migration; minorities; rehabilitation of Bosnia-Herzegovina and Croatia; science and technology; small and medium-sized enterprises; statistics; telecommunications; tourism; transport; and vocational training. The CEI's activities and initiatives for cooperation range from workshops to investment projects of specific interest to the countries of the subregion or in the broader European context. In contrast to the Alpe-Adria group (which has not been wholly subsumed in the CEI and continues to operate in a low-key manner in fields such as culture, sport, education and media), the emphasis in the CEI is on practical cooperation. At the CEI summit meeting in 1993, Vaclav Klaus, the Czech Prime Minister, pleaded for a concentration on concrete economic cooperation rather than a political role. This advice has, by and large, been heeded. The group acts as a forum for identifying the needs of its Member States, formulating joint decisions and exchanging experiences. In many cases, the CEI's activities and projects are designed to complement and reinforce strategic programmes pursued in Central and Eastern Europe by other international organizations, in particular the European Union. To this end the CEI maintains links with the EU, other subregional organizations, relevant United Nations bodies and international financial institutions, in particular, the EBRD. Currently the CEI's priorities are: the development of infrastructure in Central and Eastern Europe and the rehabilitation and reconstruction of Bosnia-Herzegovina and Croatia. According to the annex on the CEI's selected projects and activities issued after the meeting of Heads of Government in Graz on 9 November 1996, the group sees as its task in both these areas (which are of interest to the EU and the international community at large) as being 'to mobilise the economic potential of its own member countries in terms of expertise, goods and services, with special emphasis on strengthening the private sector and small and medium-sized enterprises in the context of project implementation'.

In the CEI's operational work in these economic areas, an important role is assigned to cooperation with the Chambers of Commerce of CEI Member States through the joint CEI-EBRD Secretariat in London combined with the CEI Centre for Information and Documentation in Trieste. The CEI Secretariat, situated at the offices of the EBRD in London, advises CEI committees on investment projects, develops methodologies and technical cooperation, and supports CEI strategies for economic sectors

and infrastructure. It is answerable, on a day-to-day basis, to the EBRD's Vice-President. The Secretariat's main task is to produce project ideas and develop them into bankable projects for the benefit of CEI Member States, and also to facilitate the investment promotion and implementation work of the EBRD. Once CEI project ideas seem certain to lead to bankable projects, they are directed by the Secretariat to the appropriate desks at the EBRD or other institutions for further development and implementation. In its work, the Secretariat draws upon three kinds of support:
- experts employed by the Secretariat and seconded, in most cases, to those EBRD teams which are directly responsible for the projects in which the CEI has an interest;
- funds for administration and operational activities;
- technical cooperation to initiate the larger technical and financial studies necessary for project preparation or implementation.

The Secretariat employs about five experts in the EBRD teams and maintains links with the CEI structure and Working Groups through regular meetings, documentation and papers, and computer information networks.

The initial preparation and implementation of large projects may start independently of the CEI. However, the CEI may become involved at a later stages in which case the Secretariat can provide additional support and facilities during implementation. Where institutional projects are not directly linked to specific investments, the CEI Secretariat advises on technical and organizational matters, but agencies other than the EBRD are approached for assistance and the Trieste Centre assumes a leading role in development and implementation.

The Centre in Trieste, which opened in March 1996, was given a mandate by the CEI summit in Warsaw in October 1995, to 'further intensify the cooperation among Member States and associated countries, on the basis of a minimal structure'. The Centre's structure is indeed minimal. Its office, staff and infrastructure are funded by the Autonomous Region Friuli-Venezia Giulia in agreement with the Italian Foreign Ministry. Its Director-General, an Austrian diplomat, is funded by the Austrian government. The Centre's primary objective, as explained in a speech at the Centre's opening on 15 March 1996 by Ambassador Paul Hartig, its Director-General, is 'to circulate information and maintain an archive of CEI documentation', as well as to fulfil 'other tasks assigned to it by the Heads of Government, the Foreign Ministers, the Chairman in Office and the Committee of National Coordinators (CNC)'. A permanent unit for the rehabilitation and reconstruction of Bosnia-Herzegovina and Croatia has been attached to the Centre. Its aim is to link the beneficiary countries' rehabilitation needs with the funding potential of the donor countries and international financial institutions. Two other CEI units will be attached to the Centre: the Central European Transport Reporting (CETR) and the Central European Combined Transport Information Centre.

National Coordinators are appointed to each Working Group. Working Groups identify technical cooperation and investment opportunities, or project ideas, which might be of interest to the EBRD and other financial institutions. Those that the EBRD accepts are known as investment project ideas. The next stage is to turn investment project ideas into a formal proposal. Project preparation usually requires technical cooperation, including such activities as feasibility studies, surveys, the establishment of information systems, seminars, training, design work, technology transfer, environmental impact assessment and institutional strengthening (also known as implementation assistance). Where the EBRD is the lead investor, there has to be further investigation before technical cooperation can be considered. The project idea must be documented by the Working Group in order to: establish the potential sponsors and borrowers for the investment and construction stage and the managers of the finished project; estimate costs for construction and operation; calculate the potential revenues of the project; and gauge the order of magnitude of the financing gap which necessitates the assistance of financial institutions.

The CEI Secretariat keeps the CEI Project List, which provides a standard format for summarizing the essential details of each project. Projects considered for direct investment by the EBRD usually require a minimum of thirty million ECU, so the minimum participation of the Bank is about 10 million ECU. These investments are expected to produce an economic return, and preference is given to private sector projects. In a speech at the CEI summit held in Graz from 8 to 9 November 1996, Antonio Maria Costa, Secretary-General of the EBRD, revealed that since its creation the Bank had signed 300 projects worth almost seven billion ECU (over nine billion US dollars). In the CEI subregion, the Bank has a commitment of over 200 projects from a total of 300 and has committed over 4.3 billion ECU from a total of 6.8 billion. In the period ahead, the EBRD will be able to finance commitments of about $2.5-3 billion a year.

The following is a brief summary of the CEI Working Groups' structure and activities at the end of 1996:

Agriculture (chaired by Poland). This Working Group's priorities are social problems in agriculture accompanying the transformation process, especially unemployment; programmes for creating new jobs in rural areas; the development of agriculture market institutions; and experience-sharing between Chambers of Agriculture and specialist farming bodies.

Civil Defence (chaired by Italy). This Working Group oversaw the preparation of a CEI Convention on the Cooperation in the areas of Forecast, Prevention and Mitigation of Natural and Technological Disasters, which came into force on 1 August 1994. Its current priority is the compilation of a handbook of civil protection.

Culture and Education (chaired by Slovakia). The main programme in this Working Group has been the Central European Exchange Programme for University Studies (CEEPUS). The Working Group has been engaged in negotiations for the EU programme Leonardo da Vinci, PHARE programme, VET Reform in the Czech Republic and Free Movement of Labour Force.

Energy (chaired by Slovenia). Subjects within this Working Group in the past have included: various pipeline projects; safety improvements to the nuclear power industry's plans for radioactive waste management (Austria and Poland have raised objections to the involvement of the Working Group in this activity); removal of barriers in trade of energy materials and products among CEI countries; harmonization of energy policies of CEI countries and of the activities of their agencies (concentration on environmental protection, localization of energy construction and energy efficiency); and progress in approximation to the EU in the energy sector (Energy Charter Treaty and energy markets integration - supported by the PHARE Programme). In 1996 the main items for consideration by this Working Group were being dealt with in other forums, so the Working Group did not meet that year.

Environment (chaired by Austria). This is one of the most active Working Groups, whose main recent preoccupation has been the relationship between transport and environment. A special CEI meeting of Environment Ministers, held in Graz in September 1996, discussed the implications of EU enlargement for environment policies. In November 1996, the first meeting of a CEI sub-group on transport and environment discussed environmentally sustainable transport in the context of an OECD report on the same subject. Among topics for action were: a declaration on Sustainable Transport in the CEI countries; an action programme for the development of an environmentally benign transport system – especially in the field of public transport logistics and rolling stock technology; an action programme for pilot projects on sustainable transport development; and the search for environmentally benign solutions for the common problem of transit.

Information and Media (chaired by Austria). Recent activities in this

Working Group included a CEI Media Forum in Vienna in February 1996, at which representatives of news agencies expressed an interest in the creation of an 'information pool', exchange of training programmes for journalists, provision of updated technical equipment, study of media legislation and improvement of accreditation procedures (for example, in relation to visas). A follow-up meeting was scheduled to take place in Warsaw.

Migration (chaired by Hungary). The main subjects of cooperation in this Working Group are: exchange of information on asylum seekers, and refugees, legislation, policies and practice in CEI countries; exchange of statistical data; study of East-West migration, prevention of illegal migration and integration of migrants; repatriation of refugees from former Yugoslavia; cooperation with relevant international bodies; and organized crime and smuggling of drugs.

Minorities (chaired by Hungary). As early as 1990, CEI countries agreed that it was essential to the peace and stability of Central and Eastern Europe that the rights of national minorities be respected, promoted and guaranteed. An ad hoc Working Group was set up under Hungarian coordination in 1992. This was transformed into a permanent Working Group in July 1993 and given the task of elaborating an instrument for the protection of minority rights, based on internationally acceptable principles, which would also be acceptable to all member states. The result is the 'CEI Instrument for the Protection of Minorities' approved by the Foreign Ministers of the CEI in November 1994. The Instrument was published, with a Preface by the Working Group, in May 1996, by which time it had been signed by the Foreign Ministers of Austria, Bosnia-Herzegovina, Croatia, Hungary, Italy, Macedonia, Poland and Slovenia.

Reconstruction of Bosnia and Croatia (chaired by Poland). This Working Group has started preparing projects that include: Sarajevo Airport Rehabilitation with CEI technical assistance; help with Bosnia's energy programme in the shape of three CEI engineers and a special vehicle provided by the CEI Secretariat to the EBRD energy team; selected private sector projects in cooperation with Bosnian agencies; and selected environment, tourism, energy and transport projects in Croatia, in cooperation with Croatian authorities.

Science and Technology (chaired by Italy). This group had elaborated 58 projects by 1992. In 1994, the following were identified as priorities: Centre for Transfer of Innovative Technologies; Geophysical and Geological Characterization of the Central European Region; Laboratories Network of CEI Countries for Experimental Mechanics; Centres of Excellence and Physics of Matter; Meteorology Centres Network of CEI

Countries; Astronomical Observatories Network of CEI Countries; Space - Feasibility Study for CESAR Satellite (a subregional satellite for scientific tasks whose launch could take place early in the year 2000 provided a final decision on the implementation of the project is taken soon); Cooperation between CEI Research Institutes on Industrial Technology and Innovation; and Cooperation between CEI Scientific Institutes on Parallel Computing. Within the framework of this Working Group, workshops have also been held on the following subjects: Eureka Initiative, earth science, meteorological standards, technological innovation, meteorology, centres of excellence, Trieste Scientific System, technologies for rational use of energy and experimental mechanics

Small and Medium-Sized Enterprises (chaired by Slovenia). Recent activities within this Working Group have included: preparation for a workshop on credit guarantee schemes for small and medium-sized enterprises; support for pilot projects for establishing the methods and forms of funding for rapidly growing companies ('gazelles'); and the creation of a network of small and medium-enterprise national focal points via the internet, with headquarters at the UN Economic Commission for Europe in Geneva.

Statistics (chaired by Austria). This Working Group published a brochure called 'CEI in Figures' in February 1994 and has organized workshops in Prague (June 1994) and Bled (June 1995). Current activities include a project on Neighbouring Regions Environment Statistics and Migration Statistics. However, a meeting in Rome in September 1996 agreed a series of rationalizations aimed at avoiding duplication of work with institutions like OECD, EUROSTAT and others. This will mean more concentration on supplying other Working Groups with data and bringing to an end the Group's own projects on the environment and migration.

Telecommunications (chaired by Croatia). This Working Group, originally assigned to Yugoslavia, then – after the latter's collapse – for a while overseen by Austria and eventually given to Croatia, was dissolved in 1996 for lack of concrete projects.

Tourism (chaired by Croatia). Main current activities in this Working Group are: the elaboration of a 'Strategic Tourism Marketing Plan for the CEI' (including ideas on cultural and rural tourism) based on a preliminary concept prepared by the Croatian Ministry of Tourism and Institute of Tourism; the establishment of a CEI Centre for Tourism (including a databank) in Zagreb; the preparation of an 'image-brochure' to be used for the promotion of tourism in CEI countries; and the setting up of a network of tourist information centres in CEI countries.

Transport (chaired by Italy). This is a key Working Group whose current priorities are: East-West Priority Corridors (Adriatic Sea/Black Sea corridor and Trieste/Ljubljana/Budapest/Kiev); CETIR, a large technical cooperation project organized by the CEI using consultants and cooperating institutions in CEI countries to develop a comprehensive transport database and transport planning methodology suitable for the subregion; and combined transport.

Vocational Training (chaired by the Czech Republic). Recent activities in this Working Group have included seminars on the development of environmental equipment and on small and medium-sized enterprises, both held in Prague and financed by the Czech government. Both seminars are to be continued and a new project called 'Capacity Sharing in Training' is to be launched under a CEI coordinator.

RELATIONS WITH OTHER ORGANIZATIONS

In July 1992 representatives from the Council of Europe, the European Union, the European Free Trade Association (EFTA), the Danube Commission, the Black Sea Economic Cooperation, the Council of Baltic Sea States, the Alpe-Adria and the EBRD attended a CEI summit for the first time. Since then, there have been regular contacts with all of these organizations. The CEI summit in Warsaw in October 1995 recommended that the Committee of National Coordinators 'consider ways to strengthen contacts and cooperation with the Organization of Security and Cooperation in Europe (OSCE), the Council of Europe, the UN Economic Commission for Europe as well as other European organizations and institutions, particularly with neighbouring regional structures like the Council of the Baltic States and the Black Sea Economic Cooperation'. The summit's final document noted the significance of 'the CEI's close and regular cooperation with the European Commission, initiated in 1995' and mentioned, as of particular importance, cooperation in priority areas such as transport, science and technology, energy, environment, telecommunications and the promotion of small and medium-sized business. The Prime Ministers also noted that 'the Initiative's activities, especially in the above-mentioned areas, could become an advantageous platform reinforcing their pre-accession strategy'. The summit also agreed – obviously to assuage Russia's frequently voiced complaint at being left out of the CEI - to a regular exchange of information between the Troika of the CEI and the Russian Federation at Senior Officials' level. The European Union's view of the CEI is presented in a 1996 document called 'Report from the Commission to the Council on European Union

Cooperation with the Central European Initiative'.[7] An illustrated seventeen-page guide to the activities of the CEI was published by the EBRD in April 1997 under the title the 'Central European Initiative'.

At the Graz summit in November 1996, CEI Heads of Government drafted an offer of closer cooperation with the OSCE which was duly handed over at the OSCE summit meeting in Lisbon on 2 and 3 December. The CEI Heads of Government proposed to the OSCE the following steps as a basis for closer cooperation: periodic exchange of information between the OSCE and the CEI using the appropriate channels of communication; mutual invitations to OSCE and CEI high-level meetings; and contributions by the CEI to current subregional initiatives in the framework of the OSCE. The proposals emphasized that the CEI intended to realize its subregional potential as an element of a new security architecture in Europe, by means of a close cooperation with the OSCE. In his speech at the Lisbon meeting, Mr. Schussel, Austria's Foreign Minister and CEI Chairman-in-Office during 1996, pointed to the CEI's important role as a catalyst in assisting Member States in their political and economic transformation and, at the same time, providing a framework for maintaining the cohesion of the subregion regardless of the kind of relationships member states have, or would obtain, with the European Union. He recalled the CEI's recently formalized 'special relationship' with the European Union (see above), as well as its ever closer relationship with the Council of Europe and the UN Economic Commission for Europe.

FUTURE PROSPECTS

How should the Lisbon bid by the CEI to achieve a higher profile in the new European security architecture be seen? How should the CEI be rated as a bottom-up, 'soft security' body amid a plethora of other European organizations? Andreas Unterberger, a prominent Austrian commentator, claims that many subregional and international bodies that have sprung since the Second World War, both during the years of East-West conflict and during phases of euphoria about the UN, have since become redundant and need to prove that they are needed. As for the CEI, he argues that it has 'already long ago demonstrated that it is completely redundant' and goes on: 'it is only with difficulty that officials can cobble together texts with which politicians are trying to cover this piece of Central European emptiness'. The trouble is, he continues, that it is only diplomats who investigate and pronounce upon international organizations and they are, quite naturally, reluctant to stop any diplomatic activity whatsoever.

Jobs and other interests are involved – hence there is no serious discussion of the issue.[8]

It is true that in some ways the CEI can be said to be marking time.[9] To a certain extent this is due to the war in former Yugoslavia which overshadowed the work of the CEI and forced it to adopt a lower profile than might otherwise have been the case. The other major subregional group in Central Europe, at the time, the Visegrad group, concerned itself more with cooperation in foreign policy and security issues. The Visegrad group's successor, CEFTA, has made formal strides on free trade, rather than working on the unspectacular practical projects which are the CEI's bread and butter.

It is incontrovertible that the only two serious games in town are EU and NATO enlargement. In this context, bodies like the CEI can play only a modest supplementary role as bit-players. However, the CEI may yet prove to be a more significant contributor to Europe's multi-layered integration than its critics are prepared to admit: chiefly as a forum linking those already in the EU, those about to join in the foreseeable future, and those who may never join or are only likely to do so in the very distant future. Not surprisingly, this potentiality of the CEI is appreciated particularly in the countries whose chances of joining the EU soon are not good. There is, however, also a new realism among all Central European states, both in regard to the European Union and NATO and in regard to the uses to which bodies like the CEI might be put. For example, the Czech Republic and Poland, which to begin with had eyes only for the EU, seem to have become more interested in cooperation within the framework of bodies such the CEI. Hungary's interest in the CEI continues to be serious, despite its preoccupation with its entry into the EU and NATO. For a country in an exposed position such as Ukraine, CEI membership has a political value as it lessens its political isolation. In the case of Belarus, its membership of the CEI at the very least gives those who believe in reform and their country's independence a little more room for manoeuvre, and outsiders more of a chance to help them.

Italy, which provided many of the original impulses for the CEI, is still interested.[10] Its keenness on the CEI has, if anything, grown - not least owing to the important EU transport projects, such as the 1600 kilometre Kiev-Budapest-Ljubljana-Trieste-Barcelona high-speed road (Corridor 5), which have a CEI dimension. This project has led to close cooperation within the CEI between Hungary, Italy and Slovenia, although Croatia consequently feels left out. Slovenia's veto of Croatia's request for a Rijeka-Trieste connection, with a road and rail link via the Slovene Adriatic port of Koper, has led to a deterioration in Croat-Slovene relations (which were already burdened by a territorial dispute over the Piran Bay territorial waters). Croatia stayed away from the signing of a Memorandum of Understanding by Ministers of Transport of Italy, Hungary, Slovenia, Slovakia and Ukraine in Trieste on 16 December 1996. Croatia, however, is unlikely to walk out of the CEI, the only Western/Central European group (apart from the Council of Europe) to which it belongs. Slovenia has an interest in the CEI, despite the fact that it is a candidate for both EU and NATO membership. Interest in the CEI is still considerable in Austria, even after its entry into the EU, but its role as one of the two financial contributors to CEI core activities (Italy is the other one) is not popular at a time of large budget deficits and consequent cuts in public expenditure.

In this context, the CEI may be able to provide 'added value' and play a complementary role in a number of particular ways. By including those Central and Eastern European states who do not yet have Association Agreements with the EU (most of the former Yugoslav states, Ukraine, Belarus and Albania), it can help to bring these states closer to the EU (perhaps preparing them for the eventual conclusion of Association Agreements with the Union and, in the longer term, membership of that organization) while also promoting cooperation amongst this wider group of Central and Eastern European states. By bringing in the former Yugoslav states (including eventually Federal Republic of Yugoslavia), it can contribute to post-conflict peace-building and reconciliation (both in a general sense and through specific projects) and to these states gradual re-integration into the wider international community. The CEI Instrument for the Protection of Minorities can perhaps provide an additional, subregional framework for efforts to prevent, manage and resolve minority conflicts, particularly in former Yugoslavia. Given its pre-history as a transfrontier cooperation group and the continuing relevance of some of its practical projects to transfrontier cooperation, the CEI may also have some potential for promoting such cooperation, particularly in the parts of South-Eastern Europe where it is currently weak or non-existent.

Certainly, the recent arrival of so many new members has posed questions of identity for the CEI. Its flexibility and pragmatic spirit should help it to resolve them but, like the future of so many other international and subregional bodies, that of the CEI remains open. If it dies, it will be through benign neglect rather than a deliberate execution. For the time being, however, its chances of survival seem better than even.

8 The Black Sea Economic Cooperation: Will Hopes Become Reality?[1]

Oleksandr Pavliuk

As the cradle of different civilizations, located at the trade and geopolitical cross-roads between Europe and Asia, the Black Sea subregion has been, since ancient times, a place where people of different nationalities, traditions, cultures and religions lived together and intermingled. Historically, the Black Sea basin has been known for efforts to build bridges, establish rapprochement among neighbouring – and often conflicting – nations, and develop mutually beneficial trade relations and contacts. The famous Silk Road, for centuries, linked the countries of Europe and Asia. Consequently, extensive and useful experience of trade exchange, cohabitation and mutual enrichment between different cultures and beneficial contacts among neighbouring peoples have been established and nurtured. This process, however, has never been an easy and simple one: periods of intensive trade relations, peace and tranquillity were followed by mutual misperceptions and tensions, protracted conflicts and destructive wars. In particular, for many decades after the Second World War, the atmosphere and political climate in the Black Sea subregion were characterized by mutual suspicions and mistrust between the countries belonging to the two opposing political and military blocs divided by the Iron Curtain. With the end of the Cold War in the last decade of the twentieth century, the countries of the subregion have at last won a new chance to revive the cooperative spirit of the area.

THE BSEC'S ORIGINS AND BASIC FEATURES

The political initiative for the creation of the Black Sea Economic Cooperation (BSEC) group was officially put forward by the President of Turkey, Turgut Ozal, at the end of 1990. In November-December 1990, the Turkish Ministry of Foreign Affairs organized in Ankara several preliminary meetings of delegations from four Black Sea coastal countries: Turkey, Bulgaria, Romania and the then Soviet Union. These meetings confirmed the existence of political support for the establishment of economic cooperation in the Black Sea subregion, based on geographical proximity and common subregional and domestic problems (mainly of a socio-economic and environmental nature). At follow-up meetings of experts held in Bucharest, Sofia, and Moscow in the first half of 1991, a draft document on the BSEC was prepared and reviewed.

The collapse of the Soviet Union at the end of 1991 changed the scope of the initiative. The newly independent, former Soviet republics of the Black Sea subregion quickly confirmed their interest in the project, looking for various possibilities to facilitate their transition to market economies, to ensure a higher degree of integration into the world economy, and to enhance stability and security in the subregion. For most of these states, the BSEC became one of their first exposures to independent, international politics on a multilateral level. The demise of the communist superpower also gave a new political dimension to the BSEC. Azerbaijan hoped to find in Turkey a counterbalance to Russian influence. Russia, on the contrary, sought to limit the growth of Turkish power in the subregion.[2] During the spring of 1992, Albania and Greece also expressed their desire to join the emerging cooperation.

On 25 June 1992, the BSEC was formally established at the Meeting of Heads of State and Government in Istanbul. Eleven countries of the Black Sea subregion – Albania, Armenia, Azerbaijan, Bulgaria, Georgia, Greece, Moldova, Romania, Russia, Turkey and Ukraine – signed the Summit Declaration on the Black Sea Economic Cooperation and the Bosphorus Statement. These two basic documents set forth the aims and agenda of the BSEC, which were later further developed in the Bucharest Statement of 30 June 1995 and the Moscow Declaration of 25 October 1996. The main purpose of the BSEC was defined as the promotion of 'comprehensive multilateral and bilateral' economic cooperation and, on this basis, the consolidation of peace and stability in the Black Sea subregion. The statement, referring to the general principles of the United Nations' Charter and the Organization for Security and Cooperation in Europe (OSCE), defined the shared vision of the BSEC countries as the transformation of the Black Sea into 'a region of peace, freedom, stability and prosperity'. The Heads of State and Government also stressed that the BSEC 'constituted an effort that would facilitate the processes and structures of European integration'.[3]

De jure, the BSEC is not an organization and has rather been defined as a forum or process. The participating states decided that at this stage of their cooperation 'it is necessary to ensure institutional flexibility'. Consequently, most of the BSEC's decisions are of a recommendatory, rather than obligatory, nature. Decisions on all the key issues pertaining to the BSEC's functioning, including the admission of new members, the granting of an observer status, creation of new BSEC bodies, adoption of the agenda for BSEC meetings, approval of cooperative projects and financial commitments affecting all participating states, are taken by consensus. Other decisions may be taken by a two-thirds majority vote. The chairmanship of the BSEC rotates among the Member States (every six months according to the English alphabetical order) and is exercised by the Minister of Foreign Affairs of the state concerned. Since 1995, an European Union (EU) type 'Troika' system has operated as a way of coordinating BSEC activities more effectively.

The highest, regular decision-making body of the BSEC is the Meeting of the Ministers of Foreign Affairs, which is convened at least twice per year, and decides on all issues pertaining to the functioning of the BSEC. Additional meetings of the Foreign Ministers may be held upon the request of one or more of the participating states, subject to consensus. Meetings of Heads of State and Government are also held (the first three such summits were held in June 1992 in Istanbul, in June 1995 in Bucharest and in October 1996 in Moscow). The Foreign Ministerial meetings are preceded by meetings of Senior Officials of Foreign Ministries to prepare agendas and draft documents for the Foreign Ministers.[4] A Permanent International Secretariat (PERMIS) of the BSEC was established in 1993 to provide secretarial services, with its headquarters based in Istanbul. The PERMIS consists of eleven staff, including five diplomats (a director, first deputy and three deputy directors). English is the official language of BSEC documents, while English, French and Russian are the working languages.

In line with the founding documents, from the very outset, priority in BSEC activities has been given to economic cooperation in specific fields. Consequently, several specific practical programmes have been developed and twelve permanent expert Working Groups (on transport, energy, banking and finance, trade and industrial cooperation, exchange of statistical data and economic information, agriculture and agro-industry, environmental protection, health care and pharmaceutics, cooperation in science and technology, legislative information, cooperation in tourism, and communications) and six Ad hoc Working Groups have been set up. These subsidiary bodies do the bulk of the BSEC's work. In addition to Working Groups, the BSEC has a number of permanent institutions (PERMIS, the BSEC Coordination Center for Statistical Data and Economic Cooperation in Ankara, the Black Sea Regional Energy Center in Sofia, and the Black Sea Trade and Development Bank in Thessalonika) and affiliated organizations (the Black Sea Economic Cooperation Council, the International Black Sea Club, and the Parliamentary Assembly of the Black Sea States).[5]

The Parliamentary Assembly of the BSEC (PABSEC) was convened in

February 1993 as the 'parliamentary segment' of the BSEC. It was established to 'provide the legal ground for the realization of the principles and the goals of respect for human rights, rule of law and democratic values'[6] as embodied in the BSEC founding documents. The PABSEC has also aimed to give further impetus to the economic cooperation of the BSEC countries, consolidating their democratic and parliamentary systems, and boosting prosperity among the member countries. Ten BSEC countries (Albania, Armenia, Azerbaijan, Georgia, Greece, Moldova, Romania, Russia, Turkey and Ukraine) have joined the PABSEC. The highest PABSEC body is the General Assembly of representatives of the national parliaments which meets twice per year. The PABSEC's International Secretariat and its Bureau are located in Istanbul, together with three Standing Committees: On Economic, Commercial, Technological and Environmental issues; On Legal and Political Issues; and On Cultural, Educational and Social Issues.

According to the 1992 BSEC Summit Declaration, the BSEC 'is open for the participation of other interested states recognizing the provisions of this document'. As early as November 1991, the Federal Republic of Yugoslavia expressed its desire to join the BSEC, but its subsequent disintegration blocked this process. Since 1995, the ('rump') Federal Republic of Yugoslavia, the Former Yugoslav Republic of Macedonia, and the Islamic Republic of Iran have applied for membership. In addition to fully-fledged members, the BSEC also grants the status of observer. Several states have already been granted this status: Poland (1992, renewed in 1996); Israel, Egypt, the Slovak Republic and Tunisia (1993); and Italy and Austria (1995). Several others (Croatia, Bosnia-Herzegovina, Jordan, Cyprus, Slovenia and Kazakhstan) have recently applied for observer status.

The further enlargement of the BSEC has, however, proved quite problematic, and the issue has become one of the most contentious within the group. The problems with the accession of new members result not so much from an exclusionary attitude toward outsiders, but rather from the BSEC's diversity and from the political tensions in the subregion. Under BSEC rules of procedure, the admission of new members requires a consensus of all BSEC participating states. Some members (for example, Russia) believe that the BSEC should be as open and transparent as possible. Others (for example, Romania) are concerned that the growing number of new applicants could lead to a doubling of the BSEC's membership, transforming it into an amorphous structure with even less efficiency than at present. Some BSEC members are also concerned that new countries, especially those of the former Yugoslavia, could bring with them new tensions and thereby aggravate existing tensions between BSEC members themselves. The October 1996 Moscow meeting of Senior Officials which discussed the various applications for full membership and observer status concluded only that 'various views were expressed by the participants'.[7] This reflects not only the different approaches of the BSEC's members toward enlargement, but also the serious political tensions in the subregion. These prompted, for example, a Greek veto of membership for the Former Yugoslav Republic of Macedonia and a Turkish veto of membership for the Republic of Cyprus. In the absence of the required consensus, the 1996 Moscow Foreign Ministers meeting 'welcomed the interest' of other states in applying to become full members or observers in the BSEC, but decided 'to continue the assessment of the issue of the BSEC enlargement ...taking into account various positions of the participating states'.[8] It is clear that the BSEC needs to work out a common conceptual approach to the admission of new full members and observers.

ACHIEVEMENTS IN THE MIDST OF PERSISTENT CHALLENGES

In spite of many difficulties and a certain pessimism on the part of many observers, the BSEC is gradually gaining ground. The growing interest of outsiders in joining the group indicates its increasing attractiveness. In general, the BSEC has more or less successfully surmounted the first – organizational – stage of its development, when its basic structure and subsidiary bodies were established and developed. The above-mentioned elements of institutionalization and the creation of permanent working bodies have allowed for fairly systematic activity.

The BSEC has proved to be a useful forum for broad multilateral dialogue on various issues of economic cooperation. The BSEC's current activities are increasingly focused on several specific subregional projects. The first has to do with the creation of a BSEC common energy market and an interconnected power system (a memorandum on cooperation in the field of electric power industries was proposed by Russia), which would help to solve the energy supply problems experienced by many countries in the subregion. Since the break-up of the Soviet Union, the transit routes for oil and gas from deposits in the Caspian Sea to the outside world have also become a major and controversial issue for the Black Sea subregion. It could be argued that particular attention should be paid to this issue within the BSEC framework. However, strong disagreements over oil/gas pipeline routes – with Russia favouring the 'northern' Baku-Grozny-Novorossiysk route and Turkey preferring the 'southern' Baku-Ceyhan route via the Turkish Mediterranean coast[9] – make it practically impossible to discuss these issues within the BSEC framework.

The second project is directed at the development of a subregional transport infrastructure integrated into wider trans-European transport networks. A comprehensive transportation map of the subregion has been prepared, and expert discussions are underway on practical steps to simplify passenger and cargo traffic in the subregion. The BSEC members are also interested in improving subregional telecommunications, including the development of fibre-optic systems. Another project is aimed at increasing cooperation in attracting foreign investment and export credits, including the creation of a common BSEC market for investment projects and the harmonization of national legislation for the promotion and protection of investment. The BSEC Foreign Ministers meeting in Moscow in October 1996 took note of the Statement on Basic Principles of Investment Collaboration in the BSEC Region, prepared by Ukrainian and Russian experts, and recommended its use as a basis for further work in this field. In line with this, the first BSEC meeting on Capital Markets and Areas of Cooperation was held in Istanbul in April 1997.

Aside from these various economic activities, the BSEC also tends to concentrate on environmental and scientific cooperation. Protection of the environment is becoming a special area of cooperation, given the dangerously polluted state of the Black Sea which is a matter of increasing concern for BSEC members.[10] In April 1992, the Black Sea countries signed a 'Convention on the Protection of the Black Sea Against Pollution'. The first BSEC conference on environmental protection and development was held in Tbilisi in 1994. By 1997, work had also begun on a draft Black Sea Action Plan to be adopted by all the BSEC members.

Another positive feature of the BSEC is the practice of involving local authorities, non-governmental organizations and professional groups from all participating states in multilateral cooperation – something which it can also be argued enhances subregional stability. Two round tables of governors and mayors from BSEC states' capital cities have been held to discuss the problems of capital cities and to find common solutions (– the first in September 1994 in Istanbul, the second in Kyiv in September 1995). A BSEC conference of representatives of academic communities was convened in Athens in December 1996 and discussed plans for the establishment of an International Center for Black Sea Studies.

The BSEC's founding documents underlined the importance of the private sector for the development of cooperation and stated the intention of participating states 'to improve the business environment and to stimulate individual and collective initiative of the enterprises and firms'.[11] In practice, the model of cooperation is largely based on maximum support for entrepreneurship and private initiative. The participating states are supposed to contribute through the harmonization of national legislation, the adoption of necessary legal instruments and the establishment of compatible visa and residence requirements. The BSEC Business Council was established to ensure more active involvement of business communities in the BSEC process. However, due to the inadequacies of national legislation, different foreign trade regimes and generally poor economic conditions in most BSEC countries, the BSEC Business Council remains far from achieving its initial goals or hoped for impact. In April 1996, a BSEC Business Forum was held in Bucharest to further stimulate this process and a common understanding was reached that such a forum should be convened, in rotation, on a regular basis. At the end of April 1997, Istanbul hosted an international economic conference on 'The New Possibilities in the Black Sea Region' attended by the Heads of State and Government of the BSEC countries. Also in 1997, a decision was taken to establish the Association of Trade and Commerce Chambers of the BSEC members, while the BSEC Business Council decided to invite representatives of private businesses to all its future meetings.

From a political point of view, the BSEC's existence for more than four years can already be assessed as a success given the past and present differences, tensions, and sometimes even armed conflicts, between some of its members. These problems include: the uneasy relations between Bulgaria and Greece over Macedonia; the Ukrainian-Romanian border dispute; the national minority problem in relations between Turkey and Bulgaria; Russian-Georgian differences over the settlement of the Abkhazian problem; Ukrainian-Russian tensions over the presence of the Russian military and naval base in Crimea; the protracted conflict between Greece and Turkey over Cyprus; the war between Armenia and Azerbaijan over Nagorno-Karabakh; the armed conflict between the Moldovan government and its eastern region (Transdniestra) supported by Russia; and several other, less prominent, conflicts.

Despite its declared intentions and the progress described above in preparing several very promising projects, the BSEC has so far failed to achieve many of its practical goals. The major problem in the BSEC's development is its poor record in implementing decisions and failure to establish substantive cooperative activities. This serious weakness is explained primarily by the absence of mutually agreed and accepted international, legal obligations. On the whole, the BSEC's activities are limited to discussions and usually no binding document is signed. Some argue that the BSEC Working Groups, which do not have decision-making responsibilities, are 'typical debating clubs'.[12] The implementation of their recommendations, if and when they are approved by the Foreign Ministerial meetings (and again these meetings' decisions are not of a binding character), remains the responsibility of national governments. The lack of mutual, legal obligations leads to a lack of responsibility for the implementation of decisions taken. As a result, many decisions remain no more than good intentions and joint declarations.

At the same time, the structure of the BSEC subsidiary bodies has become decidedly large and complex, and streamlining them has become one of the group's concerns. In particular, there was little initial interaction between the BSEC and the PABSEC. Only in 1996 did the PABSEC and the BSEC Member States approve a paper on the two bodies mutual relations, stipulating the strengthening of cooperation through the organization of joint meetings at different levels and the undertaking of joint activities serving their common objectives. It was agreed that representatives of the BSEC and the PABSEC 'may attend' various of their respective meetings and the two bodies would exchange information on their activities. Some progress was made after this: both secretariats supplied each other with relevant documents and their representatives attended meetings of various BSEC and PABSEC bodies, discussing issues of mutual interest as well as measures to be taken.[13] However, there is still no appropriate mechanism for BSEC-PABSEC interaction, and to a certain extent the PABSEC duplicates BSEC's activities by addressing similar problems.

In addition, the BSEC still lacks a clear priority or unifying core for its activities (for example, a free trade agreement or a customs union). The development of subregional trade remains embryonic. Moreover, bilateral trade relations between most of the BSEC members are underdeveloped. Very often the main trading partners of BSEC members are outside the group. For example, aside from Russia which comprises more than 50 per cent of Ukraine's total trade volume, all the other BSEC countries together account for less than six per cent of Ukraine's overall trade. The BSEC countries' mutual investments are also insignificant. As a result, most BSEC states have substantial economic interests elsewhere and often give preference to participation in other economic institutions or customs unions. In this regard, a declaration of intent on the establishment of a BSEC free trade area – signed at a special meeting of BSEC Foreign and Economic Ministers in Istanbul in February 1997 – may provide both a new impetus and a necessary unifying core for the future development of the BSEC. The declaration appealed to participants 'to start the examination of the ways and means' of establishing a free trade area. After this, the BSEC PERMIS had relevant contacts with the European Commission and the ninth Foreign Ministers' meeting agreed to work out a special action plan. The establishment of a BSEC free trade area is, however, likely to be a long and overwhelmingly difficult process (if achievable at all), given the different levels of economic development and different trade regimes of the BSEC members, their different status and aspirations vis-à-vis the EU, as well as the need for the prior conclusion of bilateral free trade agreements between the BSEC members themselves.

Another reason for the BSEC's lack of substance lies in the sphere of finance. Most (if not all) BSEC members face economic problems and consequently lack the financial resources necessary to implement joint projects. Nine out of eleven BSEC states are former communist countries, experiencing grave economic problems in their transition to market economies and finding it difficult to fulfil their financial obligations within the BSEC. Insufficient infrastructure, poor communications and underdeveloped transportation facilities are also common characteristics of the BSEC countries. Agreement on the budget for the BSEC PERMIS meets with constant difficulties. At the beginning of 1994, the participating states reached a tentative agreement on the scale of their contributions to the PERMIS budget: Greece, Russia, Turkey and Ukraine would each contribute 16 per cent of the budget, Bulgaria and Romania would each contribute eight per cent, and the other members would contribute four per cent each. Nevertheless, in 1996, as in previous years, the Government of Turkey contributed two-thirds of the PERMIS's budget. The most economically successful among the BSEC members are Turkey and Greece, which are themselves not particularly prosperous by European standards. Hopes that Turkey would emerge as an economic leader and financial donor for the subregion have not materialized. Consequently, neither Turkey nor Greece has been able to assume the heavy burden of financing BSEC activities.

The impact of the BSEC members' financial straits was well illustrated by the problems encountered with the creation of a Black Sea Trade and Development Bank (BSTDB). The agreement on the Bank's establishment was signed in December 1993, and it was initially planned that the Bank would start operating at the beginning of 1996. As the BSEC's main financial body, the BSTDB is supposed to accumulate resources for and finance joint BSEC projects, as well as facilitating BSEC cooperation with various international financial institutions, encouraging them to participate in BSEC projects. Because of financial difficulties, the entry into force of the agreement establishing the BSTDB (its ratification by all BSEC members, the transmission of the instruments of ratification to the depository of the agreement, and the necessary financial contributions) turned out to be long and complex. Only by late 1996-early 1997 had some progress been achieved. After the expected inaugural meeting of the Board of Governors of the BSTDB, the Bank was due to become fully operational in the course of 1997. Consequently, it could well become the BSEC's first major joint project to be implemented.

The last but not least factor posing serious obstacles to BSEC activities stems from the broader political situation in the Black Sea subregion. Most of the BSEC countries are characterized by internal political and/or social instability. Their bilateral relations are characterized by political tensions and sometimes outright conflicts. Furthermore they have different (sometimes hidden) agendas and interests in the BSEC itself.

VARIED PARTICIPANTS, VARIED AGENDAS

As of today, the BSEC is the most diverse among all other subregional groups in the Barents-Black Sea belt. It unites eleven countries which differ very greatly in many areas: economic and military potential, geostrategic interests, and even simple geographic and population size (ranging from large Russia, striving to maintain its superpower status, to small Albania and the three Caucasian states). The Black Sea countries differ also in their cultural, social, and religious traditions. The BSEC includes, on the one hand, almost all the countries of the Orthodox world (Greece, Bulgaria, Romania, Russia, Moldova, Ukraine, Armenia and Georgia) and, on the other hand, Muslim Azerbaijan, Albania and Turkey. Their institutional affiliations with, and attitudes toward, the main European structures, particularly the North Atlantic Treaty Organization (NATO) and the EU, also differ greatly. The BSEC includes full members of NATO (Greece and Turkey) and the EU (Greece), EU Associates and NATO applicants (Bulgaria and Romania), others which have not formally applied but are developing close cooperation with both NATO and the EU (Moldova and especially Ukraine), the Caucasian states which are not directly involved in the disputes over NATO's eastward enlargement, and Russia (which remains opposed to NATO enlargement despite the conclusion, in May 1997, of the NATO-Russia Founding Act). In comparison to the BSEC, other subregional groups in the Barents-Black Sea area either have strong Western involvement (– the Barents Euro-Arctic Council (BEAC), the Council of Baltic Sea States (CBSS) or the Central European Initiative (CEI)) or are much smaller in size and hence more coherent (– the Central European Free Trade Area (CEFTA)).

The BSEC's broad and diverse membership and its largely consensus-based working methods, together with the subregion's long standing political and ethnic problems, affect the group's evolution and partially explain the BSEC's weakness in taking and implementing decisions. Its members' differing visions of the future of European integration have also led them to support sometimes varied agendas, priorities and foci within the group. Taking into account the combination of political influence, economic potential, and the envisaged shares of financial contributions to its core activities and joint projects, Russia, Turkey, Greece, Ukraine, Romania, and Bulgaria play the main role in the BSEC. Relations between Russia and Turkey (the BSEC's two largest states and the major players in the subregion by all important measures of power) and their attitudes toward the BSEC are of particular importance.

As noted at the beginning of this chapter, it was Turkey which put forward the initiative and took the lead in establishing the BSEC, as well as taking upon itself the major financial burden for BSEC's operation. Turkish interest in the BSEC stemmed from a variety of factors. During 1989-92, Turkey was discovering for itself a new geopolitical role. The collapse of communism in the Soviet bloc countries of the Black Sea subregion followed by the disintegration of the Soviet Union itself, opened up opportunities for Istanbul to build a new domain of political and economic influence and to realize its long-lasting hope of becoming a subregional leader and playing a major strategic role in international politics. The timing seemed to be perfect to increase Turkish influence in the Balkans and the Caucasus, as well as among the 50 million Turkish-speaking Muslims in the Central Asian republics of the former Soviet Union, by offering them the Turkish model of secular government. In contrast to the Islamic fundamentalism of Iran, Pakistan or Saudi Arabia, the Turkish model was clearly preferred by post-communist leaders, as well as by the West. Economically, hopes were raised that Turkey would 'emerge as an economic powerhouse in the region, channelling Western capital and technology to former Eastern bloc countries and making profit in the process.'[14] In 1989 and 1990, when the Soviet Union was experiencing growing economic difficulties, Turkey recorded a 9.4 per cent annual economic growth rate.[15] The fact that Turkey was refused EU membership in 1989 added to its desire to create an influential subregional structure under its own leadership, although Turkish officials indicated that the BSEC should not be perceived as an alternative or rival to the EU. Turkish support for the BSEC was also grounded in its geographical position as a coastal state and its interest in developing trade (in particular, border and off-shore trade) with its Black Sea neighbours.[16]

Soon, however, it became apparent that Turkey lacked the financial and political capacity to establish itself as the dominant power in the subregion. Istanbul was unable to provide economic aid in the quantities needed by the ex-communist countries, and by and large its attempts to extend its sphere of influence into the Caucasus and Central Asia met with only minimal success. Consequently, Turkey became less dominant in the BSEC. Some even predicted that Turkey might loose interest in the group. Nevertheless, despite their overall failure, the Turkish ambitions and intentions were sufficient to alarm Russia.[17]

Historically, the Russian-Turkish relationship has not been cordial. Mutual suspicions and misperceptions, exacerbated by competing geostrategic interests and competition for the leading role in the Black Sea subregion, continue to characterize the relationship.[18] Although weakened after the demise of the Soviet Union and overwhelmed by domestic problems, Russia has been unwilling to give up its traditional role in the Black Sea area, where it lost much of its maritime power. Viewing Istanbul as its main subregional rival, Moscow has become increasingly anxious about the newly established Turkish military and naval superiority in the Black Sea (while Turkey has 116 vessels and 16 submarines, Russia possesses 52 vessels and four submarines[19]), and growing Turkish influence in the Black Sea subregion and among the Turkish nations of the former Soviet Union.[20] As Elizabeth Fuller concluded:

> given Russia's traditional mistrust of Turkey (the two countries have fought 13 wars against each other over the past five centuries), Moscow might not have fully perceived the discrepancy between Turkey's ambitions and its ability to realize them. In other words, what matters is not so much what Turkey can or cannot achieve ... as what Russia perceives Turkey to be capable of doing, and how Russia's reactions to this misperception will influence future developments. As long as Russia fears an expansion of Turkish influence into these regions, it will continue to treat Turkey as a threat, even if that threat is minimal, and compound latent tensions.[21]

These Russian fears, together with the need to cope with domestic economic, social and ethnic challenges, also explain Russia's cautious and somewhat reluctant engagement with the BSEC during the first three years of its existence. As a result, Russia was very passive within the BSEC which could not but impede the group's evolution. Since 1996, however, when Russia held the BSEC chair, its approach to the group has changed significantly. Russia has become more proactive, and there are grounds to believe that – as Russia succeeds with its economic recovery – it is likely to further intensify efforts to regain its role and influence in the Black Sea basin and, perhaps, to establish itself as the BSEC's leader.

Turkish ambitions in the Balkans also raised concerns among other countries in the Black Sea subregion, in particular Greece and Bulgaria. The long-standing Greek-Turkish rivalry and continuing mutual distrust[22] account for the initial hesitancy of Greece about the BSEC, and especially about the PABSEC (whose establishment was another Turkish initiative). Perceiving the PABSEC as an additional political tool for Turkish influence and suspecting Istanbul of planning to turn the BSEC into a kind of mini-EU with executive and legislative bodies, both Greece and Bulgaria refused to join the PABSEC. Greece finally became a member in 1995. Bulgaria, however, remained outside the PABSEC, fearing that the structure could be used to impose on Sofia Turkey's preferred solution to the Turkish minority issue in Bulgaria.

The agendas of other BSEC states also vary. As the BSEC's only full EU member, Greece sees its main task as to take advantage of this position to serve as a link and mediator between the BSEC and the EU. In particular, this role is manifested in efforts to attract EU financial resources for BSEC joint programmes. Consequently, Greece has been an active promoter of the establishment of the BSTDB and the International Center for Black Sea Studies, which are based respectively in Thessalonika and Athens and supported by the EU. Meanwhile, other BSEC participants worry that Greece, Russia and Turkey will be the first to benefit from the BSTDB's creation, as these three countries secured the executive posts at the Bank.[23]

Having declared their first priority to be to gain membership of the EU and NATO, Bulgaria and Romania view the BSEC largely from a political point of view: as a complementary and helpful instrument for their future integration into European institutions.[24] Both Sofia and Bucharest are also in favour of closer cooperation between the BSEC and other subregional groups (in particular the Central European Initiative). A similar approach is taken by Ukraine. Membership of the BSEC corresponds to Ukraine's general approach of gradual integration into Europe using inter alia the possibilities offered by subregional groups. Consequently, Kyiv also considers the BSEC a necessary component of European integration.[25] In addition, all three of these countries favour the development of concrete activities for pragmatic economic reasons, hoping to increase their export capacities, improve subregional transport, energy and communication systems, and promote foreign investment (and, in Ukraine's case, diversify its energy sources). Moldova, Albania and the three Caucasian states seek economic support and benefit from the BSEC. Georgia and Azerbaijan also see the BSEC as a means of balancing Russian influence in the Caucasus, and would like the BSEC to become an additional instrument to address some of their security concerns. However, due to the economic problems of each of theses five states and their strained relations with one another and their neighbours, their contribution to BSEC activities has so far been modest.

IS THERE A POLITICAL AND SECURITY DIMENSION?

The political tensions among the BSEC members also explains their unwillingness to deal with political and security issues in the BSEC framework. Rather, economic cooperation is viewed as 'the cornerstone of lasting regional stability and as a practical mechanism for reducing political risks and preventing destabilization'.[26] Despite the fact that in the past few years the Black Sea subregion has been effected by severe armed conflicts in the former Yugoslavia, Nagorno-Karabakh, Transdniestra, Abkhazia and Chechnya, all attempts to include an explicit political and security dimension in the BSEC have failed. At the 1992 Istanbul Summit, the Georgian President, Edvard Shevardnadze, proposed the creation of a Council of Defence and Foreign Ministers to deal with subregional crises, but this idea has not been taken further. From the very beginning, BSEC members sought to avoid any political and security debates within the BSEC framework, and Bulgaria refused to join the PABSEC with its Committee on Legal and Political Issues. Consequently, the BSEC has had no interface with such European security institutions as NATO, the Western European Union (WEU) and, until recently, even the OSCE. Even if political and security issues are addressed by BSEC representatives, this is done outside the BSEC framework, as for example in April 1996, when the Bucharest Foreign Ministers' Meeting was followed by the BSEC Business Forum including a special session on Stability and Security in the Black Sea Region. In this regard, the extent to which the BSEC is able to rise above security issues and handle them through enhancing economic cooperation is any interesting question for the longer term.

Nevertheless, the BSEC does deal with security at least at an existential level and in terms of some 'soft' security issues. First, the BSEC provides additional channels for multilateral and bilateral dialogue, and brings around the table neighbouring countries which have often viewed each other with deep suspicion and distrust. In this regard, regular meetings and personal contacts between senior governmental officials provide a useful forum for discussions and exchange of opinions. This, in itself, enhances mutual knowledge, fosters interaction and cooperation among BSEC members, and contributes to an atmosphere of mutual understanding and acceptance, confidence-building and overall stability in this turbulent subregion. Moreover, most countries joining the BSEC did not have any previous experience of voluntary cooperation within international, integrated institutions based on free choice and equality. For them, the BSEC is a good opportunity to learn how to consider the interests of other countries and could serve as a sort of 'training ground' for integration. In this sense, the BSEC, which is based on the principles laid down in the 1975 Helsinki Act and subsequent OSCE documents (particularly the 1990 Paris Charter for a New Europe), plays an important political role in strengthening subregional stability and security and could be viewed as a testing ground for certain principles and mechanisms of cooperation which may be useful for the OSCE and its European Security Model for the Twenty-First Century.

The BSEC is also a multi-functional group, which includes inter-governmental, inter-parliamentary, business, finance, academic and public dimensions and deals with a wide variety of issues. Taken together, these different dimensions contribute to subregional stability by improving each country's economic conditions, developing subregional infrastructure and communications, promoting human and sectoral contacts, encouraging cooperation between local authorities and supporting multi-dimensional approaches to subregional problems. The BSEC also attaches particular importance to the protection of the Black Sea environment and the joint handling of emergencies and accidents. By 1997, a draft Black Sea Action Plan was being elaborated and a draft agreement on cooperation in managing the effects of natural disasters and industrial calamities (initiated by Russia) was being considered. The 1996 Moscow Declaration emphasized the BSEC's intention to promote 'cooperation in coping with consequences of natural disasters and technogenic accidents and ensuring ecological and nuclear security, as well as the safety of maritime and other transport'.[27]

Due to its diversity and the political tensions among its members, the BSEC is very unlikely to agree a coordinated approach to peacekeeping or crisis management, to elaborate a common position within wider groups or to coordinate security policies towards its neighbours. There is even less prospect of any 'hard' security measures being undertaken jointly by BSEC members. At the same time, the BSEC has become increasingly proactive in tackling such non-military security threats as organized crime; terrorism; trafficking in illicit drugs, weapons and radioactive materials; and illegal migration. Thus, in October 1996 the Ministers of Internal Affairs of the BSEC countries held a meeting in Yerevan, Armenia, to discuss the possibilities for expanding multilateral cooperation in combating such threats. The ministers called upon national parliaments 'to formulate an approach to the elaboration of appropriate national legislations'. They also adopted a joint statement, calling for: the strengthening of the legal basis for cooperation between law-enforcement agencies of BSEC states; the introduction of mechanisms for the implementation of bilateral agreements, including the establishment of direct contacts between the heads of the relevant national operational services; the holding of expert meetings on a regular basis; cooperation in the sphere of personnel training; and the exchange of experience and legislation regulating relations in the sphere of combating crime.[28]

Some believe that the BSEC has some potential as a framework for developing subregional confidence-building measures. In November 1993, Ukraine put forward an initiative 'Towards Economic Cooperation through Confidence Building', proposing the development of measures to strengthen military and naval confidence around the Black Sea. Five other BSEC countries (Bulgaria, Georgia, Romania, Russia and Turkey) supported this idea but insisted that the initiative be explored outside the BSEC framework. The expected result is a political document regulating military and naval activities on the Black Sea, establishing a mechanism for the exchange of relevant information and promoting contacts among naval forces of the participating states. The document is expected to confirm such basic principles as the inviolability of sea borders, the commitment not to make one's territory available for use by other states for the purpose of aggression against any country of the Black Sea basin, the non-use of military and naval forces against each other, and the reduction of military and naval tension in the subregion through enhanced transparency. Several rounds of expert consultations took place after June 1994, but without any tangible results by 1997. Further elaboration of the document was blocked by the Ukrainian-Russian dispute over the Russian military and naval presence in Crimea, which was only resolved in the spring/summer of 1997. The signing of the Ukrainian-Russian Black Sea Fleet agreements in May 1997 might well open the way for further work on the document.

There is some hope that in the security field, the BSEC might be able to deal with the subregional aspects of certain pan-European initiatives. The Ukrainian Foreign Minister, Hennadii Udovenko, in particular, expressed his view at the 1996 Foreign Ministers' Meeting in Bucharest that the BSEC's geographical expansion and the recognition of its stabilizing role in the subregion may necessitate its more active participation 'in the solution of security problems and economic progress in the pan-European context'.[29] This, however, would require not only the general consent of all BSEC members and perhaps the further development and modification of BSEC bodies, but also a closer interaction with other subregional groups and European institutions.

BSEC AND OTHER SUBREGIONAL GROUPS AND EUROPEAN INSTITUTIONS

The October 1996 Moscow Declaration of the Heads of State and Government emphasized that the BSEC participating states share the common vision of the BSEC as 'an integral part of the European architecture'.[30] From the beginning, BSEC members decided to develop their cooperation in a manner not contravening their obligations and not obstructing their relations with third countries, international organizations or subregional initiatives. Most BSEC countries stress the connection between the development of subregional cooperation and the process of European integration and would like to see the BSEC as a kind of collective institutional mediator between themselves and various international multilateral structures.

Despite this emphasis, however, BSEC participants have avoided any discussion of the issues of European integration, afraid of further exacerbating the already existing tensions in the subregion. In fact, in the first years of the BSEC's existence there were only irregular contacts between the BSEC and other international institutions and subregional groups. From time to time, representatives – principally from such structures as the CEI, the World Bank, the International Monetary Fund (IMF), the United Nations Development Programme (UNDP) and the European Bank for Reconstruction and Development (EBRD) – were invited to BSEC gatherings. In turn, the IMF, the EBRD and the World Bank showed some interest in the BSEC after its establishment, but on the whole remained cautious given the BSEC's failure to demonstrate real economic cooperation and the continuing political instability in the subregion. By 1996-97, however, the BSEC's interest in interaction with other international institutions had grown significantly, especially as regards economic bodies. Lacking the necessary financial resources themselves, BSEC members are looking for partners who are able to provide financial support. There is particular interest in attracting concrete assistance for the BSEC's joint multilateral projects.

Both the sixth and seventh BSEC Foreign Ministerial Meetings (in Chisinau in November 1995 and in Bucharest in April 1996) requested the PERMIS to develop an exchange of information and experience with subregional and international organizations and institutions interested in the BSEC. These exchanges were especially intensified after the April 1996 meeting in Bucharest. Upon the invitation of the PERMIS, representatives of the United Nations Economic Commission for Europe (UN ECE), the European Commission, the CEI, the Organization for Economic Cooperation and Development (OECD) and the International Labor Organization held working consultations in Istanbul with the Directoral staff of the PERMIS. Some specific BSEC activities took place in collaboration with international organizations (for example, an OECD-BSEC workshop on actions for combating corruption). The United Nations Industrial Development Organizations (UNIDO) proposed the conclusion of a cooperation agreement with the BSEC and a draft was circulated among BSEC participating states. Proposals for cooperation with, and assistance to, the BSEC were put forward by the UN ECE and by the United Nations Conference on Trade and Development (UNCTAD) in such fields as transport, energy, environment, trade facilitation and the simplification of border crossing procedures. The October 1996 Foreign Ministers Meeting in Moscow, expressed an intention to develop appropriate interaction and further cooperation in fields of common interest with the EU, the UN ECE, the League of Arab States, the Economic Cooperation Organization, as well as with the OSCE and the Council of Europe. The decision to establish a free trade area resulted in increased contacts with the World Trade Organization (WTO).

By 1997, closer cooperation between the BSEC and the EU was becoming a priority for most BSEC members, driven by the growing need for EU support in implementing BSEC projects and their increasing interest in joining the EU in the future (– Turkey, for example, renewed its efforts to gain EU membership and Ukraine sees its strategic goal as integration into European/Euro-Atlantic institutions, with priority given to EU membership). The 1996 Moscow Foreign Ministers Meeting appealed, in particular, to the EU 'to work out a common platform for developing closer contacts and mutual cooperation'. Representatives of the European Commission are now regularly invited to BSEC gatherings, and the first BSEC/EU joint initiative – a workshop on border crossing improvement and trade facilitation in the Black Sea subregion – took place in November

1996 in Istanbul. The ninth Foreign Ministers Meeting in April 1997, in Istanbul, took a formal decision to establish regular working contacts with the European Commission.

At the same time, the EU also became much more attentive to, and supportive of, the BSEC and its activities. Within the EU, there was a growing realization of the crucial importance of the BSEC as a stabilizing factor in a fragile geopolitical area and of the Black Sea's importance as an access route to Caspian and Central Asian energy resources (– hence also the EU's interest in infrastructure and transport issues in the Black Sea subregion). The European Commission contributed to the elaboration of a BSTDB business program; planned to increase its participation in BSEC activities in the areas of transport, infrastructure, and environmental protection; and was by 1997 preparing a draft document on the possible establishment of formal institutional links with the BSEC. This increased support of the EU for subregional cooperation in general, and for the BSEC in particular, contributed significantly to the increased activities of the BSEC.

As a group focused on economic cooperation, the BSEC has no institutional relationship with NATO or WEU. Greece and Turkey, however, are NATO members. Romania and Bulgaria are candidates for NATO membership and, along with other BSEC members, participants in the Partnership for Peace (PfP) Programme. Russia and Ukraine signed special cooperation agreements with the Alliance in 1997: the NATO-Russia Founding Act and the NATO-Ukraine Charter on a Distinctive Partnership. In the summer of 1997, NATO and some BSEC members (Ukraine, Romania, Turkey and Greece) planned to hold multilateral PfP naval exercises in the Black Sea. Russia, however, objected to these exercises.

More steps were also taken to cooperate with other subregional groups, especially the CEI. A joint Conference of the Ministers of Transport of the BSEC and CEI countries, sponsored by the European Commission, took place in Sofia in November 1996. In May 1997, Kyiv hosted the Ministerial Conference on Transport of Countries of Central and Eastern Europe and the Black Sea Region. Both conferences were perceived as preparatory steps toward the Third Pan-European Transport Conference in Helsinki in June 1997. It was also agreed that a regular exchange of relevant information would be developed between the BSEC and the CEI through direct contacts between the BSEC Coordination Center for the Exchange of Statistical Data and Economic Information in Ankara and the CEI Center for Information and Documentation in Trieste. The BSEC also exchanges information with the CBSS. In addition to the CEI and the CBSS, the 1996 Moscow Declaration called upon the BSEC to develop relations with the EU's Euro-Mediterranean Initiative.

All BSEC members seem to realize that there are still unexplored opportunities to develop in BSEC cooperation with other subregional and international institutions. To facilitate the existing interaction as well as to extend it to new institutions, an appropriate formal framework may be required, based on bilateral documents such as a memoranda of understanding or joint action programmes. When the BSTDB becomes fully operational, this may help to solve the problem of the BSEC's relations with international financial bodies. So far, the latter have found it difficult to deal with the BSEC which is not an organization with consolidated responsibility for its members. Many hopes for the effective functioning of the BSTDB have been placed on support from the EBRD and the European Investment Bank, which were invited by the BSEC to consider the possibility of developing co-financing programmes and to eventually participate as members in the BSTDB. Much more activity and initiative will also be needed from those BSEC countries which are simultaneously members of other international or subregional structures: for example, Russia is a member of the BSEC, the CBSS and the BEAC; while Albania, Bulgaria, Romania, Moldova and Ukraine participate in both the BSEC and the CEI. These states may and should serve as links between these various groups, facilitating interaction among subregional groups from the Barents to the Black Sea. In this regard, a regular exchange of information among permanent secretariats (or other appropriate bodies) of relevant subregional groups could be very useful.

PROSPECTS FOR THE FUTURE

In June 1997, the BSEC celebrated its fifth anniversary. Having passed the organizational stage of its development, the BSEC is entering a second stage which is already marked by the increased activities of its members and should be further characterized by a new qualitative level of BSEC cooperation.

Five years of the BSEC's existence have supplied enough fuel for both sceptics and optimists with regards to the group's prospects and future. Optimists point to the BSEC's recently increased dynamism and its achievements to date, as well as to the fact that BSEC countries represent a subregion with a population of more than 300 million people (and a Black Sea 'littoral population' of about 100 million[31]), a potentially huge consumer market, a wealth of natural resources (most importantly, oil and gas), large agricultural potential, certain advanced technologies (for example, in nuclear energy and space programmes), a qualified and well-educated but also cheap labour force, an attractive tourism/resort area, a geographical location at the trade and geopolitical cross-roads of Europe and Asia and unlimited opportunities for Western investment. Sceptics point out that existing BSEC mechanisms are inefficient and implementation of decisions is weak; the participating states are financially poor and economically unstable; their interests vary; their national legislations are underdeveloped; approaches to foreign trade, tax regulations and the use of convertible currency differ significantly; while political instability prevails throughout the subregion.

It is clear, however, that the further successful development of the BSEC will require the fulfilment of at least three inter-related conditions. First, most experts and observers recognize that more fundamental economic links can only be developed within the BSEC if the individual economies of the BSEC countries are strengthened and the profound discrepancies and differences in their economic development are reduced. Thus, the continuation of economic reforms in the former Soviet bloc countries and, at least, their initial success will be of key importance, since most BSEC participants have so far been more preoccupied with their domestic economic challenges than with the development of BSEC activities.

Second, further successful development of the BSEC requires financial support. As recognized at the April 1996 Bucharest Foreign Ministers Meeting, 'a search for financial resources for implementation of the programs of cooperation remains the most urgent problem'.[32] In this regard, Western governments and international financial bodies would do well to consider what practical help, including financial assistance, they can offer the BSEC to support subregional cooperation in the Black Sea basin. The EU's role could be of particular importance in this regard. Given the fact that (unlike the BEAC or the CBSS) the BSEC has no wealthy Western near neighbours, a concerted EU approach might also encourage individual EU members to support the BSEC and its specific projects more actively.

Third, the BSEC's future will largely depend on the group's ability to develop effective mechanisms for implementing adopted decisions. Accordingly, the question of strengthening the institutional and legal basis of the BSEC, to enhance its effectiveness and to ensure better interaction among its inter-governmental, inter-parliamentary, business, finance, academic and public dimensions, has appeared increasingly often on the agenda of BSEC meetings. With this in mind, BSEC members are now seriously considering the possibility of transforming the BSEC from a loose group into a formal subregional organization through the adoption of a

BSEC statute. As an organization, the BSEC should be able to formulate clear, international obligations for its Member States, thus heightening their responsibility for implementing BSEC joint projects. Such a step would also enhance the BSEC's international identity and improve its interaction with other subregional structures and international institutions, including financial bodies.

As has often happened with its development, the initiative for transforming the BSEC into an organization was put forward by Turkey, which prepared and presented a statute for the organization in January 1996. An ad hoc Working Group on Organizational Matters was set up to consider the issue. Initially, other BSEC members were cautious, if not sceptical, about the idea. Russia, in particular, believed that although this question was important, the practical needs and realities of the participating countries, as well as the possible financial implications of such a decision, should be taken into account. The issue was reviewed at the seventh Foreign Ministers Meeting in Bucharest in April 1996, which stressed the importance of the BSEC's further institutionalization. Most BSEC states supported the idea of its transformation into a subregional organization, although some preferred this to be gradual in order to minimize its possible financial costs. The Moscow Foreign Ministers Meeting and the BSEC summit in October 1996 underlined the need to continue the process of the BSEC's transformation into a subregional economic organization and authorized Senior Officials to further consider the issue, to reconcile the approaches of the member states, to examine all aspects and repercussions of this process, including the financial ones, and to elaborate, by the end of 1997, a draft report on the necessary legal procedures and prepare the appropriate draft legal documents.[33] A special drafting group was set up and the process of drafting the necessary legal documents to transform the BSEC into a subregional economic organization was launched.

The BSEC's further institutionalization also requires the streamlining of its structure and a serious re-examination of the working methods of its subsidiary bodies. In consequence, the task of reform and modernization of BSEC executive structures has become one of the group's priorities. In particular, Georgia argues that the PERMIS should not only perform technical functions, but should also become a source of new initiatives, lobbying for their promotion and implementation.[34] A decision was taken to reduce the number of BSEC Working Groups from eighteen to twelve. In order to enhance efficiency in decision-making and implementation, BSEC members also agreed that more regular meetings of national representatives at higher – ministerial – level should be held to take specific decisions in fields under their competence.

Given the BSEC's diversity and the fact that its members often have an unequal interest in different BSEC projects, it is also believed by many that BSEC members should focus more on projects involving sub-groups of the BSEC (i.e., involving some but not always all BSEC members), which will facilitate practical decisions and enhance the effectiveness of their implementation. Consequently, the BSEC itself could serve as 'a facilitator and organizational framework for these subregional projects'.[35]

If successfully implemented, all these steps should lead to the BSEC's gradual evolution towards a more efficient subregional organization. The BSEC is very likely to remain predominantly an economic group, with probably a strong environmental component. There is practically no likelihood of it assuming a 'hard' security role, given the varied agendas of its members as well as political differences between them. The possibility of certain security initiatives being taken by smaller sub-groups of states within the BSEC, rather than by the whole group, however, cannot be excluded. Stronger economic ties and trade exchange, in any case, would enhance the BSEC countries' mutual interdependence, which in turn would have a positive spill-over effect on subregional peace and stability. Further development and consolidation of the BSEC could also significantly contribute to the creation of a future Europe-wide economic zone and exert a favourable influence on the situation in adjacent regions of the Middle East and Central Asia. As such, the BSEC could be viewed as a promising model of subregional cooperation which, together with other subregional structures, may become an important element of the new European security order of the twenty-first century.

Part III
Subregional Cooperation and the New European Security Order

9 The Role of Subregional Cooperation in Post-Cold War Europe: Integration, Security, Democracy[1]

Alyson JK Bailes

ORIGINS AND MOTIVES

In 1989-90, the strategic geography of continental Europe lay open for change and free creation to a degree that was most unusual in the region's history. In Central and Eastern Europe, the bonds of the Warsaw Pact and COMECON were dropping away, Soviet forces were gone or on their way out, and the level of strategic tension along what used to be the Central Front had fallen from one of the world's highest to one of the lowest in human memory. For the new (or more properly, restored) democracies to the east of the old Iron Curtain, there was both internal motive and external opportunity to revel in national independence and explore the full uniqueness of national identity. Our familiarity, in hindsight, with the choices these states made should not blind us to the wider range of options which was theoretically available, and actually debated, at the time. Nor should it blur recognition of how remarkable, in some ways, their choices were.[2]

One scenario which was never seriously on the cards – though it was at least floated in Poland and Ukraine – was the reconstruction of a region-wide security system special to Central and Eastern Europe, either with or without the Russian Federation. The attraction of the Western-based integrative organizations, however, was too strong and there was no alternative that could offer anything like their potential, both for defence protection and economic regeneration. There were obvious psychological and practical obstacles to the idea of a 'doubly guaranteed' status between the West and Russia. Though the exact form taken by the successively developed mechanisms for extending the West's mentor role – through the North Atlantic Treaty Organizations (NATO)'s North Atlantic Cooperation Council (NACC) and Partnership for Peace (PfP), the European Union (EU)'s Association Agreements and the Western European Union (WEU)'s Associate Partnership – was not predetermined, the emergence of an essentially uni-polar system from the Atlantic to the east Baltic and the Black Sea probably was.

Given that the new strategic choices would be concerned with Westward integration, its price and its limits, states' options were still relatively open with regard to how to organize their relations with smaller and closer groups of neighbours. In a fluid and complex security environment, coloured by bad memories, lingering mistrusts and elements of competition vis-à-vis potential protectors, there were (and still are) pressures on nations to avoid systematic subregional ties. Strong countries may hope that the free play of forces gives them best hope of manipulating their environment. Weaker states may fear that inter-state agreements will risk legitimizing such manipulation. Medium-sized countries are reluctant to be

Figure 9.1. The 'Down-Side': Possible Reasons for States to Resist Subregional Cooperation

Political and security factors

Preference for an unregulated environment
- Desire to maintain maximum flexibility for future changes in relations and realignments.
- For large states, power may be more easily exercised in an unregulated environment.

Preference for bilateralism
- For large states, bilateralism may make the exercise of leverage easier.
- For small/medium states, bilateralism may make it easier to balance threatening neighbours, practice 'divide and rule' tactics or auction favours freely.
- Dealings can more easily be kept confidential.

National concerns
- Large/medium states may be reluctant to assume security responsibility for others.
- Small/medium states may fear licensed 'encroachment' or subregional domination by larger states.
- Fear of encroachment in sensitive border zones; preference for a national 'free hand' and military secrecy in such regions.

Relations with outsiders
- Feeling that local cooperation is being enforced 'against the grain' from outside and/or could be exploited by outsiders for subregional domination
- Preference for partnership or integration with outside partners or organizations; fear that close subregional cooperation could conflict with this (– fear that apparent 'self-sufficiency' will discourage help from outside or reduce chances of integration with larger groups; fear that states will be judged by their local group identity and therefore have less freedom to compete for outside favours; fear that

political energy/resources will be diverted away from more important relationships).

Domestic factors

- Distrust of provincial authorities and/or minorities in border regions and reluctance to allow them free contact with neighbours (– fears of loss of control, interference by ethnic kin states or mass migration).
- Historically inherited/grass-roots dislike/mistrust of neighbouring countries/nationalities.
- Inexperience (particularly of multilateral cooperation); cost/difficulty of reorganizing internal policy machinery and developing communications.

Economic and financial factors

- Protectionist attitude to national economy and/or economy of frontier zones; desire to see frontier zones integrate/adapt to the national economy rather than seek cooperation with neighbouring states.
- Preference for freedom to compete with neighbours for aid/trade from outside states and institutions.
- Bureaucratic costs of hosting/attending/servicing subregional activities (especially fixed secretariats and other organs).
- For large/wealthy states, fear of being drawn into 'subsidizing' weaker neighbours.
- For smaller/poorer states, fear of economic dependence on larger/wealthier states.
- Inequalities in capacity and performance may be highlighted.

drawn into an implied protective or 'buffer' role which compounds their own burdens or in the case of non-aligned states may prejudice their traditions of neutrality. Another common concern is that formalizing the existence of a specific multi-state 'neighbourhood' will complicate and perhaps damage the locals relations with partners and institutions further afield. It may cut them off from potential sponsors whose strength they feel they need to balance larger and closer neighbours. It makes it harder to compete, both for such friends' favours (including trade and investment) and for entry – if desired – into wider continental bodies. Another set of concerns can arise when the proposed local cooperation involves freer intercourse across frontiers and/or contact between provincial authorities on each side. Central governments may fear the light shed on their security arrangements in sensitive border areas, the necessary transfer of power to sub-state levels in those areas, and the way a neighbouring state could exploit such changes to foster centrifugal forces (especially if it has an ethnic tie with minorities living across the border). Finally there are practical costs to consider: time and money to be spent on meetings, coordinating structures to be financed – all of which can be just as unappetising for a strong state, apprehensive of being called upon for resource transfers, as it can for a fragile new democracy with limited bureaucratic means. The various factors which might discourage states from engaging in subregional cooperation are summarized in figure 9.1.

In short, it was not predestined that independent states in the new Europe should opt for developing additional subregional networks and there were more than trivial reasons for them not to. The fact that within four years, these networks had nevertheless covered Europe from the Barents to the Black Sea cannot simply be attributed to outside compulsion. The individual Western countries who led the way in developing the Council of Baltic Sea States (CBSS), the Barents Euro-Arctic Council (BEAC) and the Black Sea Economic Cooperation (BSEC) – Sweden, Norway and Turkey – were not strong enough themselves to coerce unwilling neighbours, nor were they perceived as proxies for other dominant powers. One of the most prominent groups in the early stage of transition from Cold War conditions – the Visegrad group – had no Western members at all.[3] Russia, while ending up as a member of the BEAC, the CBSS and the BSEC, was not the prime mover of any of them and would have generated counter-productive resistance if it had tried, from its side, to impose such devices against others' wills. While Central and Eastern European states have varied all along in their degree of liking for subregionalism, and some have yet to reconcile themselves fully to its cross-border aspects, it does seem that the roots of the post-Cold War subregional movement found rich soil in the terrain previously most scarred by the weight of the Iron Curtain.

One explanation for this outcome is offered by earlier history. Traditions like the Hansa, the far northern 'Pomor' coastal trade or the Habsburg Empire, were drawn upon, more or less openly, by the founders of the CBSS, the BEAC and the Central European Initiative (CEI) to legitimize what they were doing. Such 'stories' had value for mobilizing populations, reassuring neighbours about the naturalness and inoffensiveness of the groups and convincing their members that no diminishment of their national identity – rather, an enhancement of one of its layers – was intended. As many analysts have pointed out, however, these 'stories' had little constituent force of their own and became significant only when consciously manipulated or embellished by political leaders.[4] To some extent they were used to avoid dwelling too much on stronger but less easily articulated motives provided by recent history. Overcoming Cold War dividing lines that had been drawn between natural neighbours was a concept easy enough to explain. Less easy to admit (and still difficult to quantify today) was the persistence of habits of multilateral dealing formed among the Central and Eastern European states themselves in the Warsaw Pact/COMECON era, facilitated by shared experiences and a Russian lingua franca, built in some cases (like that of the Visegrad group) upon habits of ganging-up that had developed quite far even before the collapse of Soviet power.

There were more immediate practical concerns for the new Central and Eastern European leaderships which subregionalism could ease: the concern to pre-empt destructive competition among neighbours, to provide a civilized framework for handling minority issues, to avoid the operation of brute power factors and the spiralling of tensions vis-à-vis Russia, to ensure that the wished-for influx of models and resources from the West came as a transaction between equal partners and not in neo-colonial style. Learning from the mistakes of the inter-war period, many leaders also grasped the dangers of economic fragmentation and protectionism, the advantages of a region-wide infrastructure and the opportunity to seek a more genuine economic complementarity than COMECON ever offered. For the Central and Eastern European states, subregional ties offered a quick, simple and non-prejudicial way of filling a diplomatic vacuum that had daunting as well as liberating aspects. Subregional groups working by free consent provided an arena for exploring national roles and identities, for seeking a new non-zero-sum relation between the 'self' and the 'other'. For the smaller or most remote states, lacking powerful sponsors or early prospects of NATO or EU membership, they brought comfort which was hard to find elsewhere and some assurance of maintaining titular equality, self-respect and a hedge against isolation.

SUBREGIONALISM AND INTEGRATION

If even part of this account is correct, it brings out one first important point: the impulse to subregional cooperation was in large part an integrative one and its results have shown many of the characteristics of integrative processes. Post-Cold War subregionalism was dominated by the ideas of opening and creating larger communities: of easing cooperation across state borders and exploring links between non-state actors and populations which neither the Iron Curtain nor intra-bloc relations had permitted earlier. At the psychological level it offered a non-confrontational, open-ended way of exploring national identity and experiencing the dialectic of common interest in diversity. But also it had a practical side as a recognition of, and a way of further promoting economic interdependence.[5] It was motivated to varying degrees by hope of economies of scale, mutual profit and added value through cooperation, both in creating positive assets and warding off potential threats. To revert to a historical perspective, these late twentieth-century groups were based on assumptions and practices differing significantly from any that had been used (at least between sovereign states) in Central and Eastern Europe before. The reasons for this surely had something to do with the existence, in the same continent, of the world's most advanced – partly supranational – integrative model, as well as with 'globalizing' influences also felt beyond Europe.

Considered as a form of integration, modern subregionalism in Europe has characteristic strengths and weaknesses. It has been outstandingly flexible both in accommodating diverse groups of states – with varying sizes, security statuses, governmental systems, economies and cultures – and in finding the organizational forms best tailored to each subregion. To a remarkable extent it has also managed to accommodate different motives, allowing member states to pursue diverging and even contradictory agendas, provided only that all maintain their preference for continuing cooperation rather than reverting to the entirely free play of forces. It has managed to incorporate specific provinces of larger states (notably, Germany and the Russian Federation) without appearing to challenge those states' sovereignty or encountering significant problems in bringing together both states and sub-state actors/regions in various frameworks. It has covered a remarkably wide range of functional topics (claimed by some to be even wider than the EU's) and has found ways of drawing in multiple state, sub-state and non-state entities. It has developed its own version of variable geometry to allow for sub-group initiatives, overlapping memberships, observer relationships and ad hoc or formal partnerships between one subregional group and another. It has been typically demand-led and responsive to inner needs – which the locals should after all understand better than anyone – instead of outside pressures. In many of these respects, it provides a concrete illustration of the meaning, and benefits, of the new European concept of subsidiarity.

The limitations of the subregional model are the obverse of its strengths. With the partial exception of the free trade commitments of the Central European Free Trade Agreement (CEFTA) and specific conventions negotiated within the framework of other groups, subregional cooperation has not been based on binding international legal commitments and rarely has any direct legislative consequences within the Member States. Based as it is on political consent, it exerts no real discipline or constraint over members and lacks authority to enforce compliance. Even the execution of agreed programmes takes place very largely on an inter-governmental, state-by-state basis and is thus subject to uncertainties over capacity and will, as well as the perennial issue of funding. There is no clear view within any of the groups studied here over whether they are meant to be permanent features of the European architecture or not, and one – the Visegrad group – has in fact lapsed for most practical purposes within a couple of years of its creation. Some of the groups have reached consensus at least on the limits of their geographical identity and size, but this issue has only recently neared clarification for the CEI, remains contentious in the BSEC, and is still very open for CEFTA.[6]

The most evident weakness of the groups, however, is a comparative one vis-à-vis the EU and NATO. They have managed (so far) to hold their own against competition from those organizations' association and partnership schemes, because the latter do not bring together the same subgroups of states, reach significant parts of the subregional agenda, cater for the same sub-state elements or allow recognition of geographical group interests. The appeal of full membership is, however, a different question. No Central and Eastern European state involved in a subregional group believes that the group can (or should) offer anything like NATO's defence guarantees, or that it can go beyond freer trade to a true single market and other profound integrative effects similar to those of the EU. For states convinced that they need those deeper forms of integration, a number of potential tensions between their desire for integration and any interest in subregional cooperation may be identified (– see also figure 9.1). A number of Central and Eastern European states have felt concern at different times about committing themselves too fully to subregional cooperation lest it should hamper them in the NATO and/or EU accession stakes. They have feared that current members of NATO and the EU would use the very success of subregional cooperation as an excuse for delaying or denying membership to its beneficiaries, claiming that what was already available to them was good enough, and thus trapping them for ever within a second-rate substitute (or 'grey zone'). Another concern has been that the EU and NATO would see candidates only in the context of their subregional groups and handle accession also on a group basis, thus condemning the strongest local candidates to wait for the 'slowest' and stifling performance-based competition. At a purely practical level, subregional cooperation eats up time, resources and political capital that could otherwise be devoted to lobbying the larger organizations and their members. In specific collaborative fields, there may also be a real or perceived conflict between the measures that can best serve immediate subregional purposes and those needed to 'pre-adapt' or prepare for wider integration.[7]

Though less widely noted, there have also been some cross-currents in subregional development because of participants' fears that the process may bring too much integration, rather than too little. One set of concerns, relating to the intrusive and subversive effect of cross-border cooperation, is addressed in more detail below. Others have mainly been expressed by smaller states and relate to the risk of subregional groups being commandeered for purposes of local hegemony, either by Russia or by Western powers whose vision of their neighbours' future may not coincide with the neighbours' own. Even without such cause to apprehend imbalances of power, some members have been less than enthusiastic simply because they do not much like the partners available in their vicinity. Some (Western) non-aligned states, finally, have been through considerable heart-searching about the proper limits of subregional groups' evolution and their own involvement, because they do not want to get dragged 'through the back door' into a degree of commitment they have deliberately avoided elsewhere.[8]

The historical dynamic which threw up these contradictions had also, by 1996-97, begun to reveal some solutions. It is noteworthy that most of the subregional groups under study here experienced a new lease of life and/or a productive 'course correction' during the period 1996-7, precisely when NATO and the EU were drawing close to their first fateful decisions on post-Cold War expansion. This had something to do with national dynamics within the groups (notably, a positive learning curve on the Russian side). It was also made possible, however, in part because the larger institutions concerned and their influential members had offered important clarifications. It would be a rare Western policy-maker today who tried to claim that subregionalism could provide a lasting alternative for a state with its heart set on joining the EU or NATO. The EU and NATO themselves have repeatedly stated that they will assess each candidate state in its own right, not as part of any neighbourhood group.[9] At the same time, the growing interest shown by the Organization for Security and Cooperation in Europe (OSCE) in defining and maximizing the value of subregional groups in a pan-European context – together with a similar Council of Europe focus on cross-border cooperation – has de facto increased the degree of normative scrutiny over these bodies.[10] The clearer the expectation that subregional groups should conform to United Nations (UN) and OSCE principles, the less cause their members should have to fear a sudden lurch into non-voluntary integration (and the better right they will have to withdraw from membership if it happens). The way has thus opened for a more constructive reading of the interplay between subregionalism and deeper integration, which at the same time stresses their complementarity and their autonomy. Once it is recognised that subregional groups need neither dictate nor obstruct the entry of their individual members into any other institution, they should not only cease to be feared as a 'trap' by states who have a strong hope of early integration, but can be explored by states of all kinds as a useful extra tier of European architecture and a way of bridging enlargement's 'dividing lines'.

The inter-relationship of subregional groups with other European organizations is discussed in detail in the next chapter. The generic scope for complementarity may be explored here by looking at three main kinds of potential interaction: the subregional group as a complement to EU/NATO integration and a buffer for enlargement-related tensions; the use of subregional approaches as a path to integration; and the survival of subregional identities within the larger integrated groups.

The six groups in the Barents-Black Sea belt can be sub-divided, on the grounds both of membership and motivation, into two types. The northern and southern groups – the BEAC, the CBSS, the CEI and the BSEC – have relatively large memberships, encompass a diverse range of states (EU and NATO members, leading candidates for EU/NATO membership, candidates who may be disappointed in the first round, non-applicants including Russia and other Commonwealth of Independent States (CIS) states, and non-aligned states). CEFTA and the former Visegrad group are distinctly smaller and consist only of states with real hope of reasonably rapid Westward integration. Clearly, a group of the first kind will not have a joint integration strategy but it might develop some shared views on how to manage the process of phased integration in its subregion. By its very existence – despite all that was said before about the lack of true substitutes – it can relativize the loss felt by those who do not get into the EU or NATO at first attempt, and mediate some of the tensions between existing members of those groups, applicants and local powers opposed to enlargement. Specifically, the members of such subregional groups could use the framework they provide to:

- maintain a flow of information from 'insiders' to 'outsiders' on what is happening in the EU and NATO, thus providing an opportunity for debate and feedback and combating tensions fed by uncertainty or misunderstanding;
- encourage the maintenance and strengthening of cooperation between

countries left on opposite sides of an enlargement 'dividing line', and exert peer pressure for them to handle any concomitant tensions in a peaceful and sensible way;
- consolidate norms of conduct for the subregion which inter alia militate against the mis-use by successful EU/NATO members of their new-found strength, and the risk of retaliation by opponents of enlargement against their neighbours;
- doubly underwrite the OSCE and Council of Europe obligations which should prevent any mistreatment of ethnic minorities, or subversive exploitation of minorities by neighbouring states whose relations are tense as a result of 'first-wave' divisions;
- preserve confidence and cooperative relations within the group as a whole by continuing to develop new programmes and activities for mutual benefit;
- devise ways of extending some of the benefits of enlargement to non-participating states, for example, by further developing infrastructure and communications links to channel traffic from/to the integrated region or tailoring cross-border cooperation to exploit assets created by EU structural funds;
- produce ideas for EU and/or NATO assistance to the subregion as a whole which the EU/NATO members of the subregional group can promote within their parent organizations.

The combination of all these measures would provide an optimum model for handling the phased enlargement of NATO and the EU as it affects specific subregions – and perhaps, by the same token, an unreachable ideal. Such a model, however, may run counter to the instincts of many states displeased by 'first wave' enlargement decisions and may be hard to sell to their publics even if leaders can grasp how it serves their interests. It will certainly not succeed unless the long-term members of the integrated organizations who take part in subregional processes – and even more crucially, the first new entrants – commit themselves to it wholeheartedly and comport themselves beyond reproach. The attention of new NATO and EU members may be focused on their integration with those bodies and their may be temptations to 'turn their backs' on their neighbours who have not joined NATO or the EU. Given this, the EU and NATO should have clear collective policies designed to support, where necessary stimulate, and provide the material backing for the further development of subregional cooperation. Any additional 'cushioning' strategies adopted by the EU, NATO and others should also be tailored to respect and not usurp or complicate the role of existing subregional bodies.

The small homogeneous subregional groups of the second type were created expressly as 'schools' for integration and devices for maximising their members' hopes of entry – to NATO in the case of the Visegrad group, and the EU in the case of CEFTA. They have pursued these aims in four principal ways: [11]

- by prior, voluntary introduction or 'trialling' among themselves of features known to be critical for membership in the institutions concerned (for example, free trade);
- by aligning and associating themselves with policy positions adopted by the target institution (for example, the Visegrad group support for various NATO and EU Common Foreign and Security Policy (CFSP) positions and NATO-Visegrad liaison on the development of European arms control);[12]
- by 'concerting' their members' pre-accession strategies (and actions within related association/partnership schemes), at least to a sufficient degree to avert destructive competition;
- by using the collective leverage of the group to influence the target institutions' pre-accession and accession policies, both in a positive sense and through counter-acting lobbying from other candidates and the opponents of enlargement.

It has yet to be seen how such groups adjust to the eventuality that some but not all of their members are included in enlargement's 'first wave'. Leaving aside the specific constitutional issues for CEFTA, there is no generic reason why a pro-integration group should not convert itself to fulfil some of the 'cushioning' roles described above for its left-out members. Such a group would have two additional options in this scenario. First, that of adopting a 'no black-balling' policy, whereby its first successful members would engage not to veto the later accession of the others. Second, that of developing measures (whether for action within the group or for adoption by the EU or NATO) specifically tailored to boost the prospects of 'second wave' entry into NATO or the EU for those states initially excluded. In practice, the possibilities open to current contenders for accession will be even more complex because of the differential timing of NATO and EU enlargement. Thus an agreed strategy by CEFTA's members to maintain and even enhance their cooperation during the early stages of the EU's enlargement process, could become a 'confidence-building measure' to offset the effects of NATO's July 1997 decision to include Poland, the Czech Republic and Hungary (but not Slovakia, Slovenia and Romania) in its own first wave of enlargement.[13] The experience of Nordic cooperation following the EU entry of Finland and Sweden suggests that an effort to maintain subregional ties in such circumstances can pay real dividends, especially for the 'left-outs'. (Admittedly, the Nordic case was a relatively easy one thanks to the European Economic Area (EEA), Nordic Passport Union and the voluntary nature of Norway and Iceland's non-entry to the EU, and even so it required considerable effort and reorientation of the cooperative venture).

Should all the members of a CEFTA-type group succeed in entering their target organization, the Benelux precedent raises the theoretical possibility of maintaining their group identity inside it. There are reasons why they might not wish this: the appeal of alignments – permanent or shifting – with more established members and the temptation (accentuated by their similar profiles) to compete for internal advantages. The Finnish and Swedish example just cited, however, shows subregional commonalty starting to reassert itself after quite a short period of adaptation, especially vis-à-vis external issues on which the new boundary states of the organization have similar interests.[14] There may be features, yet untried, of the larger EU and larger NATO consequent upon enlargement which will push in the same direction. On some issues at least, compromises between internal geographical lobbies might replace the longueurs of all-against-all negotiation. Any tendency to variable geometry or differential patterns of integration within the system would offer the chance for sub-groups already used to working together to develop their own integrated 'cores' and/or be credited with devolved responsibilities. It is likely, however, that new members in particular will be much on their guard against permanent differentiation in their status (– fearing that their status within the EU or NATO might be undermined) and that this will cause patterns of subregional specialization to be kept deliberately varied, loose and informal. Another possibility, in the EU's case, is that the new economic interactions permitted by the single market will stimulate new cross-border alignments of provinces rather than states, as has happened already within the western territory of the Union.

SUBREGIONALISM AND SECURITY

The relationship of current subregional groups to security is, at first glance, much less obvious than that with integration and more prone to be described in negatives. Some causal link may, admittedly, be traced between the subregional groups emergence and the special nature of the European security environment after the Berlin Wall fell and the Soviet Union dissolved. The scope for states to experiment with new relationships was increased and the potential risks reduced, not just by the collapse of bloc divisions but also by the generalized low level of threat which released creative energies – the 'peace dividend' was garnered in the currency of decision-makers' time as well as cash. Outside former Yugoslavia, the Central and Eastern European democracies could feel reasonably confident about conducting their relations with neighbours free from the shadow of violence. A great part of this reassurance came, whether they conceptualized it or not, from awareness of NATO's and the EU's increased strategic weight in Europe, which offered the same kind of protection for small states approaching larger neighbours that the NATO-Warsaw Pact stand-off provided for Nordic cooperation in Cold War times.

One curious feature of subregional cooperation, however, was that it flourished best in some of the parts of Europe most exposed to residual tensions and showed an ability to surmount even direct inter-state and civil conflicts among its members. The BEAC was born in a territory which, even after the Cold War, was dominated by abnormal concentrations of nuclear and conventional weapons; through which the only remaining NATO-Russia border ran; and where the maritime delimitation of that border between Russia and Norway was still under dispute. The states of the CBSS had a number of unresolved border issues among them and with Belarus, of which the Estonian-Russian has been probably the most volatile. The CEI ejected the then Yugoslavia on the outbreak of hostilities but took back several of the new former Yugoslav Republics before fighting was ended and is now looking for the right moment to readmit the 'rump' Federal Republic of Yugoslavia. The BSEC has, in its short history, survived the conflicts in Chechnya, Moldova, Georgia, Nagorno-Karabakh and the former Yugoslavia, as well as Ukrainian-Russian disputes over the disposal of naval assets and bases in the Black Sea. The survival and growing success of these groups seems to reflect, therefore, a conscious choice by (at least their leading members) to compensate for and offset security tensions by building cooperative ties in seemingly unrelated areas – a deliberate 'desecuritization' of relations within the subregional group.[15] Such an approach worked perfectly well so long as all parties were willing to compartmentalize the different aspects of their relations and/or there were other mechanisms working to control and contain such conflicts as existed.

Of the six groups in the Barents-Black Sea belt, only the short-lived Visegrad cooperation had an overt security mission – the orderly dismantling of the Warsaw Pact and the opening up of the prospect of NATO membership – and even that was of the transitional type whose success would trigger its obsolescence. None of the other groups was set up expressly for security purposes, nor were they given competence for security issues in their basic 'constitutions', nor was security placed on their inaugural agendas. None of them has instituted regular meetings of Defence Ministers or military staffs. None has operated as a framework for multinational military cooperation on defence modernization, peacekeeping, or other forms of crisis prevention and management. None of the groups has considered acting, or has been invited by an organization like the OSCE to act, as a negotiating forum for 'hard' arms control measures (in terms of quantitative reductions). Nor have they engaged as institutions in direct mediation or conflict resolution efforts in relation to disputes between their members. None has considered turning itself into a nuclear-weapon-free or de-militarized zone. As noted earlier, none of these groups has even contemplated the extension of mutual security/defence guarantees amongst it members. To avoid confusion and diversion in the NATO accession context, Member States have in fact spent a lot of time telling the world that they cannot and will not go down that track.

Their choice is rational because, objectively viewed, today's subregional groups are both too small and too large (and hence too diverse) to assume any of the classic security functions listed above. They are too small in the sense that they cannot embrace the full range of states – including Western nuclear powers – needed for credible and balanced 'hard' defence guarantees. (It is interesting that the Nordic founders of the BEAC felt a compulsion to 'balance' even their totally security-blind group by bringing in four large NATO powers – the United States, the United Kingdom, France and Germany – as observers). As a matter of record, those states within these subregions who feel a deficit in their security coverage have sought to fill it through joining larger institutions like NATO, the EU and the CIS. Similarly, the military capability of members in each group is too unbalanced to allow credible 'hard' arms control agreements to be negotiated among them. The scale of Russia's military power (and in the south, that of Ukraine), as well as these larger states' geostrategic advantages, and the absence from the groups of any nuclear-weapon state apart from Russia, make it difficult to see how quantitative controls, negotiated on a subregional basis, could have any but artificial and probably destabilizing effects. The Europe-wide framework of the Conventional Armed Forces in Europe (CFE) Treaty is commonly accepted as a better basis for tackling destabilizing imbalances and risks of surprise attack, while the OSCE has developed its own 'framework' for subregional arms control along lines independent of the membership of the six subregional groups in the Barents-Black Sea belt.[16]

Conversely, the new subregional groups have proved too large for purposes of practical military cooperation or 'real-time' crisis management. Joint military units, notably for peacekeeping, have been formed between various pairs and trios of their members and there has been wider coordination for such operations on a Nordic-Polish, Nordic-Baltic and Hungarian-Italian-Slovenian basis, but no-one has suggested it would make sense to extend such schemes to – say – all 12 members of the CBSS or all 16 members of the CEI.[17]

To date, subregional groups have played little or no role in more overt conflict management activities. Whether – and how far – they can or should play a role in direct conflict management activities in the future, however, is less clear. In any given dispute, familiarity with the relevant history and psychology gives a prima facie advantage and a group of friendly, neighbouring states might seem the most natural mediators. Alternatively, experience suggests that the most decisive tools for ending entrenched conflicts are significant leverage, a degree of objectivity and the capacity to operate discreetly when required. It is hard for a heterogeneous group of neighbouring states with no formal competences for conflict management, no shared military resources and no large economic sticks or carrots to meet this prescription. It is also hard, though not impossible, for a nearby state to be truly objective and to avoid possible negative implications for its future relations with the affected party. It is thus reasonable to suggest that most mediation tasks in overt conflicts, especially those which shade over into the political equivalent of 'peace enforcement', are more likely to be successfully undertaken by individual powers outside the subregion, ad hoc and confidential groups of 'friends', or institutions like the EU, the OSCE and the Council of Europe, which are large enough to have both normative authority and presumptive neutrality. Where an individual state of the subregion does find itself well-placed to intervene it will generally do it better alone than in formal consultation with the group. The fields where subregional institutions should have real comparative advantages are those of crisis prevention, conflict containment and post-settlement reconstruction – which are examined in more detail below.

The limitations of subregional cooperation outlined above, however, reveal only a part of the total security picture for Europe's subregions, and they show it in a very deceptive light. The avoidance of 'hard' security tasks, and the habit of conflict-blindness, were in reality tactics adopted quite knowingly by the framers of the post-Cold War subregional groups to enable them to serve security in broader and more subtle ways. The concept of a 'non-security but pro-security' organization should be familiar from earlier times: it can convincingly be applied, for instance, to Cold War Nordic cooperation. All the groups studied here – with the possible exception of CEFTA – were created, at least partly, for security ends. The Visegrad group was the strongest example, reflecting not just the (original) three members' concerns about their security relations with larger neighbours, but also a well-directed urge to 'end history' by ruling out from the start any possible armed conflict with each other. The case of the BEAC is also relatively clear. Norwegian Foreign Minister Thorvald Stoltenberg hoped that the BEAC would achieve a number of aims: multilateralizing Norway's local relations with Russia (as the strategic relationship had already been multilateralized through NATO); reducing threats to Norwegian territory and resources from civilian and defence-related pollution; speeding defence conversion in northwestern Russia and thus helping to pre-empt as well as control potential mass migration; and creating new linkages (with security as well as political and economic significance) between north Norway and the European mainland.[18] The Western founders of the CBSS were interested in consolidating the sovereignty and independence of the Baltic states, stabilizing relations with the new Russia and providing a cooperative setting for the economic development of Kaliningrad, as well as in the group's overt economic and functional benefits. Turkey, the driving force in the early stages of the BSEC, hoped to seize post-Cold War opportunities to extend its strategic influence southwards and eastwards and saw the subregional forum as one tool to achieve this while avoiding open confrontation either with Russia or Greece.[19] The fact that these national motives might not have been shared by, and were even contrary to the interests of, some other participants did not matter so long as every participant saw at least some net advantage – and no existential threat – from regulation of the subregional environment.

This last point is the clue to understanding the primary security function which all the groups have in fact performed, whether their members planned and understood it or not. They are all building security at what might be called the existential level because, as already noted, they offer an arena (particularly valuable for new states) where nations can learn to express their identity in non-adversarial terms. Simply put, they allow people at several levels to meet, know and eventually understand each other better – although informed dislike may be an intermediate step. Their agendas and underlying 'stories' foster consciousness of shared group interests vis-a-vis outsiders. Thus, they may unconsciously reinforce the taboos against the use of force between adjoining states and the matching principle of peaceful resolution of disputes. Other useful by-products of their meetings are the informal contacts they allow in the margins, where specific inter-state problems may be discussed more directly: the CBSS appears to have helped in this way to manage the 'loophole' fisheries dispute between Norway and Iceland and to keep open communication between Russia and the Baltic states when their official relations were tense. Finally, the networks of personal contacts they establish become available for communications in a crisis, providing a low-key and more complex, but still useful, counterpart to the traditional 'hot-line'. In all these ways, subregional cooperation helps to strengthen the fabric of inter-state relations to the point where, while it may not entirely stifle disputes, it becomes increasingly capable of cushioning them and resisting any break-through into violence.

The second type of security contribution these groups all can make, and have made, lies in the realm of so-called 'soft' security. Without any overt defence elements whatever, their activities can help both to remove possible sources of conflict (both international and internal) and to avert threats of a non-military nature to human welfare and survival. The simplest way they can do this is by raising living standards (and narrowing variations in standards) through more effective economic cooperation, making the prosperity of states and cross-border regions more interdependent, and raising awareness of this interdependence and of common interests (through cultural/educational/social exchanges and the improvement of intra-regional and trans-regional transport and communication links). These 'socializing' effects, and the development of habits of free movement across frontiers, have particularly clear value for easing tensions when there are national minorities living within the border zones. In a well-functioning subregional group, such communities should come to be seen as bridges rather than as hostages or security liabilities. Migrant labour can develop on an economically rational, sustainable and properly regulated basis. Cooperative cross-border management of natural resources like water supplies can contribute both to prosperity and to conflict prevention.

The security value of such 'soft' cooperation becomes most evident when it develops into the fields of pollution and disease control, joint handling of accidents and emergencies, and cooperative management of borders to 'let the good through and keep the bad out' (visa abolition and rapid transit on the one hand and anti-smuggling, immigration and refugee control measures on the other). Finally, the multi-functional nature of these groups' agendas opens up new possibilities for solving problems between states because a concession made in one field of activity can be balanced

Figure 9.2. The 'Security Spectrum': The Spectrum of Security Roles Open to Subregional Groups

Existential	*Soft*	*Explicit*	*Hard*
Personal contacts	Multi-dimensional problem solving	Co-ordinated approach to peacekeeping/crisis management	De-militarized/ de-nuclearized zones
Mutual knowledge	Emergency and accident handling	Collective mediation/ multi-lateralization of disputes	Quantitative arms control measures
Understanding			
Symbolic creation of local community	First feelings of solidarity		
	Functional contributions to security	Confidence-building measures	Military co-ordination: —joint crisis management forces —joint PfP contributions multilateral training schemes
Consolidation of non-use-of-force principle	—economic cooperation/raising of living standards (inc. defence conversion)	Qualitative arms control measures	
		Cooperation on verification/ monitoring	
Learning of non -adversarial ways to define/express national identity	—human, sectoral, cultural, educational contacts	Common positions within wider groups (UN, OSCE, PfP, Association schemes, arms control and export control bodies)	
	—inter-ethnic links across borders		

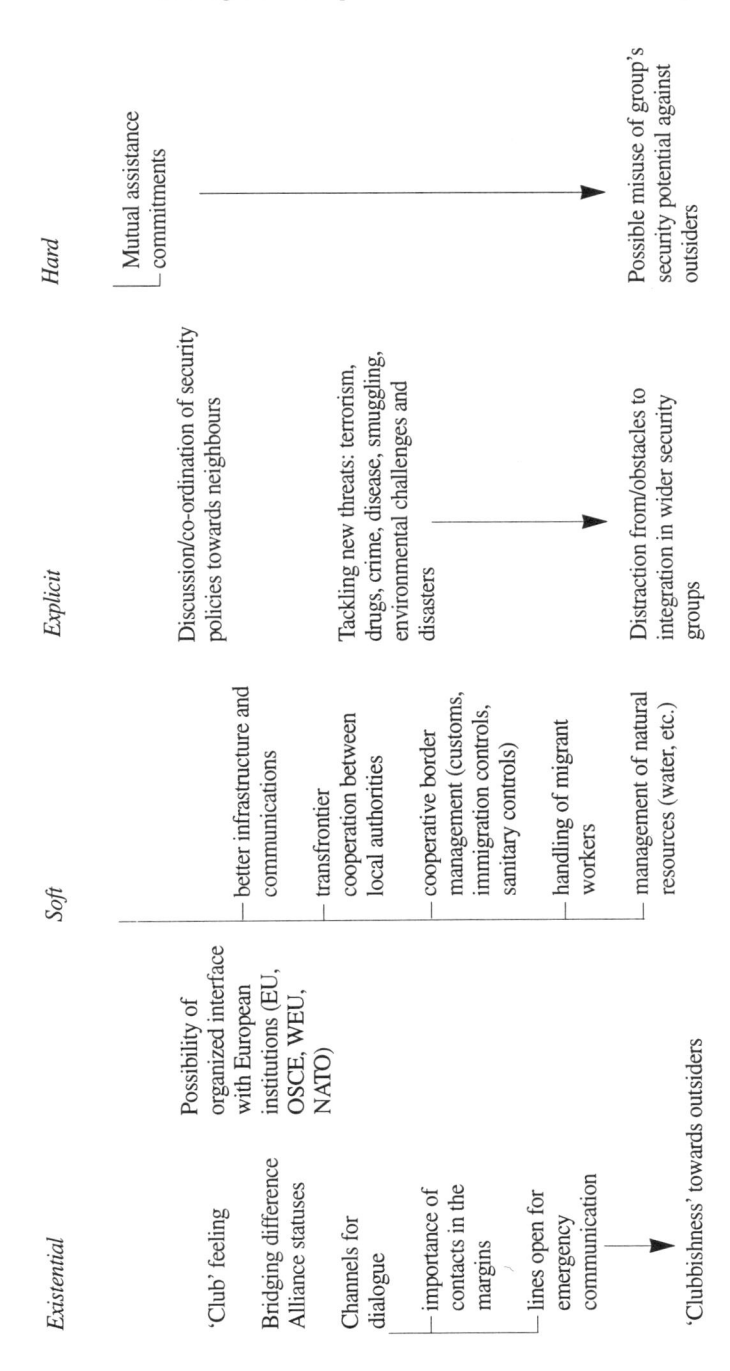

Subregional Cooperation in Post-Cold War Europe 171

Existential	Soft	Explicit	Hard
			Mutual assistance commitments
'Club' feeling	Possibility of organized interface with European institutions (EU, OSCE, WEU, NATO)	Discussion/co-ordination of security policies towards neighbours	
Bridging difference Alliance statuses			
Channels for dialogue	— better infrastructure and communications	Tackling new threats: terrorism, drugs, crime, disease, smuggling, environmental challenges and disasters	
— importance of contacts in the margins	— transfrontier cooperation between local authorities		
— lines open for emergency communication	— cooperative border management (customs, immigration controls, sanitary controls)		
	— handling of migrant workers		
	— management of natural resources (water, etc.)		
'Clubbishness' towards outsiders		Distraction from/obstacles to integration in wider security groups	Possible misuse of group's security potential against outsiders

by benefits gained in another, including inputs offered by other members which might create a better balance than the two disputants could create alone.

Aside from CEFTA, with its highly focused economic agenda, all the groups in the Barents-Black Sea belt have been involved to some degree in building cooperative security by these 'soft' and indirect means. The BEAC offers rather clear examples: the establishment of a joint Russian-Norwegian border post, joint programmes to tackle specific and general environmental challenges, and numerous schemes for economic development which have done something to ease the pain of 'defence conversion' in both Russian and Nordic provinces. The resultant drop in tension along this NATO-Russia frontier has been real, if difficult to quantify. Such disputes as have meanwhile arisen – for example, over exercises in sensitive sea and land areas – seem to have been quite successfully compartmentalized. The BSEC has had high ambitions in all the relevant fields but more difficulty in attaining them, because of lack of local financial resources and rather slow progress in getting grants from outside institutions. On the other hand, the CBSS, the CEI and the BSEC have gone further than the BEAC in launching discussions and initiatives of an overtly 'security' character. The CBSS has a Commissioner for Democratic Institutions and Human Rights with competence to address minority issues which might otherwise lead to conflicts, for instance in the Baltic states. This gives it a hands-on mediating capacity (and potential for synergy notably with the OSCE High Commissioner on National Minorities) which no other group possesses in such an explicit form. It has paid particular attention to issues of nuclear safety (on which it has a separate working group), to the handling of accidents and other emergencies, to environmental challenges affecting the Baltic Sea, and to cooperative border control. CBSS communiques have also addressed a range of issues involving European security institutions and general and specific crisis management.[20]

The CEI counts the protection of the human environment and the cooperative management of borders among its goals. It has produced a document on the protection of the rights of national minorities and a working group on the civil defence of populations in 'peacetime' emergencies. It has been directly involved in efforts for post-crisis reconstruction in the former Yugoslavia and has set up its own assistance programme and permanent coordination unit for this purpose, taking advantage of the presence in its membership of all the post-Yugoslav republics except the 'rump' Federal Republic of Yugoslavia. The BSEC has placed subregional security issues on the agenda of its Parliamentary bodies and of a recent Business Forum. Its Ministers of the Interior have adopted a range of cooperative measures to combat the transnational threats of crime, terrorism, smuggling and illegal migration. It has initiated work on accident and emergency management and there has been some discussion of military and naval confidence-building measures in the Black Sea (although most members preferred not to pursue these within the BSEC framework itself).

Thus, despite their non-involvement in most overt security issues, the subregional groups in the Barents-Black Sea belt have effectively contributed to security in a wide range of different ways. These are summarized in the 'security spectrum' outlined in figure 9.2 (which also includes for comparison a list of the 'harder' security functions which subregional groups have not tried, and probably should not try, to perform). Beyond the various roles summarized in the 'security spectrum', subregional groups have also interacted positively with the other, larger European security organizations and processes. In particular, as discussed earlier, they have relevance for handling strains related to the enlargement of NATO and the EU. The generic model set out above for considering how subregional groups can help in managing integration's 'dividing lines' is entirely relevant to the security sphere. These groups can offer no realistic substitute to disappointed NATO candidates and they would be very ill-advised to try to intervene directly in tensions between the beneficiaries of enlargement and its opponents. Their indirect confidence-building and normative effects are, however, highly relevant to containing the damage these strains could cause to subregional security. The opportunities they offer for low-key, egalitarian dialogue may be particularly valued at a time when national relations with NATO are under stress. Ideally, their continued activity should underline the right of all states, whatever their Alliance position, to participation and influence and respect for their sovereignty in the regulation of security relationships. This would provide an extra line of defence against the development of new 'coercive' pacts, shielding the smaller and more peripheral states from isolation, and providing the ideal framework for active security contributions from the non-aligned. The elements of economic interdependence, cross-border cooperation, easing of minority conditions and cooperation on 'new threats' which subregional groups are so well equipped to promote could also gain new significance as a way of stabilizing relations between neighbouring pairs of successful and unsuccessful NATO applicants.

Each group's members must decide for themselves how overtly they want to address the implications of NATO's new policies for their subregion. Some observers of the BEAC have suggested, cogently, that the best thing that group can do for Russia-West relations in the post-enlargement years is to maintain the exclusion of overt security themes from its agenda, thus preserving the 'benevolent blindness' to local defence challenges which has so far served it so well.[21] The BEAC's role in this area will be eased by the fact that none of its members is likely to change its status with regard to NATO during the Alliance's 'first wave' enlargement. The Visegrad group and CEFTA provide a special case of another kind. Within the tight-knit group of their member states, a reassessment of neighbourhood relations in the light of NATO's verdict can hardly be avoided. As suggested above, however, its most productive outcome may be to strengthen and/or extend CEFTA's non-military competences, as well as prompting efforts in other frameworks to maintain civilized cross-border and minority conditions.[22] The remaining three groups (the CBSS, the CEI and the BSEC) have a somewhat wider range of choices, and some of their members may be interested in using them consciously to offset enlargement's strains and raise the profile of non-NATO-related security endeavours. Measures to this end could include the intensification of all aspects of 'soft' security work mentioned above, an increased focus on cooperative border management and the discussion of general codes of conduct or specific confidence-building measures to give additional assurances about security-related behaviour. Local armed forces could work together on a group-wide or variable geometry basis in such fields as search and rescue, mine clearance, emergency-handling and coastguard or fisheries enforcement operations and could sponsor appropriate joint exercises. Group members could offer political and perhaps practical support for more localized measures taken in the subregion to ease any particularly sensitive 'dividing lines', to settle outstanding disputes and to protect the interests of potentially exposed territories like Kaliningrad.[23] They could also discuss and address security challenges spreading into their members' territory from non-European regions, to remind themselves of the underlying interests they have in common - this could be a particularly fruitful theme in the Black Sea context. Further development of the theme of assistance and rehabilitation for former Yugoslavia could serve a similar consolidating purpose in the CEI, above all when and if the 'rump' Federal Republic of Yugoslavia rejoins the group.

Enough should have been said here to show that subregional groups do, in reality, have extremely broad, subtle and positive security effects and that they have not just profited from the benign qualities of the post-Cold War security environment but have done much themselves to improve it. If their contribution has not so far been widely recognized, that has something to do with their own members' delicacy of approach – a well-founded preference for doing good by stealth – as well as the relatively early stage of implementation of many of their most pertinent programmes.

However, the problem is also partly in the eye of the observer. Theorists today are unanimous about the need for wider definitions of security, and serious international work has been undertaken, notably in the OSCE framework, to identify the pattern of 'multi-dimensional' contributions in a 'multi-institutional' Eurasian security system.[24] Yet the stridency of the NATO enlargement debate has kept popular perceptions and domestic debates fixed on a narrow, historically conservative and essentially Eurocentric set of security issues.

It is unclear at the time of writing whether the outcome of NATO's July 1997 decision to invite Poland, the Czech Republic and Hungary to join the Alliance will perpetuate this focus, at least for some time, or whether it will clear the way for an eventual widening of the security debate. If the latter, the subregional groups examined here should begin to reap more widely the kind of appreciation they enjoy already from European cognoscenti. In particular, there is scope for much greater recognition of their complementarity with other organizations and processes. They are demonstrably building security in areas and in dimensions – internal and international – which very few other institutions have managed to reach. The discreet and often indirect nature of their contribution is a comparative advantage insofar as it helps them to avoid the fears and jealousies attached to more powerful organs and to embrace a wider range of states than any other integrative groups. In the near term, their value could be enhanced by greater recognition for, and protection of, their specific place in the multi-institutional pattern of subsidiarity, not excluding the possibility of express 'delegation' to them from other groups (as has already happened in a limited way with the CEI in the former Yugoslav context). In the longer term, there is reason to hope that the story may come full circle as the success of subregional groups paves the way for solving those very 'hard' security questions which they at present ignore.

SUBREGIONALISM AND DEMOCRACY

Another comparative advantage of the new subregional groups, again reflecting the changed historical environment that produced them, is their ability to blend different levels of action: collective 'outputs' as international bodies, the development of cooperation between their member states and the involvement of sub-state actors. One of the notable features of the new subregional groups is that they have encouraged and facilitated various forms of 'bottom-up' cooperation involving a wide variety of non-governmental/non-state bodies (for example, businesses, chambers of commerce, universities, cities, environmental groups, tourist boards). In particular, they have supported the development of cross-border (or transfrontier) cooperation between neighbouring regions/ provinces of states. While the impact of such 'bottom-up' and cross-border cooperation cannot easily be measured, a strong case can be made that it contributes to the development of democracy within and stable relations between the states concerned. By facilitating the development of a wide range of social groups, encouraging a suitable balance of power between central and local authorities within states and supporting economic development (especially in isolated border regions) it contributes to the strengthening of democracy and prosperity. By promoting domestic stability and interdependence with neighbouring states, such 'bottom-up' cooperation may also contribute to improved international relations within a subregion.

The exact degree of 'bottom-up' cooperation varies from group to group. It is institutionally strongest in the CEI and the BEAC, both of which 'captured' pre-existing sub-state networks (Alpe-Adria and Nordkalotten cooperation), perpetuated them through general-purpose sub-state architecture within the subregional construction, and recognized the need for some kind of secretariat to help keep the levels in synch. The Barents group has accorded perhaps the strongest role of all to its sub-state 'Council of the Regions', where a clearly defined consortium of provincial authorities can jointly manage their own resources and there is separate representation for the Sami ethnic community. The CBSS and the BSEC came into being in subregions where elements of non-governmental networking and functional cooperation did already exist, but on a somewhat fragmented basis. The path they chose was not to attempt to tidy all these into a single sub-structure – which would have risked local displeasure, the loss of existing grantor relationships and foregoing the subtle political benefits of varied geometry – but to accept a proliferation of subregional bodies under relatively loose coordination. Bodies like the Baltic university network and group of municipalities, or the BSEC's Parliamentary Assembly, Business Forum and Black Sea University, clearly serve the goals of the subregional endeavour but operate independently for most purposes and with some significant variations in membership.[25] A further practical distinction between the CEI/BEAC model and that of the CBSS/BSEC is that the first two groups operate over a contiguous land area and the latter two around a sea – posing obvious difficulties for the latter in establishing a 'hard core' of province-to-province cooperation (though Norway has recently proposed attempting something of the kind for the south Baltic shore in the CBSS). Finally, neither the Visegrad group nor CEFTA has attempted to develop 'bottom-up' elements, partly because of the dominantly governmental nature of these groups' agendas, but also because their subregion has been well supplied with such mechanisms from other sources. The Transcarpathian Euroregion linking provinces of Hungary, Poland, Slovakia, Romania and Ukraine has been the most elaborate cross-border initiative running parallel with the growth of CEFTA, but there are numerous other bilateral or trilateral initiatives designed to fill similar needs.[26] It is also a function of these states' truly 'central' location that some of their most politically significant cross-border relationships have been with neighbours outside the Visegrad/CEFTA core (for example, the Polish-German, Polish-Lithuanian, Polish-Ukrainian and Romanian-Bulgarian relationships).

For analytical purposes, therefore, subregional and cross-border (or transfrontier) cooperation in Central and Eastern Europe are best seen as separate, though overlapping and ideally synergistic processes.[27] It is worth, however, briefly noting here the main features which have determined the growth, struggles and impact of transfrontier networks. The successful development of cross-border cooperation depends on support from central (i.e., national governmental) authorities, local authorities and groups, and the overcoming of various practical problems. At all three levels, there may be serious obstacles. Reservations at central government (and perhaps parliamentary and party) level have most often arisen from fears about loss of control, compromising of security, the fragility of state authority in border regions, the loyalty of ethnic minorities living there (or even of native populations when the province is perceived as having political/economic grievances), and anxiety that all these might be exploited by neighbouring states or supra-national organizations to detach the areas concerned from the parent country. Such fears are clearly born in part of ignorance, but they are easier to understand in view of the luggage of experience and national feeling which Central and Eastern European leaders first brought to the issue at the end of the 1980s. The newer a given state's sovereignty (or restored sovereignty) and the larger the proportion of minorities on its territory, the sharper such worries tended to be. There were real doubts about internal control and solidarity even within smaller and superficially more 'manageable' states, given the lack of experienced representative bodies, the weakness of civil society, and (often) the rifts between town and country inherited from the Communist era. Consciousness of practical shortcomings in border management were sometimes a factor, especially if compounded by disputed or non-demarcated frontiers. All these factors could be doubly troublesome because by definition a cross-border scheme needs equal support from all the states concerned to function properly. It only took one unwilling state to hamper seriously the growth of any given initiative. In the case, for example, of the Transcarpathian experiment there were initial reservations from both Slovakia and Romania.

At the local level, mistrust of central motives and mistrust of foreigners' intentions were both liable to dampen local actors' enthusiasm, but political and international inexperience was perhaps an even larger obstacle. The issue of who should run cross-border cooperation and who should profit from it could be tricky, especially in ethnically diverse communities. The need for advance education and training of local elites, and also the need to reach beyond elites to give the wider population a sense of trust and ownership, was often neglected in the early days. Yet if the locals were not genuinely given greater control of their own affairs through the process of cooperation, the impact on democratic development could be very limited or even negative – merely replacing one form of tutelage by another.

Practical factors often held the key because they could either compound other problems to the point of making them insuperable, or provide new ways to circumvent them. On the negative side were such factors as lack of communications and infrastructure, non-comparability of administrative (or social, educational or commercial) structures on the two sides of a border, lack of a common language, absence of internal legislation providing vires and a reliable framework for the international transactions of sub-state powers, and plain lack of funds. If the latter problem could be overcome, either by intra-state transfers or (much more often) by inputs from rich neighbours and international institutions, all other difficulties - including psychological and political ones – could be relativized because it was a rare player who would resist the prospect of (privileged) material gain. Thus, the willingness of the Norwegian state to finance, almost single-handedly, the first two years' project work under the BEAC had a bracing effect on the attitudes of Russian players both in Moscow and Murmansk.[28] Similarly, the BSEC can hope for a quantum leap in cooperation if its new bank enters successful operation.

As a matter of record, the transfrontier dimension of subregional cooperation seems to have developed more smoothly in the years since 1994 than in the immediate post-Cold War period, and to have put on a new spurt since 1996. It is no accident that the late-launched BEAC achieved the most sophisticated combination of top-down and bottom-up elements, or that – in another context – the network of Baltic-Polish-Ukrainian cross-border cooperation has grown fastest and won broadest domestic support in the later 1990s. This is just what one would expect if the initial problems were partly bred of inexperience, insecurity and inadequate preparation. But the recent growth of transfrontier cooperation also has something to do with the changing attitudes and inputs of external authorities. It took some time, and growing consciousness of the possible negative side-effects of NATO and EU enlargement, for Western states' attention to be drawn to the importance of transfrontier relations among their Central and Eastern European partners (and of these states' corresponding relations with Russia and other CIS states). It took time also for the European Union, the European Bank for Reconstruction and Development (EBRD) and other leading funders to adapt their policies and mechanisms to the complexities of multi-nation projects involving non-state actors. Earlier, the rigidity of divisions between the EU's PHARE and TACIS assistance programmes (for the Central and Eastern European Associates of the Union and the CIS states respectively) was a serious irritant, and the EBRD had no procedures for lending, for example, to municipal authorities. These problems have steadily been overcome and the EU, in particular, now possesses a well-adapted armoury of instruments which it is constantly refining. Tribute is also due to the Council of Europe's growing role in promoting new transfrontier relationships, which has not only helped to develop local competencies and spread 'best practice', but has also introduced a normative overview valuable for combating fears of exploitation.[29]

The prizes, if these positive trends can be maintained, are considerable. The security relevance of stable, interdependent, self-assured, cross-border communities has already been noted above. The value of such cooperation for conflict prevention – pre-empting disputes over resources, easing ethnic tensions, providing transparency and predictability in militarily sensitive frontier zones – is particularly clear. It also improves the prospects for effective, collaborative border management to 'let the good through and keep the bad out', which cannot be assured through central diktat alone but depends also on the compliance of local populations and motivation of local officials. At best, solid partnerships in frontier regions could even help offset and overcome tensions arising between central governments. Economic benefits are equally plain: shortfalls and disparities in provincial development can be reduced and comparative advantages exploited by those who know them best. An economically porous frontier also allows the whole state to profit from freer international intercourse and greater receptivity to global processes. Threats to prosperity from energy and water shortage, pollution, environmental change and natural disasters can also be combated on a broader basis and with a better hope – thanks to coherent, non-competitive planning – of drawing in outside aid.

The implications for internal democratic development, pluralism and civil society are perhaps most interesting of all at a time when the Central and Eastern European democracies are still searching for prescriptions to cure their inherited ills. A well-conceived transfrontier cooperation scheme places the periphery in the centre of attention, with important psychological as well as practical benefits. It should make local communities both more self-reliant and more satisfied with their lot and their say in the state, thereby strengthening – not sapping – national cohesion. From the point of view of the state as a whole, successful transfrontier cooperation combats excessive centralism, promotes decentralization, devolution and representative pluralism. By drawing in new actors (– a remarkable range of commercial, professional, social, religious, educational and cultural groups, as well as local officials have taken part in these schemes) it helps re-create civil society from the bottom up. It also promotes consciousness of local and national identity while proving that adversarial nationalism, quite literally, does not pay. It is worth underlining once again, however, that none of this potential can be explored so long as the centre itself is not persuaded of its merits. Policies to foster transfrontier cooperation must be designed from the outset to offer reassurances, normative safeguards and tangible advantage to central governments as well.

While this does not imply that every subregional group must have 'bottom-up' elements, it does suggest that groups incorporating such elements are likely to gain more popular acceptance, mobilize broader energies in their support and have better chances of long-term survival. Equally, those groups which choose to remain purely governmental may be frustrated in some of their aims – for example, the general bolstering of stability and integration – unless a cross-border network of some kind is simultaneously active in the subregion.

A number of steps may be taken to further improve and extend transfrontier cooperation in the context of subregional groups.[30] A clear legal and normative framework, consistent across the whole region, is a useful starting-point. All states concerned should sign the Council of Europe's 'European Outline Convention on Transfrontier Cooperation Between Territorial Communities and Authorities', if they have not already done so. This document not only offers organizational guidelines but also contains provisions ensuring that cross-border ties will not be misused against national sovereignty and territorial integrity.[31] Second, states can include commitments to foster transfrontier cooperation in their bilateral treaties and other, especially sectoral, agreements, including agreements with international entities like the EU. Third, national governments should provide a clear basis in internal legislation and/or administrative regulations for the international activities of sub-state authorities (bearing in mind the importance of structural compatibility with neighbours). Transfrontier and subregional goals should also be built into national economic and development planning. The same clearly goes for environmental policies and the design of measures for handling emergencies. All these steps have resource implications which must be duly considered and provided for, and governments should give thought to the practical needs of competence-building, institution-building and information exchange for sub-state and non-state actors engaged in transfrontier work. Non-governmental organizations both within and outside the country can also contribute to the development of transfrontier cooperation.[32]

At the level of subregional groups themselves, the amount of attention paid to 'bottom-up' aspects during inter-governmental meetings has been varied. The BEAC has gone about as far as any such group could go in institutionalizing, supporting, and building organizational bridges to the sub-state level. The CBSS, CEI and BSEC have for various reasons (including the lack of direct authority over some related bottom-up networks) at times seemed to take a more laissez-faire approach. Since 1996, however, there has been a notable trend in all three of them to re-address the issue of coordination, streamline their own subordinate structures (working groups and so on) and exploit more directly the economic, political and even presentational value of specialized subregional organs. Provided it stops short of harmful 're-centralization', this approach is to be welcomed. All the groups can do something to encourage bottom-up cooperation, if only by devoting adequate attention to such cooperation, offering political recognition and making information more freely available. (The use of electronic networks within, as well as between, subregional groups is well worth considering). They should encourage cross-regional ties between sub-state constituencies, such as contacts between the various business forums and university chains. They should help these bodies meet resource needs either by direct support or, if this is inadequate, by including their requirements in bids made for assistance to outside sources of funding.

CONCLUSION

Post-Cold War subregional groups in Europe have embodied some of the last decade's most forward-looking and positive trends: the integrative impulse, the non-zero-sum reading of national interest, cooperative multi-functional security, democratic pluralism and the empowerment of non-state actors. They have returned valuable nutrients to the friendly soil from which they sprang and they have played a role, which in the nature of things can never be quantified, in averting or cushioning both bilateral disputes and and those related to the enlargement of NATO and the EU. Like NATO, the EU and the OSCE, they have also mirrored the imperfections of the new and incomplete post-Cold War European order. They have witnessed conflicts where they could offer little but damage limitation and 'clean-up' services. They have been hobbled by conflicts of national interest, expressed or unexpressed. They have drawn up plans which foundered for lack of resources or support. However, and almost alone among today's institutions, they can at least claim to have observed, so far, the good physician's rule of 'First, do no harm'.

From their origins in 1989-90, these new groups have responded to two sets of dynamics, from inside and outside. The internal urge to normalize bilateral and group relations and to tackle local problems with local know-how, has been complemented by motives related to larger European institutions: the hope of using group leverage to gain membership, the willing or grudging acceptance of palliatives for exclusion, the concern to reduce local damage from enlargement's 'dividing lines'. Another way of putting this would be to distinguish the motivation and policies associated with 'the subregion in itself' from those associated with 'the subregion in Europe'. As a very rough generalization one might say that up to 1994 the latter dynamic was decisive for Visegrad/CEFTA, while the former did more – at least overtly – to guide the evolution of the other groups, not least because their Western leadership came from states themselves not fully integrated (the non-aligned states and NATO members outside the EU). During 1995-96, the growing focus on NATO and EU enlargement created mixed motives and hesitations within several subregional groups. However, while their development may have slowed, all of them proved secure enough in their local roles to survive the competition offered by region-wide schemes like PfP and EU/WEU Association. From 1996 onwards, the value of 'the subregion in Europe' could be more clearly and positively described. As enlargement approached, these groups' ability both to prepare for it and to soften 'dividing lines' was better grasped and the other European institutions (particularly the OSCE and the EU) sought more openly for ways to support them. However, certain changes could also be discerned in local dynamics which brought new openings for compromise and cohesion in terms of the 'subregion in itself'. In the case of the BSEC, these included greater Russian confidence, Russian-Ukrainian rapprochement and fading concern about Turkish domination. For the BSEC and the CEI, the end of open fighting in the Transcaucasus and the former Yugoslavia opened up new prospects for small-state activism. There were subtle shifts of balance in the BEAC as Norway handed the baton to the new EU members Sweden and Finland. There were similar shifts in the CBSS as the Nordic states swamped the initial influence of Germany.

The latest injection of fuel through these two complementary channels should be sufficient to keep all the currently active groups in the Barents-Black Sea belt driving ahead at least to the end of the twentieth century. After that, their survival may be calculated as a function of three factors: the genuineness and solidity of their local motivation; the extent to which they straddle and ease the 'dividing lines' of NATO and EU enlargement; and their relevance to further strategic divides of the future. If enlargement proves to be a continuing process, most of the members not just of CEFTA but also of the CEI may, within the foreseeable future, find themselves within the EU and/or NATO. In this case, the odds are that their sense of subregional identity will not prove strong enough to survive on the inside as more than informal and irregular 'caucusing'. The northern European groups have a stronger sense of locality to build on (although one might speculate on whether the separate embodiment of the Barents and Baltic elements will make sense indefinitely) and are likely to preserve their 'divide-crossing' rationale for much longer because of the difficulty of stretching integrated institutions – at least in their present form – to incorporate Russia. This last point is, of course, true of the BSEC as well but this south-eastern group could also have a longer-term role as a bridge from continental Europe into the 'new frontiers' of the Middle East and Eurasia. It is the only existing group which could end up sharing some members with, and providing elements of a model for, new subregional groups established on and beyond the eastern territories of the OSCE. In conclusion, there seems to be good reason for some, at least, of Europe's new subregional groups to survive well beyond 2000 in any scenario other than that of a renewed East-West military confrontation.

10 Subregional Cooperation and the New European Security Architecture[1]

Andrew Cottey

Since the early 1990s, there has been general acceptance that the new European 'security architecture' should be defined by an inter-locking framework of institutions, with differing institutions playing differing roles, but also cooperating with one another to enhance general European security, as well as in the management of specific problems. Critics argue that the differing views amongst European states and the interests of competing beauracracies have meant that the new European architecture has been defined by competition between different organizations and the absence of any real consensus on how Europe's security institutions should be re-organized. Nevertheless, a new, multi-institutional security architecture is emerging and – despite differences amongst European states on the future of that architecture – certain divisions of labour have become clear. The European Union (EU), the North Atlantic Treaty Organizations (NATO) and the Western European Union (WEU) continue to provide political, economic and military security for their members, but have also taken on new tasks: expanding their memberships to include countries from Central and Eastern Europe; developing cooperative ties with both prospective members and those states not likely to join these organizations; and developing operational conflict management and peacekeeping roles. The Organization for Security and Cooperation in Europe (OSCE) and the Council of Europe continue to provide broad normative frameworks for European security (through the principles of democracy and human rights which they enshrine), but have also taken on new operational roles in areas such as election monitoring, support for democratization, conflict prevention and post-conflict peace-building. The various organizations, further, have begun to acknowledge their comparative advantages and to cooperate with one another (particularly in relation to the peace process in the former Yugoslavia, which has highlighted the strengths and the weaknesses of the various organizations).

The growing recognition of the contribution of subregional cooperation to European security raises the questions of what place subregional groups may have in this new European architecture and what constructive forms of interaction may be developed between subregional groups and the larger European organizations. The first years of the subregional groups in the Barents-Black Sea belt suggest a number of initial answers to these questions. First, subregional cooperation cannot be seen as an alternative to any of the larger European organizations, nor to membership of NATO or the EU for countries seeking that status. Thus, while Central and Eastern European states have actively supported subregional cooperation, they have only done so to that extent such cooperation does not contradict or undermine their strategic objective of integration with the West. Second, subregionalism has the potential to contribute to European security by bringing together diverse groups of states in cooperative frameworks and by tackling specific security problems (often of a 'soft', non-military nature). Third, in the context of NATO and EU enlargement, subregional cooperation can contribute to European security by sustaining cooperation between NATO/EU members, those states seeking NATO/EU membership and those states uninvolved in or wary of the enlargement processes, while also helping some states to prepare for integration with NATO and/or the EU. There are, however, also tensions between NATO/EU enlargement and subregional cooperation. In particular, Central and Eastern European states fear that engagement in subregional cooperation may delay (or, at worst, permanently postpone) their integration with NATO/EU by condemning them to wait for their 'slower' neighbours or if such cooperation comes to be seen as an alternative to NATO or EU membership. Fourth, various forms of cooperation have begun to emerge between subregional groups and the larger organizations, as illustrated by the EU's involvement in most of the groups in the Barents-Black Sea belt.

This chapter examines the role of subregional cooperation in the new European security architecture. In particular, it explores two questions: how the larger organizations can help to promote subregional cooperation and how subregional groups can support the larger organizations. It suggests that, as pan-European organizations, the OSCE and the Council of Europe can provide important normative frameworks for subregional cooperation and play a role in encouraging dialogue on subregional cooperation and the interchange of experience between subregions. The EU has significant potential to act as a 'driver' for subregional cooperation, providing political, economic and material support for multi-functional, subregional cooperation. Although NATO and the WEU are developing subregional dimensions to their own eastern outreach policies, as primarily military security organizations they are perhaps less likely to engage directly with the Barents-Black Sea groups (which have to date remained oriented more towards 'soft' security issues).

THE OSCE: A PAN-EUROPEAN FRAMEWORK

Historically, the OSCE's primary role has been as a pan-European framework for the negotiation of agreements on human rights, confidence-building and arms control. Since the Cold War, however, Europe's security problems have become increasingly diverse and often subregional in character. Subregional conflicts have broken out in the former Yugoslavia, Moldova, Nagorno-Karabakh, Georgia, Chechnya and Tajikistan. As a consequence, much of the OSCE's operational conflict management work has a strong subregional dimension (through the activities of the Chairman-in-Office, the High Commissioner on National Minorities (HCNM), OSCE Missions, the Office for Democratic Institutions and Human Rights (ODIHR) and more ad hoc bodies such as the 'Minsk group' on the Nagorno-Karabakh conflict). This has been extended further in the context of the Dayton/Paris peace process in the former Yugoslavia, where the OSCE has been involved in monitoring elections, facilitating subregional military confidence-building and arms control agreements and monitoring human and minority rights.

In terms of substantive engagement with the subregional groups in the Barents-Black Sea belt, the OSCE has been slower in developing a role. The OSCE's 1992 Helsinki summit document welcomed 'regional and subregional cooperation', referring to it as a valuable means of multiplying 'the links uniting OSCE participating States ....promoting pluralistic structures of stability ...uniting us and promoting comprehensive security', and 'an effective form of promoting CSCE principles and objectives as well as implementing and developing CSCE commitments'. It specifically mentioned as examples the Council of Baltic Sea States (CBSS), the Visegrad group, the Black Sea Economic Cooperation (BSEC) and the Central European Initiative (CEI).[2] The December 1994 Budapest summit declaration stated that 'regional and transfrontier cooperation has a definite role in promoting good-neighbourly relations' and welcomed 'the development of an increasing number of regional groupings'; cited the BSEC, the Barents Euro-Arctic Council (BEAC), the CEI, the Central Europe Free Trade Agreement (CEFTA), the CBSS and the Danube River Protection Convention as 'positive examples'; and declared the OSCE 'ready to act as a repository for freely negotiated bilateral and multilateral arrangements and agreements and to follow their implementation if requested by the parties'.[3]

In terms of a more direct role in promoting subregional cooperation, OSCE efforts focused on the possibility of subregional arms control or confidence and security-building measures (CSBMs). The 1992 Helsinki summit established the Forum for Security (FSC) as a new framework for discussions on arms control and confidence-building. The FSC's mandate referred to the possibility of 'regional' measures and its Programme for Immediate Action specifically included regional arms control, disarmament and confidence and security-building measures, as well as more vaguely defined 'regional security issues'.[4] The 1994 Budapest and 1996 Lisbon OSCE summits both stressed the possibility of subregional arms control, confidence-building and cooperation.[5] Despite this, the OSCE still has little to show in the way of specific new subregional arms control or confidence-building measures. The issue has been discussed at the OSCE in Vienna at various points since 1992, but states in subregions such as Central and Eastern Europe, the Baltic Sea and the Caucasus have been reluctant to develop arms control or confidence-building measures with a specifically subregional character.[6] These states are wary of having arms control/confidence-building measures imposed upon them which might not fully reflect their national security concerns. They are averse to being 'singularized' as deserving 'special treatment', different from that of their neighbours or the West. Central and Eastern European states fear that subregional measures (particularly if 'too' successful) might be seen as an alternative to their full integration with NATO and the EU. Small and medium-sized states (particularly the neutral and non-aligned states who rely on the mobilization of territorial armed forces for their national defence) argue that only a small part of the territory and armed forces of larger powers (effectively Russia) would be covered by subregional arms control or confidence-building measures while the whole of their own territory and armed forces would be included, making such agreements one-sided and undermining their ability to defend themselves.

What progress has been made in subregional arms control and CSBMs has either taken place outside the OSCE framework, been rather limited in character or resulted from unique circumstances. NATO's Partnership for Peace (PfP) eastern outreach programme has developed a significant subregional dimension (– see below), but this has been driven by the political impetus of NATO's direct involvement and involves practical elements of military cooperation (such as joint exercises) which the OSCE could not easily replicate. Bilaterally, various pairs of states (particularly in Central and Eastern Europe) have undertaken security policy discussions, military-to-military contacts, joint exercises, the development of joint military units and, in some cases, specific CSBMs (such as 'hot lines', notification of military movements, neutral airspace corridors along borders or bilateral 'open skies' inspection agreements).[7] These bilateral measures have, however, been undertaken at the initiative of the states concerned, with little or no OSCE role.

The OSCE CSBM regime (as summarized in the 1994 'Vienna Document') includes various 'options' which might be used bilaterally or subregionally, particularly in the context of crises.[8] These options have, however, been relatively little applied – reflecting the general reluctance to engage in subregional arms control noted above. The adaptation of the Conventional Armed Forces in Europe (CFE) Treaty mandated by the December 1996 OSCE Lisbon summit also appeared likely to include a subregional dimension, in the form of a new Central European zone with specific force limits. This, however, was only contemplated in the context of substantive renewal of the CFE Treaty proper (which would continue to impose strict limits on the armed forces of all its signatories) and, more importantly, the likely accession of the first Central European states to NATO. The only more direct success for the OSCE in facilitating multilateral, subregional arms control has been in the former Yugoslavia in the context of the Dayton/Paris peace process. Here, the OSCE played a major role, providing both political impetus and technical expertise for the CSBM and 'CFE-type' agreements concluded by the former Yugoslav states. These dimensions of the Dayton/Paris peace process, however, resulted from the unique circumstances of an externally imposed peace, facilitated by strong external political and economic pressure and the deployment of the NATO-led Peace Implementation/Stabilization Force. While this model of OSCE-facilitated CSBMs/arms control might be conceivable in other similar circumstances (such as a possible settlement of the Nagorno-Karabakh conflict), it is unlikely to provide a more general model. Given these realities, the prospects for wider OSCE facilitation of subregional arms control or political-military CSBMs seem limited.

The OSCE was given a further subregional dimension when it was entrusted with following up the March 1995 Pact on Stability in Europe. The 'Stability Pact' was initiated by the EU in 1993-94, aiming to facilitate cooperation among Central and Eastern European countries. It was subregional in the sense that discussions took place in two round tables (Central Europe and the Baltic) and that various bilateral agreements were appended to the March 1995 concluding Pact (which re-iterated the principles of respect for international borders and minority rights).[9] The March 1995 Pact entrusted the follow-up of the agreement to the OSCE. Since then, while there have been various discussions of the Stability Pact at the OSCE in Vienna, there has been little inclination – and some resistance – shown by Central and Eastern European states to revive or further develop the process.[10] By 1996-97, there appeared little prospect of significant new developments within the Stability Pact framework. The OSCE, lacking the political or economic leverage of the EU, found itself at a disadvantage in attempting to 'encourage' similar solutions for outstanding subregional problems.

By 1996-97, however, a combination of concern over the near-exhaustion of these traditional subregional approaches and the rising profile of the independent subregional groups in the Barents-Black Sea belt had stimulated new interest – across a wide range of OSCE states – in exploring what the OSCE might do directly for and with the existing subregional groups. In conceptual terms this could be seen as a return to Helsinki 1992. In practical terms the subject had much larger resonance than before because of the multiplication of such groups, their expanding membership, their new potential for 'cushioning' NATO/EU enlargement and progress made within the OSCE in developing the concept of 'mutually reinforcing institutions'. As the broadest pan-European institution, the OSCE includes all states which are members of existing European subregional groups, as well as most of their immediate neighbours – making it the most appropriate framework both for inter-group liaison and for wider discussion of the place of subregionalism in European security. The basic principles which the OSCE defines for member states' international and domestic behaviour – respect for international alignments, democracy, respect for human and minority rights, respect for the security of other states – also provide an important normative framework for subregional groups. OSCE principles and norms are relevant both to states' behaviour within subregional groups and to such groups' relations with their neighbours. In their internal relations, such groups should clearly be based on respect for borders and sovereignty, the non-use of force, and the free choice of states to join (or leave) them. In dealing with neighbours, the most vital OSCE guideline is that such groups and their activities should not be directed against the security of any other state. The OSCE's pan-European character, its on-going discussions on relations between the various European security organizations and its practical cooperation with other international bodies – for example, in the context of its involvement in the Bosnian peace process – also make it the ideal framework for discussing subregional groups' relations and practical cooperation with other European organizations.

The potential synergy works both ways because subregional groups have also shown that they can give practical substance to the OSCE's efforts to build a common, cooperative and comprehensive European security order. While the OSCE can provide high-level, pan-European support for these goals, its large membership and mainly consensus-based decision-making sometimes makes it difficult for it to translate such objectives into concrete terms. The smaller size and often more functional orientation of subregional groups has evident advantages here. Subregional groups have the potential to give substance to general OSCE commitments to common, cooperative and comprehensive security by bringing together diverse groups of states to engage in practical cooperation and address security in a broad sense.

During initial work in 1996 on the idea of a new 'Common and Comprehensive Security Model for Europe for the Twenty-first Century', this fresh approach to subregional security emerged as one area commanding support among member states. The theme was given considerable prominence in the separate Declaration on the Security Model made by the December 1996 Lisbon Summit:

> interaction with regional, sub-regional and trans-border cooperation in the economic and environmental field should be enhanced, as they contribute to the promotion of good-neighbourly relations and security. ...We encourage bilateral or regional initiatives aimed at developing relations of good neighbourliness and cooperation. In this context, the OSCE could explore a menu of confidence and security-building measures in support of regional security processes. ...Regional round tables can be a useful means of preventive diplomacy. ...European security requires the widest cooperation and co-ordination among participating States and European and transatlantic organizations. The OSCE... is particularly well suited as a forum to enhance cooperation and complementarity among such organizations and institutions. ...the OSCE will strengthen cooperation with other security organizations which are transparent and predictable in their actions, whose members individually and collectively adhere to OSCE principles and commitments, and whose membership is based on open and voluntary commitments.[11]

As part of the follow-up to the Lisbon Declaration, it was agreed that an official OSCE seminar on 'Regional Security and Cooperation' should be held in Vienna in June 1997. The seminar was attended by representatives of all OSCE states and observers, the main subregional groups within the OSCE area, the EU and NATO, plus non-governmental and academic representatives. The proceedings included presentations on the BEAC, the CBSS, the BSEC, the CEI and CEFTA and discussion of Central Asia and Bosnia-Herzegovina as case studies.[12] The Chairman's summary of the seminar recorded agreement among participants that subregional groups 'contributed significantly to cooperation, confidence-building and addressing new security challenges', dealing with new non-military security risks, 'counteracting the establishment of new dividing lines by creating multi-layered, transboundary cooperative networks' and helping to prepare for 'the integration of their members into broader fora'. It argued that 'closer links between the OSCE and subregional groupings would facilitate the overall objective of a Common and Comprehensive Security Model. At the same time, the development of further links should be pursued in its own right as a useful supplement to existing cooperative arrangements. The relationship should be non-hierarchical and of a mutually re-inforcing nature'. The seminar also discussed a wide range of possibilities for the enhancement of subregional cooperation and for the development of relations between the OSCE and subregional groups.[13] The seminar was an important step because it reflected the growing interest among OSCE states in subregional cooperation and highlighted the potential of the OSCE as a framework for discussion and interchange on subregional cooperation and for cooperation between the OSCE and existing subregional groups. Whether and how OSCE support for subregional cooperation might be translated into concrete elements for eventual inclusion in the 'Security Model' and/or a possible new OSCE Charter was less clear.[14]

In terms of the future, there would appear to be a number of areas in which the OSCE might support subregional cooperation and develop its own relations with subregional groups.[15] First, the OSCE might be developed more explicitly as a normative framework for subregional groups and for their relations with the other European organizations. As was noted above, the OSCE's 1992 Helsinki, 1994 Budapest and 1996 Lisbon summit documents all referred to the positive value of subregional cooperation but they did so in brief and relatively neutral terms. A stronger formal statement defining and expressing OSCE support for the contribution of subregional groups to European security – in a future Security Model text, summit declaration and/or OSCE Charter – would give greater political salience to subregional cooperation, encouraging those states involved in subregional groups to further develop them, other European organizations to give greater support to them and other states to consider whether similar efforts might be possible in their own subregions.

Beyond this, the OSCE might also consider going further in defining the principles which should guide subregional groups and their relations with other European organizations. The Lisbon summit's Security Model declaration contained suitable formulae, even if not always expressly applied to the subregional context, when it spoke of 'the inherent right of each and every participating state to choose or change its security arrangements'; stated that OSCE members 'will not strengthen their security at the expense of the security of other states' and that 'no state, organization or grouping can have superior responsibility for maintaining peace and stability in the OSCE region, or regard any part of the OSCE region as its sphere of influence'; and (as noted above) declared that in the interests of European security OSCE would strengthen cooperation with 'other security organizations which are transparent and predictable in their actions, whose members individually and collectively adhere to OSCE principles and commitments, and whose membership is based on open and voluntary commitments'.[16] It would be a further step forward if the OSCE could find a suitable context in future to state specifically that these and other relevant OSCE principles apply to subregional groups as they do to other institutions. It might note in the same context that transfrontier and non-governmental cooperation may be valuable components of subregional cooperation, and that the same norms of conduct should apply to the actors involved at all levels. At the same time, those subregional groups which have not already done so should consider re-affirming their own commitment to relevant OSCE principles and to cooperation with OSCE and other European organizations on the basis of non-hierarchical, mutually re-inforcing relations. Such statements could have two benefits. First, they would help to reassure all states (whether involved in subregional groups, neighbouring such groups or considering the prospects for such cooperation in their own subregions) that such cooperation will only be undertaken on the basis of OSCE principles and will not threaten their security. Second, they would provide a political basis for the further development of cooperation between subregional groups and the larger European organizations – again, with the reassurance that such cooperation will eschew hierarchy and subordination.

While statements of political support and normative guidelines can help to encourage subregional cooperation and cooperation between subregional groups and the larger organizations, they are likely to have a rather limited impact unless they are followed up by more practical steps. As a pan-European 'umbrella' framework, the OSCE could play a significant role in this area also, by providing a forum for exchange of information between the various subregional groups and the larger European organizations and for discussing the possibilities of further generic and task-related synergy between them. Such information exchange and discussion would: help to raise the profile of existing subregional groups; encourage more supportive policies towards such groups by the larger organizations and the development of practical forms of cooperation; encourage the transfer of 'best practice' between existing subregional groups; and promote interest in subregional cooperation in countries which are not yet involved in such efforts. The June 1997 seminar on 'Regional Security and Cooperation' was a valuable first step in this direction.

The OSCE could facilitate information exchange and discussion of subregional cooperation in a number of ways. On the model of the June 1997 seminar, the OSCE could hold an annual meeting on subregional cooperation, bringing together representatives of subregional groups, the larger European organizations, non-governmental organizations and the academic community, and including annual reports by existing subregional groups (with a focus on lessons and successes). A smaller 'group of groups' (with each subregional group represented by its President/Chair) or 'friends of subregional cooperation' group could meet in Vienna to continue more regular discussions. Subregional groups could agree to exchange all major documents systematically with other subregional groups and the larger European organizations and could invite representatives of neighbouring/overlapping groups and the larger organizations to observe their high-level meetings. The larger organizations could invite representatives of subregional groups to attend their own high-level meetings and other relevant meetings as appropriate. To facilitate this interchange, the Chairman-in-Office or Secretary-General of the OSCE could compile, distribute and keep updated a list of relevant contact points. To maximize the availability of information, the OSCE could establish a written archive on subregional cooperation, publish a one-off or annual handbook, and expand its Internet/WorldWideWeb/ on-line information facilities to include a dedicated Web page, data-base and ideally discussion group on subregional activities. In order to strengthen the OSCE Secretariat's capacity to work with other organizations, a new post of liaison officer has been suggested. As noted by the OSCE Secretary-General at the June 1997 seminar, such an officer could also take charge of ties with subregional groups.

Another option under discussion within the OSCE is the establishment of a 'menu' of subregional confidence-building measures, designed to encourage the adoption of subregional or bilateral CSBMs by maximizing states' awareness of the range of options open to them and the experiences gained by other states. This idea was proposed by the Dutch delegation to the OSCE in 1996 and (as noted above) the Lisbon summit document stated that 'the OSCE could explore a menu of confidence and security-building measures in support of regional security processes'.[17] There has, however, been some resistance to this idea, with states fearing that they might have CSBMs imposed on them against their will and that the exercise might merely repeat the so far fruitless debate on subregional arms control or military CSBMs.[18] The conclusions from the June 1997 OSCE seminar endorsed the idea of continued work on a menu of CSBMs, but also sought to address these concerns, noting that a menu should be 'based on a comprehensive review of existing measures, beginning with "soft" measures ...the menu should be dynamic and illustrative of the range of options, not prescriptive or normative'.[19] A menu of this more novel type – particularly if it highlights the very wide range of non-military measures states have already undertaken without detriment to their security or independence, and is clearly based on an à la carte approach – could offer real practical help in expanding the gamut of means for subregional and bilateral cooperation.

There may also be potential for more substantive practical cooperation, and division of labour, between the OSCE and individual subregional groups in relation to specific issues. Subregional groups might work with the OSCE, provide information/resources for the OSCE or be delegated tasks by the OSCE in relation to areas such as early warning, conflict prevention, conflict resolution, post-conflict peace-building, support for democratization, election monitoring and the promotion or monitoring of respect for human and minority rights. In this context, there may be particular scope for cooperation between subregional groups and the various operational components of the OSCE (ODIHR, the HCNM, OSCE Missions, OSCE election monitoring activities). In the Baltic subregion there is obvious potential for greater cooperation between the CBSS (particularly its Commissioner for Democratic Institutions and Human Rights) and the HCNM and the OSCE Missions in the Baltic states. In Central and Eastern Europe, there may be similar potential for expanded cooperation between the CEI and the HCNM, given the CEI's attention to (and explicit commitments on) minority rights. In the former Yugoslavia, the CEI might conceivably take on some post-conflict peace-building and human/minority rights monitoring tasks (particularly if the Federal Republic of Yugoslavia rejoins the CEI before it rejoins the OSCE). Subregional groups may be particularly suited to these tasks because states within any subregion will have a particular interest in subregional stability, may have more detailed knowledge of the local situation and may be more willing to commit resources to promote stability within their 'neighbourhood'. The OSCE, with its limited financial/manpower resources, could in turn benefit from the practical, material inputs that subregional groups can offer. At the same time, it can provide wider European legitimacy for and oversight of activities undertaken by subregional groups, helping to ensure that they respect OSCE norms and have proper regard for the competencies of other organizations active in the field.

By mid-1997, such practical cooperation had barely begun. How far it would develop might depend on the willingness and ability of subregional groups to take on some more directly security related tasks than they had to date. It would also depend on general support within the OSCE – including from states outside the most active cooperation zone – and might raise some tricky (though hardly insoluble) issues over the high-level political control of such activities. The diversity of the different existing subregional groups and of tasks facing the OSCE suggested that such practical cooperation would best be undertaken on a flexible, ad hoc, case-by-case basis.[20] Differing subregional groups might engage in cooperation with the OSCE to differing degrees and in differing ways. In short, there appears to be significant potential for the OSCE to further support subregional cooperation and for the development of practical cooperation between the OSCE and subregional groups – potential which was only beginning to be explored by 1997.

THE COUNCIL OF EUROPE

With its enlargement to include the majority of Central and Eastern European states, including Ukraine, and the Russian Federation, the Council of Europe has become another 'pan-European' organization, paralleling the OSCE. Like the OSCE, the Council of Europe also has potential to support subregional cooperation in its own areas of competence. The Council of Europe's primary function is to support democracy and human rights (including minority rights) and it is here that the Council has the most potential to support subregional cooperation and develop relations with subregional groups – particularly those such as the CBSS and the CEI which have explicitly sought to support democratization and human and minority rights. Other Council of Europe functional objectives, such as the promotion of a common European cultural heritage, youth cooperation and the development of transfrontier cooperation also mesh well with the 'soft security' concerns of the subregional groups in the Barents-Black Sea belt. Since the end of the Cold War, the Council of Europe has developed a wide range of programmes to support democratization and respect for human and minority rights, as well as cooperation in a number of non- or 'soft' security areas, in the countries of Central and Eastern Europe and the former Soviet Union.

The Council of Europe has also played a particular role promoting subregionalism in the specific form of transfrontier cooperation. In 1980, the Council adopted an 'Outline Convention on Transfrontier Cooperation' which legitimated the general concept of ties between sub-state regions, defined some basic principles for such cooperation and included a number of 'model agreements'.[21] A number of transfrontier cooperation schemes established in Western Europe since 1945 (the Upper-Rhine 'Regio' linking Switzerland, France and Germany, the Meuse-Rhine Euroregion and the Working Community of the Pyrenees) provided examples of what could be achieved in this area. Recognizing the vast new opportunities for such cooperation in Central and Eastern Europe, at its fortieth anniversary summit in Strasbourg in 1989, the Council's Committee of Ministers adopted a Declaration on Transfrontier Cooperation calling for a special effort to be made to develop new ties with the frontier regions of Central and Eastern European states.[22] The Council gave practical force to this new emphasis, not just by promoting specific transfrontier schemes in Central and Eastern Europe (– such as the Transcarpathian Euroregion bringing together border regions of Poland, Slovakia, Hungary, Romania and Ukraine), but also by taking further steps to strengthen the legal and normative underpinnings for such initiatives. Thus, in October 1995 an Additional Protocol to the Outline Convention on Transfrontier Cooperation was opened for signature by parties to the Convention.[23] The Additional Protocol defines a specific 'right' for territorial communities or authorities within a state to enter into transfrontier arrangements on their own initiative and clarifies the legal status, effects of and constitutional controls upon any obligations or mechanisms created in the course of such cooperation. The Council has also supported transfrontier cooperation in Central and Eastern Europe by providing technical expertise and facilitating the exchange of information between frontier regions in Central and Eastern Europe and existing transfrontier cooperation efforts in Western Europe.[24]

In both the general area of the Council of Europe's work for democracy and human rights and the specific area of transfrontier cooperation there is obviously significant potential for cooperation and synergy between the

Council and subregional groups. Various examples of such synergy already exist, as with the parallel work of the Council, the OSCE and the CBSS in support of minority rights and conflict prevention in the Baltic states. Nevertheless, there remains potential for further developing synergistic cooperation between the Council of Europe and subregional groups. Further information exchange and discussion of possible forms of cooperation and divisions of labour would appear to be a sensible starting point. One possibility would be for the Council and particular subregional groups to discuss the relevance of Council norms and standards to the maintenance and enhancement of cooperation in the particular subregion concerned. Subregional groups could also explore how the implementation of Council norms might best be supported in their subregion, perhaps making specific suggestions to the Council. Specific joint Council of Europe-subregional group programmes might also be possible.

THE EUROPEAN UNION

While the OSCE and the Council of Europe have the potential to act as normative frameworks and fora for information exchange on subregional cooperation, they lack the more substantial political and economic resources necessary to act as driving forces for such cooperation. In significant part, this role has been played by individual states: Norway in the BEAC; Germany, Denmark and Sweden in the CBSS; Italy and Austria in the CEI; and Turkey in the BSEC. At the same time, however, the European Commission is a member of the BEAC and the CBSS and the European Union has played a significant role in providing political support, ideas and material resources to support the activities of these and other subregional groups. In the context of prospective enlargement, and alongside the Union's Association Agreements with the countries of Central and Eastern Europe, Partnership and Cooperation Agreements with the former Soviet states and the PHARE and TACIS aid programmes, subregional cooperation is a useful means of developing the EU's ties with its eastern partners.

The EU has supported subregional cooperation in a number of ways. At a high political level, EU Council summits have endorsed efforts at subregional cooperation – providing an important signal of Western support. The Commission's membership of the BEAC and the CBSS and its attendance at CEI meetings allows it to directly input policy ideas and expertise. Elements of the EU's aid programmes – PHARE, TACIS, the Interreg programme for support of regional development – have been directed to support subregional cooperation. Individual Member States of the Union (as well as non-members such as Norway and Turkey), however, provide the larger part of economic support for subregional cooperation. It can be argued that the Union's provision of material economic support to the BEAC and the CBSS has helped to turned these groups from rhetorical commitments into more substantive cooperative frameworks. More generally, it may be argued that the EU provides an important multilateral framework for the integration of the policies of individual states in support of subregional cooperation.

Reflecting the EU's growing interest in subregional cooperation, the European Council has since the mid-1990s directed the Commission to develop detailed proposals for increased support for specific subregional groups. So far, these include the CBSS, the CEI and the BSEC. The December 1995 Madrid European Council directed the Commission to develop a 'regional cooperation initiative' for the Baltic subregion to be presented to the CBSS Visby summit in May 1996. The Commission's 'Baltic Sea Region Initiative', completed in April 1996, identified three areas for further action (strengthening democracy and political stability; promoting economic development; and promoting transfrontier and sub-state cooperation), with specific, detailed proposals in each area.[25] The initiative helped to shape the subsequent Visby summit statement and CBSS 'Action Programmes' – which are generally seen as having given CBSS activities a more concrete and focused character. Since then, the Union/Commission has played an active role in supporting the CBSS and more general cooperation in the Baltic subregion: through aid from the PHARE, TACIS and Interreg programmes; chairing the CBSS Working Group on Economic Cooperation; establishing a Baltic Cross-border Cooperation Committee (to select projects for EU funding); and funding two staff members for the CBSS Commissioner on Democratic Institutions and Human Rights.[26]

The June 1996 Florence European Council asked the Commission to report on the Union's relations with the CEI, with the aim of defining possible ways of stepping up cooperation with that group. The Commission's report to the Council, completed in December 1996, supported the CEI as a framework for fostering good-neighbourly relations, encouraging political stability, strengthening human rights and democracy and boosting economic and trade cooperation. It also noted a number of areas for possible EU-CEI cooperation or EU support of CEI activities: strengthening democracy and stability, boosting economic development and free trade, the development of trans-European transport networks, protection of the environment, fostering closer economic links between businesses, guaranteeing individual and collective rights, cooperation on justice and home affairs and extending cross-border cooperation. Unlike the Baltic initiative, the report did not propose any specific priority areas for EU-CEI action, anything akin to the CBSS's 'Action Programmes' or any new institutional role for the Commission or the Union in relations with the CEI. Indeed, it stated that 'it is up to the countries participating in the CEI to take the lead by developing concrete forms of cooperation, which could benefit from complementary support by the European Union'.[27] While the Union has continued to support CEI activities, it does not appear that the Commission report resulted in a significant upgrading of EU-CEI relations or of EU support for CEI activities. The Commission is invited to attend relevant CEI meetings, but it is not a member of and has no permanent institutional relations with the CEI. Thus, the Commission/Union has no direct means of inputing ideas or proposals into the CEI. A possible next step would be for the Union/Commission to propose an initiative/action plan along the lines of the Baltic initiative and the CBSS's 'Action Programmes', with specific priority areas and institutional mechanisms for action and follow-up. Commission membership of the CEI could also be considered as a means of upgrading the relationship.

The European Council also requested the Commission to prepare a communication on EU relations with the BSEC, which was due to be published in the second half of 1997 or 1998. Since the Council requested a communication (rather than an initiative along the lines of the Baltic initiative), the Commission was somewhat limited in what it might propose. Nevertheless, the communication had the potential to provide a further endorsement of the BSEC and identify possible priorities for cooperation with and support from the EU. To the extent that the Commission communication provided a focus for practical EU support for BSEC activities it might give an important boost to the group. Commission/Union financial support, however, was likely to be limited to existing programmes. In the longer run, a Union/Commission proposed Black Sea initiative or action programme and Commission membership of the BSEC might again be further means of supporting the BSEC.

Although the Commission is a member of the BEAC, the Union/Commission has played a less substantial role in that group than in the CBSS, nor has the Council asked for a Commission communication or initiative on the BEAC. Norway has been the driving force behind the BEAC and the primary relationship within the group is the Norwegian-Russian one. Since Norway chose not to join the Union, the opportunities for EU involvement in the BEAC have been limited. Through the TACIS and Interreg programmes the EU has played a role in supporting BEAC activities, particularly transfrontier cooperation.[28] Since substantial cooperative activities/programmes have already been established within the BEAC, however, and Norway, Sweden and Finland have been able to commit substantial funds to these activities, there appears to be less need or demand for EU support for the BEAC than in the CEI and BSEC cases. Nevertheless, an EU initiative/action programme for the Barents subregion might be a longer term possibility even without Norwegian membership of the Union, particularly if Finland and Sweden give priority to this area and/or the Union perceives it as a useful channel for consolidating relations with Russia.

The EU's relationship with the Visegrad group and CEFTA has been very different from its relationships with the larger subregional groups. The Visegrad group and CEFTA have been defined by their character as relatively exclusive Central and Eastern European groups, with their members amongst the primary candidates for membership of the EU and NATO. For the Union, this has raised the sensitive question of how far it should develop special relationships with defined sub-groups of Central and Eastern European states and the relationship between subregional cooperation and the EU's own enlargement. The signing of Association Agreements with Poland, Czechoslovakia and Hungary in 1991 helped to define the Visegrad group, giving the three countries closer ties with the EU than their neighbours and special access to the EU. By December 1992, the European Council was specifically calling for the development of closer ties with the Visegrad countries.[29] The longer term direction of EU policy, however, has been to develop 'bilateral' relations with individual Central and Eastern European states, while judging all Central and Eastern European states by the same criteria in terms of access to Association Agreements, PHARE aid and EU membership. Thus, no formal EU-Visegrad/CEFTA relationship ever developed and once other Central and Eastern European states concluded Association Agreements with the Union the special status of the Visegrad states ended. Further, although Central and Eastern European states may be invited to join the Union in groups, the EU also made clear that membership decisions will be made on the basis of the individual readiness and merits of each state (rather than their involvement in any subregional group). This became absolutely clear in July 1997, when the Commission's 'opinions' on the readiness of Central and Eastern European states for membership of the Union suggested that accession negotiations be opened in the first place only with

Poland, the Czech Republic, Hungary, Slovenia and Estonia (as well as Cyprus)[30] – excluding Slovakia despite its membership of the Visegrad group and CEFTA, Romania despite its membership of CEFTA and Lithuania and Latvia despite their tri-Baltic cooperation with Estonia.

The Union's development of 'bilateral' relations with each Central and Eastern European states and assessment of their readiness for membership on a case-by-case basis, while sensible (and probably inevitable), created certain disincentives for subregional cooperation in Central and Eastern Europe. It encouraged the Central and Eastern European states to compete with one another in their relations with the Union and down-played the Union's support for subregional cooperation. Central and Eastern European states were also reluctant to engage 'too closely' in subregional cooperation in case this should condemn them to wait for their 'slower' neighbours before they might join the EU and/or be seen as an alternative to EU membership – despite signals from the West that this would not be the case. Thus, if the EU wishes to further support subregional cooperation in Central and Eastern Europe, it will need to emphasize its support for such cooperation and show that there is no contradiction between such cooperation and rapid integration with the Union. In particular, as enlargement moves ahead, it will be important for the Union to encourage the maintenance and deepening of cooperative ties between those states which join the Union first, those which join later and those which are unlikely to join at all.

The accession of some but not all CEFTA members to the Union may have particular implications for that subregional group. Since the EU has common external trade arrangements, new members have to join these arrangements and leave any other separate trade agreements. As Austria, Sweden and Finland had to leave EFTA when they joined the Union, so Central and Eastern European states will have to leave CEFTA when they join the Union. To the extent that the EU's external trade policies are more restrictive than those between the CEFTA countries, this could lead to the introduction of new trade barriers (or at least the slowing of trade liberalization) between those CEFTA members which join the Union and those which do not. Given that CEFTA is modelled on the Central and Eastern European states Association Agreements with the EU and both EU-CEFTA and intra-CEFTA trade relations are moving in the direction of liberalization, however, this problem should not be insuperable. The political effects of some CEFTA members joining the EU and therefore leaving CEFTA could also be negative, undermining the group and creating a further 'dividing line' between those states which have joined the Union and those which have not. As enlargement proceeds, attention therefore needs to be given to enhancing economic and political cooperation between those CEFTA states which join the Union and those which do not. In economic terms, something akin to the European Economic Area (which brought those EFTA states which had not joined the EU – Norway, Iceland and Lichtenstein – into Union free trade arrangements) might be possible for those CEFTA states which do not initially joining the Union. Politically, one way of sustaining CEFTA cooperation would be for those states which join the Union to remain 'honorary' CEFTA members (for example, by participating in higher level meetings). In this context, CEFTA could be a useful framework for discussing the on-going process of EU enlargement and the first Central and Eastern European states to join the Union might also act as advocates of their neighbours within the Union. Assuming that all CEFTA states join the EU in the medium term, however, it may only be natural that CEFTA disappears.

Aside from its relations with the existing subregional groups, the EU has also taken three major initiatives of its own to promote subregional cooperation on its periphery: the Stability Pact (– which, as noted earlier, has now been placed under OSCE auspices), the Royaumont process for stability and good neighbourly relations in South-Eastern Europe and the Euro-Mediterranean Barcelona process designed to promote cooperation between the EU and its Mediterranean neighbours (– these latter two are examined in more detail in the next chapter). While the Stability Pact produced some positive results (in particular, encouraging the signing of the 1995 Slovak-Hungarian Treaty), its overall impact was limited, producing few substantive new agreements between Central and Eastern European states. Thus, even with the strong support of the Union, the utility of such 'grand conference' approaches to preventive diplomacy – seeking to resolve many complex disputes in a short space of time – is limited. Further, as was noted above, since the Union disengaged from the Stability Pact the process has effectively ceased. In the cases of the Royaumont and Barcelona initiatives, while both have been welcomed by states in the subregions concerned and initial meetings have made some progress, they remain to be filled with more substantive cooperation. Overall, this suggests three lessons for the Union – with relevance not only for EU initiated processes, but also for EU support of existing subregional groups. First, subregional cooperation should be seen as an on-going process which promotes stability in the long term, rather than a means for resolving serious, high-level disputes in the short term. Second, initiatives required sustained, long-term political support from the Union. Third, in order to develop, subregional cooperation requires practical cooperative projects (often of an economic nature) which can become a focus for activities, give substance to political commitments to cooperate and promote mutual confidence and trust in the longer term.

NATO

NATO's relationship with subregional cooperation has been more tangential than those of the OSCE and the EU and prone to certain tensions. NATO members, ranging from Norway to Turkey, belong to and have often been driving forces behind the BEAC, the CBSS, the CEI and the BSEC. Unlike the EU, however, NATO has not developed formal relationships with or sought to directly support any of the subregional groups in the Barents-Black Sea belt. NATO has historically been averse to subregional security arrangements, fearing that these would create different 'statuses' among its members and undermine the Alliance's unity and the credibility of its core mutual defence guarantee. There have been elements of subregionalism within NATO's military command structure and the Alliance's military arrangements were significantly affected by acceptance of subregionally-based 'zonal' provisions in the Conventional Armed Forces in Europe (CFE) Treaty. Neither of these sets of dividing lines, however, coincides at all closely with the subregional groups in the Barents-Black Sea belt. Despite certain new elements of subregionalism in NATO's post-Cold War eastern policies and internal reforms, further, there remains opposition to any subregionalization which might undermine Alliance unity or the credibility of the NATO defence guarantee. At the same time, the largely non- or 'soft' security focus of the groups in the Barents-Black Sea belt has meant that there has been little opportunity or interest in cooperation with the political-militarily oriented NATO.

NATO's post-Cold War outreach policies to the countries of Central and Eastern Europe and the former Soviet Union, however, have gradually developed a significant subregional dimension. Initially, NATO was wary of 'differentiating' between its eastern partners, fearing that this would risk excluding or alienating those states with less close relations with the Alliance (above all, the Soviet Union and then Russia). The North Atlantic Cooperation Council (NACC) – established at NATO's December 1991 Rome summit – was thus open to all former Soviet bloc states on an equal basis and most NACC meetings included all members, with decisions made on a consensus basis. NATO's then Secretary-General Manfred

Woerner, however, noted that the NACC did 'not exclude the possibility of separate consultations with one or two or three (NACC members). We remain very flexible. It is not necessary in every instance for everybody to be present.'[31] Under the NACC's March 1992 work plan 'cooperative activities' might involve 'only some' NACC members and in April 1992 NACC defence ministers agreed that 'small teams of civilian or military defence experts ...could be sent, on request, to countries desiring advice'.[32] Within this context, NATO began to develop particularly close cooperation with the Visegrad states, often on the basis of NATO-Visegrad discussions and meetings. Nevertheless, the pan-European structure of the NACC limited the possibilities for subregional cooperation.

The limitations of the NACC led NATO to establish the Partnership for Peace at its January 1994 Brussels summit. Unlike the NACC, PfP is based on 'bilateral' relationships between NATO and individual eastern partners. Individual partners determine the extent of their cooperation with NATO, allowing a substantial degree of 'self-differentiation': those states most interested and able to cooperate with NATO have subsequently developed close relations with the Alliance, while others have not. Though much of the focus of PfP has been on individual states' partnerships with NATO, a significant subregional dimension has also developed. First, multilateral peacekeeping and crisis management exercises have become an important feature of PfP – and many of these have taken place on a subregional basis (bringing together, for example, states in Central Europe, in South-Eastern Europe and in the Baltic Sea). One of the implicit purposes of these exercises is to act as subregional confidence-building measures – using the incentive of cooperation with NATO to encourage states to cooperate with one another. Second, various PfP activities helping states to reform/ develop their armed forces have also taken place on a subregional basis – for example, encouraging the Visegrad states to cooperate with one another in air defence management or supporting the establishment of the tri-Baltic BALTBAT peacekeeping battalion. Despite these dimensions, however, the 'bilateral' character of PfP also to some extent acted as a disincentive for subregional cooperation:

> Because each partner sees its relationship as being directly with NATO, though not with other partners, PfP does not offer incentives for the emergence of mechanisms for regional cooperation. On the contrary, the efforts of some partners to qualify for future NATO membership through active participation in PfP has led to some kind of 'competition' within PfP ...a tendency of countries to make their case for joining

NATO by emphasizing their potential contribution to strategic, rather than regional stability.[33]

As with the EU, certain tensions emerged between NATO enlargement and subregional cooperation. By 1993-94, the intensifying cooperation between NATO and the Visegrad states raised the question of how far enlargement would take place on the basis of bringing pre-defined subregional groups of states into the Alliance. NATO's 1995 study on enlargement, however, rejected a group-based approach: 'enlargement will be decided on a case-by-case basis and some nations may attain membership before others. New members should not be admitted or excluded on the basis of belonging to some group or category. ...the timing of future accessions could be sequential or in one or more simultaneous sets'.[34] This was confirmed in July 1997 when NATO invited Poland, the Czech Republic and Hungary, but not the fourth Visegrad state Slovakia, to join the Alliance. As with EU enlargement, such an approach was sensible and probably inevitable. However, in the absence of any balancing statement by NATO – at least in the same context – about the desirability of sustaining and developing subregional cooperation, there was some risk of encouraging leading applicants to press their case in an excessively selfish, competitive spirit. As with the 'bilateral' approach of PfP, the enlargement of NATO on a case-by-case basis gave aspiring Alliance members and invitees no particular incentive – and perhaps some disincentive – to strengthen subregional cooperation with their neighbours.

By 1996-97, there was growing recognition within NATO both that the nature of PfP and the enlargement process to date had perhaps inadvertently discouraged subregional cooperation and that subregional cooperation could play a valuable role in reassuring and enhancing cooperation with those states excluded from the first or subsequent waves of enlargement. Thus, as NATO sought to strengthen its overall cooperation policies towards its eastern partners, efforts were made to enhance the subregional dimension of these policies. The Euro-Atlantic Partnership Council – the EAPC, the successor to the NACC, established in May 1997 – includes a significant subregional dimension. The EAPC Basic Document states that, while the EAPC will be an 'overarching framework', an 'expanded political dimension of consultation and cooperation which the Council will offer will allow partners, if they wish, to develop a direct political relationship either individually or in smaller groups with the Alliance.' The EAPC may also meet 'in a limited format between the Alliance and open-ended groups of Partners to focus on functional matters or, on an ad hoc basis on appropriate regional matters'. 'Regional matters' may also be the subject of specific EAPC consultations.[35] In strengthening PfP, NATO also agreed to 'increase scope for regional cooperation activities in the context of the Partnership including both consultations on regional security matters and practical cooperation'.[36]

At their Madrid summit in July 1997, NATO Heads of State and Government acknowledged the 'need to build greater stability, security and regional cooperation' in South-Eastern Europe, the 'progress achieved towards greater stability and cooperation by the states in the Baltic region which are also aspiring members' of the Alliance, and the need for the EAPC to 'increase the scope for consultation and cooperation on regional matters and activities.'[37] Of two specific topics discussed at the first meeting of EAPC Heads of State and Government the next day, one was 'how practical regional cooperation could contribute both to strengthening stability and security in the respective region concerned and in the Euro-Atlantic area as a whole. A number of contributions highlighted the need to complement the work of the OSCE and other relevant institutions in these fields.'[38]

The internal reform of NATO's own military structure has also developed in an increasingly subregional direction – a trend likely to increase as a result of the Alliance's widening mission, enlargement and expanded outreach activities. At their January 1994 Brussels summit, NATO leaders endorsed the concept of Combined Joint Task Forces (CJTFs): flexible military formations for peacekeeping and other missions, which might not involve all NATO members and might involve non-NATO partners.[39] NATO subsequently agreed 'to take further measures to increase (PfP) Partners' involvement in our efforts to promote security through regional cooperation, including through facilitating participation in CJTF at an early stage.'[40] Parallel reforms of NATO's command structure were also likely to result in fewer commands, but commands of a more subregional character and with greater responsibility for subregionally oriented planning, exercises and partnership activities. Additionally, agreement was reached on the establishment of PfP Staff Elements at various NATO headquarters'[41] – a step likely to widen the opportunities for subregional military cooperation with PfP Partners, including at important command and control levels. Thus, there was a potentially important link between the subregionalization of NATO's internal structures and the subregional dimension of its outreach policies. Indeed, some analysts have argued that these two processes should be further developed to create 'strategic homes' for Central and Eastern European countries (especially those not joining

NATO at an early stage) based on especially close cooperation with neighbouring NATO members and commands (for example, in the Baltic subregion and in South-Eastern Europe).[42]

By late summer 1997, exactly how far these subregionalizing dynamics within NATO and its relations with its PfP activities partners would evolve was unclear. They appeared likely, however, to pose a number of dilemmas. One issue was how far PfP activities include or exclude all states in a given subregion. In the Baltic, for example, close PfP defence cooperation between NATO and the three Baltic states (but excluding Russia) might maximize reassurance and support for the Baltic states, but risk alienating Russia. Baltic PfP cooperation which included Russia might help to build cooperation with Russia, but would be less reassuring to the Baltic states. Similar dilemmas might be faced with regard to Russian involvement in PfP activities in the Black Sea area or which states should be involved in PfP activities in South-Eastern Europe. The issue need not be 'black and white', since PfP and the EAPC appear flexible enough to combine both smaller group activities (for example, practical support for building/reforming armed forces) and wider confidence-building measures (for example, peacekeeping exercises). Nevertheless, the question seemed likely to pose an on-going dilemma for NATO and its Partners.

NATO also faced the question of how far it should formalize/ institutionalize the subregional dimension of its outreach policies. Some observers, for example, suggested the formation of a 'Balkan Association for Partnership for Peace', to give a higher political profile and commitment to NATO's support for subregional cooperation in South-Eastern Europe.[43] While such a step might encourage cooperation in any given subregion, it would undermine the flexibility and self-differentiation which seem to have been major parts of PfP's success to date. Certainly, such a step would seriously exacerbate the inclusion/ exclusion dilemma mentioned above and weaken the prospects for a constructive 'variable geometry' of overlapping cooperation. Central and Eastern European states might also fear – with some justification – having Western definitions of their subregion imposed on them and their prospects for membership of NATO (and perhaps also by implication the EU) undermined by being placed in a 'backward' subregion.

NATO's growing role in this area also raised the issue of whether there should be any more formal link between the Alliance's subregional dimension and the subregional groups in the Barents-Black Sea belt. The two differing forms of cooperation – the largely non/'soft' security cooperation of the groups in the Barents-Black Sea belt and the political-military cooperation of NATO's PfP/EAPC – were already relatively successful in their own right and neither seemed to 'need' the support of the other. Additionally, the Barents-Black Sea groups owed a significant part of their success to their ability to 'turn a blind eye' to contentious security issues. Developing a more formal relationship with NATO might risk undermining their successful cooperation in other areas. For Russia, in particular, an important part of the value of the BEAC, the CBSS and the BSEC was that these groups – in which it was a major partner – were not dominated by the West. Efforts to develop a formal NATO relationship with these groups might well undermine Russia's support for them and exacerbate Russian fears of encirclement by NATO. Thus, while NATO might support subregional cooperation through PfP and the EAPC, there seemed to be a strong case for the Alliance to maintain some political distance between its own subregional dimension and the existing subregional groups in the Barents-Black Sea belt and to avoid encroaching on the 'soft' security areas in which these groups were pre-eminent.

THE WESTERN EUROPEAN UNION

Although the Western European Union (WEU) is the 'defence arm' of the EU and the 'European pillar' of NATO, it has not developed an institutionalized relationship with the subregional groups in Barents-Black Sea belt, nor has it sought to develop practical cooperation with them. Like NATO, WEU's primarily political-military character has limited its potential for cooperation with the more 'soft' security oriented subregional groups. Similarly, there has – again with the partial exception of the Visegrad group – been no demand from subregional groups for closer ties with or direct support from the WEU.

WEU's eastern outreach has also been less subregionally oriented than that of either the EU or NATO. The WEU 'family' now includes its ten full Members, plus three Associate Members (Iceland, Norway and Turkey – which are members of NATO but not the EU), five Observers (Austria, Denmark, Finland, Ireland and Sweden – EU but not NATO members, except in the case of Denmark which is a NATO member) and ten Central and Eastern European Associate Partners (- the countries with Association Agreements with the EU). As the 'defence arm' of the EU, the WEU has sought to develop a special cooperative relationship with those Central and Eastern European states likely to join the EU – hence their WEU Associate Partner status. Such cooperation has gradually been expanded to include a range of meetings and activities. Associate Partners may now take part in WEU Council meetings, develop liaison arrangements with the WEU military planning cell, associate themselves with WEU decisions, participate in crisis management operations (including relevant exercises and planning) and, if they join such operations, be involved in WEU command structures and subsequent WEU Council decision-making processes.[44] Thus, in contrast to NATO, the WEU has clearly differentiated between those states likely to join the EU and those not – creating a larger WEU 'family' which is still significantly smaller than the pan-European PfP, EAPC or OSCE. Lacking the more operational aspects of PfP, however, most WEU outreach activities have taken place as discussions amongst the whole WEU 'family', rather than more subregionally oriented sub-groups.

The WEU has shown some more direct interest in subregional cooperation. The 'Common Concept' on European security, agreed by the members of the WEU 'family' in November 1995, suggested that European security might be enhanced by 'a greater emphasis on regional cooperation, including pursuing the concept of regional round tables, in particular in fields such as CSBMs, environmental protection and economy. ...the structures of regional and sub-regional cooperation will also continue to form an important element in strengthening security and stability in Europe.'[45] In April 1996, the WEU Council held a 'brainstorming' session on subregional cooperation, discussing the pre-requisites for such cooperation, contacts with subregional groups and their contribution to European security. By 1997, the WEU 'family' was also working a common 'reflection' on European security in the twenty-first century which seemed likely to note the contribution of subregional cooperation to European security, the potential for larger organizations to support subregional cooperation, and the possibility of greater WEU interest in and information exchange with subregional groups. There was, however, little interest – either within the WEU or from subregional groups – in developing much closer relations.[46]

The WEU's subregional dimension was further limited by its secondary role in the process of enlarging Western institutions. Since WEU is both the 'defence arm' of the EU and the 'European pillar' of NATO and all WEU members are also members of both the EU and NATO, it was clear that Central and Eastern European states would only join WEU once they had already joined both NATO and the EU.[47] As a consequence, the dynamics of enlargement were driven by NATO and the EU and the WEU's role in managing the tensions between enlargement and subregional cooperation was inevitably likely to be marginal.

Militarily, it was conceivable that the WEU might develop a greater subregional dimension – although even here the possibilities seem limited. In 1992, the WEU agreed that it might undertake a range of military operation known as 'Petersberg tasks' (humanitarian and rescue tasks, peacekeeping and the use of combat forces in crisis management, including peacemaking).[48] In this context, the WEU might engage in planning, exercises or real operations on a subregional basis (for example, amongst the Baltic members of the WEU 'family'). In enforcing the UN Security Council embargo against the rump Yugoslavia, for example, the WEU had already undertaken police and customs cooperation with Bulgaria, Hungary and Romania on the Danube river. Closer links between the WEU and existing subregional groups might also be possible – for example, in facilitating peacekeeping exercises under the auspices of, say, the CBSS or the CEI. A WEU role in this area might have the advantage of being more acceptable to those states (particularly Russia) wary of NATO and US domination. Equally, those states seeking close ties with NATO and the US (for example, the Baltic states) might be wary of military cooperation which specifically excluded the US – especially if it included Russia. The growing subregional focus of PfP and the EAPC also suggested that the opportunities for the WEU in this area might remain limited.

In the longer term, the possible full absorption of the WEU into the EU could also have significant implications for the EU/WEU's relations with subregional groups. The assumption of direct defence responsibilities by the EU would inter alia raise the question of whether its existing institutional relationships with subregional groups such as the BEAC, the CBSS and the CEI should also take on a defence dimension (for example, defence training/modernization assistance to countries in the subregion or preparation for joint EU-subregional group military operations). While this might seem to be a 'logical' consequence of an EU/WEU merger, bringing military/defence issues directly into subregional groups which had not so far dealt with such issues might risk undermining successful cooperation in non/'soft' security areas.

CONCLUSION

This chapter has examined role of subregional cooperation in the emerging, multi-institutional security architecture of post-Cold War Europe. It suggests that subregional cooperation has a significant place in this architecture, and that there is substantial potential for cooperation and burdensharing between the existing subregional groups in the

Barents-Black Sea belt and the larger European security organizations. The active engagement of the larger European organizations (particularly the EU and the OSCE) with the subregional groups in the Barents-Black Sea belt indicates that the larger organizations have already recognized the importance and potential of subregional cooperation and are seeking to promote such cooperation. There are, however, a number of ways in which they might perhaps do more to promote subregional cooperation. At the high political level, they could do more to emphasize their support for subregional cooperation through summit statements, declarations and so on. The OSCE has the potential to act as a framework for discussion and information exchange on subregional cooperation, thereby helping to encourage the transfer of 'best practice' between groups, the possible development of new subregional cooperation processes and cooperation with the larger organizations. The EU already provides substantial support for subregional cooperation, but could explore how it might provide further political, economic and technical support to the various subregional cooperation efforts.

There is also potential for the development of cooperative divisions of labour between subregional groups and the OSCE, the EU and the Council of Europe in a wide range of non or 'soft' security areas (conflict prevention, post-conflict peace-building, democratization, promoting respect for human and minority rights, environmental protection, economic development, transport and infrastructure). With the larger organizations facing an ever-growing range of tasks, subregional groups have the potential to share the burden of promoting European security. In the military security area, the picture is somewhat different. The subregional groups in the Barents-Black Sea belt have largely avoided engagement with military security issues. In contrast, NATO (through PfP, the EAPC and its own internal reforms), and to a lesser extent the WEU, are developing growing subregional dimensions. While connections between these two distinct levels – the existing subregional groups and the subregional dimensions of NATO and the WEU – might gradually develop, there also appear to be advantages in maintaining a certain political distance between them.

The relationship between the enlargement of the EU and NATO and subregional cooperation raises some problems. While subregional cooperation has the potential to 'cushion' tensions arising from NATO/EU enlargement, the 'bilateral' character of NATO and the EU's outreach policies and their assessment of membership candidates on a case-by-case basis have acted as disincentives for subregional cooperation. The enlargement process does also risk creating some new divisions within subregional groups such as CEFTA. In the context of enlargement, therefore, NATO and the EU could do more to emphasize their support for and encourage subregional cooperation.

The subregional groups in the Barents-Black Sea belt and the wider subregionalizing dynamic they represent are one of the newest features of Europe's post-Cold War security architecture. There is substantial potential for constructive engagement and cooperation between these subregional groups and the larger European organizations. The challenge for the future is to explore and make best use of that potential.

11 Emerging Subregional Cooperation Processes: South-Eastern Europe, The Newly Independent States and the Mediterranean[1]

Ian Bremmer, Sophia Clement, Andrew Cottey and Thanos Dokos

One of the central theses of this book is that, despite and in part because of their low profile, the existing subregional groups in the Barents-Black Sea belt are success stories. In various ways they have contributed to the development of cooperative relations and the building of shared interests and a sense of common security in their respective subregions, but also in Europe more widely. The cooperative character of these groups and their avoidance of overt, potentially divisive security issues also enables them to play an important if low key role in mitigating and cushioning the inevitable dividing lines resulting from the enlargement of the North Atlantic Treaty Organization (NATO) and the European Union (EU). The relative success of these groups clearly raises the issues of whether similar subregional groups or processes could or should emerge elsewhere in Europe, and what lessons there may be for new subregional groups and processes in Europe (and beyond) from the experience of the groups in the Barents-Black Sea belt.

In the European context, the prospects for subregional cooperation over the next decade or so may be particularly important in three areas: South-Eastern Europe, the Newly Independent States (NIS) of the former Soviet Union and the Mediterranean. During this period, these subregions – for all their differences – will pose certain parallel issues in their situation as Europe's new 'boundary zones', lying on the periphery of an enlarged European Union and NATO.[2] Apart from Slovenia, the former Yugoslav Republics can have no early hope of integration and are surrounded by other states disappointed at having to have to wait for the 'second wave'. By virtue of geography and history, the western NIS (Ukraine, Belarus and Moldova) and the Caucasian and Central Asian states will find themselves striving to balance between an enlarging West, a Russia still struggling to define its post-imperial role and other major subregional players (particularly Turkey, Iran and China). All three areas also face the problem of overcoming recent or on-going violent conflicts (in the former Yugoslavia; in Moldova, Georgia, Nagorno-Karabakh and Tajikistan; and in Algeria and Morocco). In these circumstances, it is an important explore how far subregional cooperation might help to mitigate the potentially negative consequences of these areas' peripheral status and overcome the legacies of their indigenous conflicts. In all three cases, various efforts have already been made to establish subregional frameworks. So far, however, they have made at best limited progress and remain stymied by uncertainties as to the definition of each subregion (and hence which states should be included and excluded), serious differences between states and a lack of resources to support practical cooperative projects. Against this background, this chapter examines the prospects for subregional cooperation in these areas.

Before examining the specific situations in South-Eastern Europe, the NIS and the Mediterranean, it is worth briefly recalling the generic lessons which might prima facie be carried over to them from the experience of the groups in the Barents-Black Sea belt. As was noted above, the broadest conclusion which this study suggests is that subregional groups have the potential to contribute to security in a wide variety of ways: developing cooperation amongst diverse groups of states and thereby helping to manage potential tensions resulting from the processes of NATO and EU enlargement; building confidence between states with historically inherited disputes and fears; and contributing to the management of a wide range of non-military security problems. The experience of the groups in the Barents-Black Sea belt also suggests some important lessons about what contributes to the emergence and success – or failure – of such groups. Strong high-level political support played a central role in the establishment of the groups in the Barents-Black Sea belt, with one or two states often playing a leading role in initiating cooperation. Once the existence and basic organizational structure of a group was established, however, the successful implementation of more practical projects became critical for the group's further development. The development of practical cooperative projects (often of an economic or environmental nature) and 'bottom-up' and transfrontier cooperation has played a central role in the success of the Barents Euro-Arctic Council (BEAC) and the Council of Baltic Sea States (CBSS) and seems likely to be a key factor in determining the future of the Central European Initiative (CEI) and the

Black Sea Economic Cooperation (BSEC). This in turn points to the importance of financial support for such practical cooperation – support which has come either from wealthier Western members of the groups or from international institutions such as the EU or the European Bank for Reconstruction and Development.

The development to date of the groups in the Barents-Black Sea belt also suggests some important lessons about the limitations of subregional cooperation and the problems it can run up against. While external support may be important, efforts to 'impose' subregional cooperation – whether from powers within the subregion or from those outside – are unlikely to succeed. The groups in the Barents-Black Sea belt emerged and have survived because they were initiated on a voluntary basis from within the subregions concerned, and fears of domination by a single power were limited. Notably, support for the BSEC has grown as fears of Turkish hegemony have declined. Conversely, the Visegrad group declined in part because it was perceived – rightly or wrongly – in certain quarters to have been imposed on the Central European states by the West. Thus, efforts by a single power to dominate a subregion are unlikely to result in meaningful cooperation. External (especially Western or major power) efforts to promote subregional cooperation are most likely to be successful if they work with – rather than against – the grain of relations within the subregion. The best reassurance that subregional cooperation will not involve domination by a single power, or the imposition of cooperation by external powers, may be provided by ensuring that such efforts remain based on voluntary and equal participation and on the basic principles of the United Nations (UN) and the Organization for Security and Cooperation in Europe (OSCE).

Another lesson from the groups in the Barents-Black Sea belt is that subregional groups are unlikely to be able to address 'hard' security issues (for example, collective defence, arms control, peacekeeping or peace enforcement). While the existing post-Cold War groups (and earlier ones like Nordic cooperation) have contributed to security in a variety of ways, none of them has made significant attempts to address 'hard' security topics. They appear to be too large and diverse to develop the unity of views and/or lack the power resources necessary for such roles. While the Barents-Black Sea groups' security roles may perhaps be gradually extended to include further elements of conflict management and military confidence-building, their potential in this area appears limited. The lesson for other subregions is that attempting to address 'hard' security head-on may not only fail to ease the problems in question but actually stand in the way of developing other forms of cooperation, which by indirect routes might have done more to stimulate confidence in the end.

The direct conflict resolution potential of multilateral subregional groups also appears to be limited. All the groups in the Barents-Black Sea belt are, to varying degrees, characterized by unresolved bilateral disputes between their members. Except in rather limited ways (for example, through discussions in the margins of meetings), the groups have not attempted directly to address or resolve such disputes. Indeed, one of the strengths of the Barents-Black Sea groups has been their ability to build confidence and cooperation between their members by 'turning a blind eye' to serious disputes between them – allowing states to cooperate in a multilateral framework when it might be more difficult to do so bilaterally. The experience of the Barents-Black Sea groups, therefore, suggests that direct mediation in contentious bilateral issues is something subregional groups are not well-suited to.

Continental European experience also highlights the fact that subregional groups may be very different in character and that this has major implications for their roles and limitations. The Visegrad group and the Central European Free Trade Agreement (CEFTA) are characterized by their small, relatively homogenous membership with shared strategic goals. Thus, one of their central roles has been to aid their members in achieving their policy aims vis-à-vis larger neighbours (Russia and the West). Dismantling the Soviet bloc and joining NATO and the EU, however, have been the strategic goals of the Visegrad/CEFTA states, taking precedent over subregional cooperation. Subregional cooperation has been viewed as means to an end and this has imposed limits on the extent of such cooperation. The exclusive character of such small, homogenous groups also raises another dilemma: that of undermining relations with those states excluded from the group. In contrast, the BEAC, the CBSS, the CEI and the BSEC are characterized by their large and diverse membership. The main strength of such groups is the fact that they are able to build cooperation across apparent strategic, political and cultural divides. Their strength, however, is also their weakness, since their very diversity limits the extent to and fields in which they are able to cooperate. In general, the dilemmas of these two different types of subregional groups suggest two conclusions. First, that there may be a difficult balance to be struck between homogeneity and the associated risk of alienating or provoking excluded states on the one hand, and diversity and the associated risk of ineffectiveness on the other. Second, in exploring the potential for subregional cooperation in other subregions it is important to be clear about the scope and goals of any actual or proposed group or process and to ensure that its membership and mandates are in line with the potential implications thereof.

Finally, this study also suggests that there are certain tensions in the relationship between subregional cooperation and the integrative processes of NATO and EU enlargement. The EU and NATO have sought to support subregional cooperation. At the same time, however, the 'bilateral' character of the own eastern outreach policies and the assessment of applicants for membership on a case-by-case basis has to some extent undermined incentives for subregional cooperation in Central and Eastern Europe. As in Central Europe, the West is likely to face this dilemma again in South-Eastern Europe and perhaps also in the western NIS, the Caucasus and Central Asia. States seeking closer ties with the EU and NATO are likely to be wary of being classified as members of a 'backward' subregion or condemned to wait for the 'slowest' of their neighbours. The 'bilateral'/'individual' character of the EU and NATO's outreach and enlargement policies may risk exacerbating such concerns, thereby unintentionally undermining subregional cooperation. If the EU and NATO are to maximize their support for subregional cooperation in Europe's new 'boundary zones', therefore, they will need to find ways of minimizing the tension between such cooperation and their own eastern policies.

SOUTH-EASTERN EUROPE

The outbreak of the war in former Yugoslavia, the revival of ethnic and political tensions and the depth of economic crisis have made South-Eastern Europe one of the continent's most volatile subregions. These problems slowed the transition process in a subregion already characterized by a lower economic base and weaker civil societies than in Central Europe, turning countries from the subregion into 'slow-track' ones in the NATO/EU enlargement process. For South-Eastern European countries, being the 'left-outs' of NATO and EU enlargement while needing membership the most, subregional frameworks (economic, political or military), have become an alternative if not an imperative. Defining the 'Balkans' or 'South-Eastern Europe' is inherently difficult, but broadly the subregion may be understood as including Albania, the former Yugoslavia states (except Slovenia), Bulgaria, Romania, Greece and Turkey.

A variety of subregional cooperative initiatives, addressing both political and economic issues, have been developed by the international community, as well as through local initiative, to enhance good-neighbourly relations, stability and security. The absence of any institutionalised subregional framework (a process still in the making) and the diverse degrees of integration of the South-Eastern European states with the main European organizations (full NATO/EU members, EU Associates, NATO applicants, states with little prospect of NATO/EU membership), mean that subregional cooperation is far less developed than in some other European subregions.

The challenges and incentives for South-Eastern European subregional cooperation are many. The countries of the subregion could be marginalized from both the process of Western European integration and the re-definition of the European security order. Subregional cooperation initiatives undertaken in neighbouring areas have helped the countries involved to strengthen ties and 'catch up' economically and politically with the 'West', widening the gap between themselves and their South-Eastern European neighbours. Contrary to the general view that the subregion's importance is declining, however, any instability in South-Eastern Europe will have consequences for the EU's integration process (economic costs, human costs, and in terms of undermining the Union's internal cohesion and efforts to establish a Common Foreign and Security Policy).

Despite its diversity and variable geometries, South-Eastern Europe should be considered an important subregion, and, as such as, a genuine part of Europe's new security arrangements, and not simply a disparate collection of states. The wide range of common problems, implying common solutions, make the subregion, though not entirely coherent, at least distinct.

In the past, there have been various attempts to construct cooperative frameworks in South-Eastern Europe. Usually occurring after periods of political instability (in the inter-war period and in the 1970s), such initiatives were designed to reduce tensions and facilitate rapprochement between the countries of the subregion. Seeking to be realistic in what they might achieve, they addressed only 'low politics' (such as economics, transport, energy and the environment), leaving aside political, security and military issues, and aiming, in the long run, to have positive spillover effects in these more controversial areas.

In the 1930s, the Balkan Conferences, although primarily focusing on economic issues, included more ambitious attempts to develop a Balkan Federation or Union, based on economic integration, but which would later include a political dimension on minority and border issues. These efforts failed due to national differences and the emergence of 'dividing lines'. For Bulgaria and Albania, the prior resolution of minority issues was a precondition for participation. The persistence of antagonistic blocs culminated in the mid-1930s in the Balkan Pact (a security agreement between Greece, Romania, Yugoslavia and Turkey in 1934 against Bulgaria and Albania) and the Little Entente (between Yugoslavia, Romania and Czechoslovakia in 1933, directed against Hungary).

Initiatives proposed during the Cold War addressed the security dimension more explicitly, aiming to overcome military alignments at a subregional level. A Romanian initiative in the late 1950s proposed the creation of a Balkan Nuclear Weapons-Free Zone which would develop into a regional disarmament treaty (or Peace Zone).[3] This proposal failed due to Cold War considerations. Greece and Turkey rejected any agreement which would remove the US military presence, perceiving the proposal as a Soviet attempt to enhance its influence. Yugoslavia's vulnerability between the two alliances left it undecided about the proposal.

In the 1970s and 1980s, during the period of détente, efforts were revived through Greek initiatives with the support of other South-Eastern European countries. In the same spirit as the initiatives of the 1930s, these efforts (organized at a political and expert level as a forum for subregional consultation and cooperation) focused on 'low politics', leaving aside the political dimension. Although basically driven by internal considerations[4], these initiatives were designed to move the subregion away from bloc divisions and external influence. They culminated in a series of conferences in Belgrade in February 1988, Tirana in January 1989 and October 1990. Although brought to an end by the dissolution of Yugoslavia, this initiative had already been seriously weakened by political tensions (primarily between Greece, Turkey and Yugoslavia).

In terms of lessons to be drawn from these past efforts, it appears that, in view of the deep animosities within South-Eastern Europe, subregional cooperation was able to develop because it initially addressed only 'low' security issues. Political tensions, however, were the recurrent cause of failure. Any initiative which avoids addressing political and security issues seems bound to fail in the long run. Thus, subregional cooperation should be understood as an incremental process. Subregional cooperation, further, will not succeed if it excludes or is directed against one or more countries within the subregion, or if it is tied to external 'interference' which disrupts the subregional balance of power and exacerbates existing divisions within the subregion.

With the end of the Cold War, integration with 'European' organizations such as the EU, the Western European Union (WEU) and NATO is the primary objective for most of the countries of South-Eastern

Europe. Fearing any subregional framework that might be considered a substitute for integration (a 'waiting room') and thereby impede or delay integration with the West, South-Eastern European countries have opposed anything more than bilateral and loose multilateral ties. Being the 'left-outs' of NATO and the EU's 'first wave' enlargement decisions and given the subregion's instability, however, the South-Eastern European countries are beginning to perceive subregional cooperation as a means of filling the political and security vacuum in the subregion, avoiding further marginalization and providing channels for closer cooperation and interaction with Western organizations. Subregional economic, political and security cooperation could also help them to meet the criteria for accession to NATO and the EU. Subregional cooperation should thus be understood as an integral part of the wider European integration process. The South-Eastern European countries see the development of close multilateral ties on a subregional basis as an inherent part of the broader European integration process, rather than as a distinct and separate subregional integration process.

From the Western European perspective, South-Eastern European subregional cooperation and its linkage to the broader European integration process were not envisaged a few years ago. The absence of a defined approach to the subregion stemmed from a lack of knowledge, as well as negative perceptions of the subregion and geographic/cultural prejudices – all exacerbated by the Yugoslav war, the Macedonian issue and the nationalist attitudes and policies prevalent in South-Eastern Europe. The economic, political and security consequences of instability in South-Eastern Europe for the West, however, made the formulation of a more coherent approach towards the subregion necessary. There is also now an explicit acknowledgement that subregional cooperation cannot constitute an alternative to accession to the EU or NATO.

The 'subregional approach' of the EU is mainly directed towards former Yugoslavia, particularly Bosnia-Herzegovina, Croatia and the 'rump' Federal Republic of Yugoslavia (FRY) – that is countries without Associate Agreements with the EU (neighbouring countries like Albania and the Former Yugoslav Republic of Macedonia being given at least the possibility of eventual Association Agreements). The EU's 'Royaumont Initiative', launched in December 1995, is essentially political, aiming to promote stability and good-neighbourliness in South-Eastern Europe. It follows the guidelines of a subregional approach recommended by the European Council and based on the Dayton peace agreement. It makes ties with the EU conditional on compliance with the Dayton agreement (particularly its civil dimension, such as respect for human rights and free movement of goods, people and services) and on cooperation with neighbouring countries. The Royaumont process is also related to the Stability Pact, the French EU initiative (now under OSCE auspices) designed to promote stability in Central and Eastern Europe by encouraging the conclusion of bilateral agreements on borders, minority rights and transfrontier cooperation. The Royaumont process will be brought under OSCE auspices once FRY's suspension from that organization is ended and thus included in the Stability Pact.

The American inspired Southeast European Cooperation Initiative (SECI, or 'Schifter Initiative'), established in December 1996, primarily addresses the economic dimension, aiming to promote and better coordinate private sector aid and investment in the subregion, thus leaving aside the political dimension. The main areas of focus within SECI are border crossings, infrastructure, support for investment, energy and environmental protection. Interestingly, SECI includes a wider range of countries than a narrow interpretation of South-Eastern Europe/the Balkans might imply, specifically Hungary, Slovenia and Croatia (– although these countries were initially reluctant to join the initiative). While the US sought SECI's eventual fusion with the Royaumont Initiative, the EU rejected this option because of uncertainties about financing, fears of interference in the EU's affairs and a preference for closer coordination with the OSCE.

The Conference of the Ministers of Foreign Affairs of the Countries of South-Eastern Europe, re-established by the Sofia Declaration of July 1996, originates from within the subregion itself and implicitly draws on the Balkan Conferences of the 1930s. Designed to promote stability, security and cooperation in the subregion, these meetings focus on 'low' security issues such as political cooperation through promoting good neighbourly relations; democratization and human rights; economic cooperation, particularly trade liberalization and infrastructure projects; and cooperation in the fields of justice and preventing terrorism and drugs and arms trafficking. A minimal degree of institutionalization is planned, with ministerial meetings and the creation of a series of coordinating bodies dealing with the respective fields in the national capitals.[5]

Thus, there have been a multiplicity of initiatives to promote subregional cooperation in South-Eastern Europe, but lacking a coherent, overall approach. Although these separate initiatives are often claimed to be complementary, they risk duplicating one another. Although priority is given to economic issues, the means to be employed, the time-scale envisaged and the hoped-for political impact are vaguely defined at best. Certain approaches such as the Royaumont process also suffer from a lack of leverage, as the EU is not holding out the offer of membership to all former Yugoslav countries.

The range and the depth of subregional disputes (the strained relations between Greece and Turkey, the fragility of the Bosnian peace process and the still unresolved Albanian question) further limit the prospects for cooperation. Any economic approach is unlikely to overcome political obstacles without a concurrent political confidence-building process, and, especially as ethnic and territorial conflicts could easily escalate before economic measures have an impact, there is a need for political confidence-building measures parallel to economic ones.

Furthermore, economic measures alone are likely to have only a limited impact on the essentially structural problems of the subregion: gross domestic product amounts to only 25 per cent of the EU average, South-Eastern European lacks opportunities for economic growth compared with Central European, and structural problems have meant that financial assistance from the West has been limited. Piecemeal Western investment along bilateral lines would only fuel competition. Any crisis, as in Bulgaria and Albania in 1997, only makes the situation worse.

A combination of 'bottom-up' and 'top-down' approaches seems to be the most appropriate way to promote cooperation. A 'bottom-up' approach implies a clear definition of subregionalism and a clear response by Western European states to progressive cooperation between the South-Eastern European states. Such an approach could be based on a clear statement of intent to draw the South-Eastern European states into European integration processes rather than using subregionalism to isolate them. Associating South-Eastern European countries with the European integration process would make subregional cooperation a means of fulfilling the primary objective of European integration, rather than an alternative to integration. Furthermore, subregional cooperation could act as an essential element of conditionality. Cooperation at the subregional level could be considered a way of achieving the conditions for future EU membership, thereby acting as an incentive for reform. Building security in South-Eastern Europe also needs a broader approach that makes use of non-military organizations and stresses a combination of complementary means. Western European policy and responsibility is, therefore, essential. An inward-looking Europe favouring a 'security vacuum' in South-Eastern Europe is likely to lead to further instability in the subregion.

Preferential treatment and discrimination should also be avoided in

Western approaches towards the South-Eastern European countries. Any subregional process must include all South-Eastern European states on an equal footing, avoiding the exclusion of any state. Without rejecting the need for some 'freedom of manoeuvre', too much flexibility could have negative consequences for subregional cooperation. In South-Eastern Europe, an 'a la carte' approach of the BSEC type could harm subregional cooperation by exacerbating divisions instead of bridging them, as it would imply a degree of exclusivity and competition that would impede the poorest states from participating in all undertakings. As a more coherent subregion than the Black Sea, and with political issues high on the agenda compared with the CEI, South-Eastern Europe is not well-suited to differentiation as a means of promoting subregional stability and European integration or ensuring coherent policy implementation at the subregional level and a sense of common subregional identity.[6]

Inter-linkage and interaction between the various subregional cooperation initiatives is also important. First, there should be no 'splitting off' of some South-Eastern European states into the Central European sphere. The specific problems of South-Eastern Europe have to be addressed in common. This does not mean, however, that there should be no cross-participation in other subregional groups where there is complementarity and interdependence. The political and security vacuum in Central and Eastern Europe, however, will not be filled by large numbers of interlocking security arrangements unless these groups have some political and economic coherence. Without advocating strict, rigid subregional groups, singling out only some countries as 'Central European' would undermine the potential for tackling the problems South-Eastern Europe faces. Relations with the CEI and the BSEC should be explored, especially after NATO and EU enlargement. South-Eastern European cooperation can be established only on the basis of a 'whole Balkans', including the successor states of Yugoslavia and Turkey.[7] Second, subregional cooperation frameworks should not be used by external countries, especially major Western European states, for asserting their own position by enhancing their economic interests in the subregion or their own bargaining position within the EU.

Greater coordination of policies is thus needed. A joint economic plan would avoid subregional competition over resources and promote economic equality within South-Eastern Europe. The possibility of addressing economic and political issues jointly through ties with the EU, subregional tables within the OSCE or the South-Eastern European Conference should be considered.

Finally, a better division of labour and coordination between institutions is needed. The major economic and security problems in South-Eastern Europe require substantial outside involvement – an 'entry strategy' for the major Western organizations. The European Union could focus on economic issues and reconstruction plans. The OSCE could address 'soft' security issues such as borders, minorities, transfrontier cooperation and 'new' security risks, as well as softer arms control measures (such as transparency and advanced notification) and the extension of the Conventional Armed Forces in Europe (CFE) Treaty to the whole subregion. NATO could develop a 'PfP-plus' for South-Eastern Europe, dealing with military issues, inter-operability and civil-military relations. This implies a combination of more traditional confidence and security-building measures (such as partial disarmament and information exchange) and greater transparency in relation to political issues such as minorities and borders.

A 'bottom-up' approach is the second dimension of this two-fold strategy. In the long run, the problems of South-Eastern Europe can only be resolved by the countries involved themselves. The South-Eastern European countries must take the initiative to make use of existing international organizations (for example, by using international conflict resolution mechanisms) and to develop subregional interdependence through a network of economic and political links. In South-Eastern European, there can be no single means of organizing subregional cooperation and existing models must be adapted to local conditions.[8]

THE NEWLY INDEPENDENT STATES

To date, relatively little interest has been shown in exploring the relevance of subregional cooperation to the Newly Independent States of the former Soviet Union. The most significant subregional player in the NIS is the former hegemon, Russia. Since the Soviet collapse, Moscow's relations with its neighbours have been complicated. Russia's initial NIS strategy was to treat the non-Russian states as monolithic – the 'Near Abroad' over which Moscow held a monopoly interest. Russian policy was consistently conceived and applied throughout the NIS, as evidenced by the creation of the Commonwealth of Independent States (CIS), within which all the countries of the 'Near Abroad' were to develop strong economic, strategic, and, eventually, political ties to Russia. Russia's strategy ran into difficulty in practice, as policies that worked well for one state were profoundly inappropriate for others: countless policies failed, as the steps to political, economic and military integration favoured by some states were opposed by others. Underlying the problem was a polarity of views regarding the CIS's purpose. For Russia, the Commonwealth was the institutional framework that permitted continued hegemony over the former Soviet space. For Ukraine, it was a transition mechanism enabling breakaway Soviet republics to attain full independence. Armenia viewed the CIS as an opportunity to ensure its own national security, particularly vis-à-vis Azerbaijan in the war over Nagorno-Karabakh. Kyrgyzstan saw membership as a vehicle for keeping its troubled economy afloat. Over time, the CIS fell more and more clearly into two competing camps: one favouring closer integration (Armenia, Belarus, Kazakhstan, Kyrgyzstan) and one against (Azerbaijan, Georgia, Moldova, Ukraine, Uzbekistan). This process did create or re-create some sets of ties with real integrative significance, but they tended to link states in geographically scattered coalitions, and this lacy geometry was more and more plainly at odds with the Russian 'all or nothing' approach.

The widening gap between Russian goals and the reality of the CIS led the Russian Federation towards a more differentiated, bilateralist strategy. This dramatic, if long unavowed, change in Russian policy has in turn profoundly affected the environment for NIS subregionalism. Overall, Russian policy has been straightforward: actively strengthening relations with those states most favourably disposed towards Russia, while tolerating higher levels of autonomy from others, and building in added safeguards for Russian national security by 'leapfrog' alliances with non-CIS States on the far side of less amenable neighbours. The ultimate intention – tightly-knit and comprehensive Russia-led integration – remained the same, but the process and near-term expectations were quite different. Accordingly, Russia signed landmark political and economic agreements with Belarus – creating a titular political union and real strategic dyad of the two nations – but accepted more modest economic agreements with neighbouring Ukraine. Russian President Boris Yeltsin expected relations with Kazakhstan to proceed 'along the Belarus model', but voiced no such inclination vis-à-vis Uzbekistan.

When Russian policy has been interventionist, it has, again, been adjusted subregion-by-subregion rather than mechanically consistent. Most expected a hands-on Russian policy to be driven by issues of 'the greater Russian nation' – intervening in those subregions with the highest concentrations of Russian minorities. Moscow's grip could then be expected to tighten in a consistent pattern, focusing on Transdniestrian Moldova, southeast Ukraine and Crimea, northeast Estonia, and northern Kazakhstan. In reality, the Russian approach was more reactive and pragmatic, and has moved sharply in the direction of caution over time (especially following the Chechnya experience). Direct interference was witnessed when the opportunity arose to maintain influence in a subregion thought to be important – on strategic or economic as well as ethnic grounds – and when the risk of counter-involvement by outside powers was low. This effectively limited Russian options in most cases to the manipulation of power balances in the 'Southern Tier' (the Caucasus and Central Asia) by playing major protagonists against one another. This has essentially been the Russian role in Nagorno-Karabakh, Abkhazia and South Ossetia. Moscow's change of strategy strengthened Russian relationships with several key post-Soviet countries. More direct and specific calculations of national interest cut across the conventional subregional categories of the western NIS, the Caucasus and Central Asia to create unorthodox new 'axes' such as the Belarus-Kazakhstan-Kyrgyzstan connection.

The 'bottom-up' conditions for creating positive subregional mechanisms among the NIS are also dogged by a unique combination of difficulties. The NIS as a group are largely characterized by weak traditions of statehood and a lack of international experience. The harsh environment of their recent development has accentuated tendencies to autocracy and centralization on the one hand, secessionism and ill-controlled frontiers on the other, and sometimes a daunting combination of both. This is not a hospitable climate for cross-border cooperation. Inchoate notions of statehood also make it hard for governments to grasp the 'everybody wins' thinking underpinning the Barents-Black Sea subregional groups so that such initiatives as have been launched for (especially) 'Southern Tier' cooperation have too often been competing, duplicatory and designed to please outside patrons' – more than neighbours' – eyes. Inter-state relations have also been riven by conflict. Civil and external wars raging throughout the 'Southern Tier' have gravely set back the chances of 'normal' international relations. Between Chechnya and its subregional fallout, the struggle for independence in South Ossetia and Abkhazia, and the wars in Nagorno-Karabakh and Tajikistan, there has been little leisure or incentive to invest in subregionalism.

The case of Nagorno-Karabakh has clearly demonstrated how political conflict can poison a rational course of subregional cooperation. Efforts to develop an Azeri oil pipeline through Armenia, forging regional economic ties and, accordingly, interdependence, have foundered on the Armenian occupation of roughly one fifth of all Azeri territory. Russia's own attitude to distributing the economic spoils of the subregion has compounded the problem through its mercantilist nature and divide-and-rule tactics. In hopes of securing influence over energy exploitation and transport in the Caspian Basin, Russia has cut deals with Turkmenistan, Iran and Kazakhstan, designed inter alia to isolate Azerbaijan from its neighbours and to queer the pitch for Azeri exploitation of its offshore oil reserves without Russian participation.

The prospects for subregional cooperation in the NIS are also undermined by the absence of rich neighbours and the relatively weak role of European integrative bodies. The EU's normative pull does not extend much further east than Ukraine, nor does its significant spending in support of economic reform and interdependence. The powerful effect exerted by hopes of eventual EU membership on states' subregional behaviour in Central and Eastern Europe, thus, cannot be duplicated in the NIS context.

Russian policy, further, has effectively discouraged subregional cooperation. Russian attempts to assert a hegemonic role have lead other NIS countries to conclude that EU-style integration among equals is unattainable, while Russian-dominated integration is not in their interests, and the best option, therefore, is to keep all ties to a minimum. So long as countries' integrative choices are for or against Russia, insurmountable barriers between the NIS's differently-thinking neighbours will remain.

Despite the serious obstacles to subregional cooperation amongst the NIS, there are also some seeds of hope. Positive pre-conditions for subregionalism in the NIS, especially the 'Southern Tier', have sources that are special to the subregion: the higher salience of non-traditional security threats, the scope for and attraction of cooperation with non-NIS neighbours and the scale of involvement by outside capital with its 'globalizing' side-effects. The geostrategic shadow of Russia also creates a predisposition to diversify local ties even while it places obstacles in their way.

Non-traditional security issues (the environment, water management, drug smuggling, organized crime, migration and refugees) provide a fruitful area for NIS discourse because threats in these areas neither flow primarily from, nor can uniquely be resolved by, Moscow. Different as the needs and aims of states may be on specific resource or pipeline issues, they all have a prima facie interest in avoiding conflict in these spheres which would merely aggravate the challenges to their fragile statehood. Accordingly, there have been a number of voluntary moves to set up regimes for controlling organized crime, drug trafficking, international terrorism and illegal migration, as well as supporting economic development and environmental protection. For example, a series of Central Asian summits on water management and the Aral Sea crisis (leading to an agreement by which each state has pledged a percentage of its gross national product to an environmental fund) has advanced Central Asian state cooperation without raising the ire of Russia. So too has the recently-formed Central Asian Battalion, composed of forces from Kazakhstan, Kyrgyzstan and Uzbekistan and designed to enhance local peacekeeping capabilities.

Another area of growth has been opened up by the blurring of borders between the NIS and their subregional counterparts outside the former Soviet Union. The obverse of intra-CIS differentiation and the breakdown of the old Caucasus/Central Asia divide has been a growing diversification of NIS cooperative links with non-Soviet neighbours such as Poland, Hungary, Romania and Turkey in the west and Iran, India and China in the south and east. Examples include numerous economic agreements between Ukraine and the states of Central and Eastern Europe; the development of economic infrastructure and a flourishing trade between Azerbaijan, Kazakhstan, Uzbekistan and Turkey (and parallel arrangements between Armenia and Iran); and various steps to political and military cooperation between Uzbekistan and Afghanistan. Similarly, 'piecemeal integration' has developed through cross-border agreements between provinces of NIS countries and their neighbours – linking countries together through customs checkpoints, cultural and educational ties, and special economic zones.

Arguably, none of these relationships has been as critical for the survival of independent sovereignty in the non-Russian NIS as will be the role of foreign – primarily American, Japanese and Korean, but also European – capital. Multinational companies bring to the region a mentality that de-mystifies borders. By definition, their interest is in the 'Southern Tier' as a subregion of transit as well as resource origin. Particularly through the side-effects of their dealings in the financial and services sector, they are exposing NIS economic and civic life to globalizing influences and stimulating transnational thinking and cooperation.

A further influence too often overlooked is the involvement of several NIS states in existing subregional groups in the Barents-Black Sea belt. Belarus is a member of the CEI; Ukraine belongs both to the CEI and the BSEC, and is probing the possibility of CEFTA membership; Moldova, Georgia, Armenia and Azerbaijan are also members of the BSEC. By this token, all the Western NIS and Caucasian states have committed themselves to the cooperative policies of the relevant bodies and, in the case of the BSEC, have done so sitting alongside Russia as partners of equal status.

Any analysis of future policy options must start by recognizing the different environments for subregionalism in the western NIS and in the 'Southern Tier'. In the west, the conditions for benign, truly integrative subregional relations will hinge essentially on economic factors. The fundamental challenges to Ukrainian stability are not so much whether the Russians in Crimea will secede, or how to divide the rusting Black Sea fleet, but rather the problem of raising the morale of Donbas miners while managing inflation and increasing productivity. Crimea could become a threat of international proportions, but only if the Ukrainian economy deteriorates to the point where Russian activism offers profits exceeding the evident risks. Similarly, Belarus's hunger for political union with Russia has less to do with dubious nationhood than the risk of starvation in its imploding economy. The longer-term survival of Minsk as a European capital will also demand greater Western (including Central European) stimulus to Belarusian economic development – which need not conflict with Russian interests so long as the West respects Belarus's strategic allegiance and the transit routes through Belarus can be opened up for both sides' advantage. Only if the economic equations turn negative will new political scope and motive be opened up for Russian intervention.

That said, the fate of subregional relations in this area will also inescapably be a function of Russia's relationship with the 'wider West'. The debate over NATO's first enlargement has shown how hard it is for Russians to accept that even the nations of Central Europe can move closer to the West without turning hostile backs on Moscow. To accept any degree of 'both-and' solutions – both Russian influence and permanent EU and NATO influence, if not membership – for territories previously within the Soviet Union is a severe test for even the most modern-minded Russian patriot. If Russia-West relations were to worsen, the degree of tolerance so far extended by Moscow to Ukraine, Moldova and Belarus's subregional forays could be called in question. Conversely, if a modus vivendi can be sustained at the higher Euro-Atlantic strategic level, there should be scope for using the familiar and non-threatening devices of subregional and transfrontier cooperation to strengthen integrative and democratizing influences over all the western NIS, to Russia's ultimate advantage as well. The risk of Russian misapprehension can be minimized if this process is carried on transparently in fora where Russia already belongs. In this context, the CBSS needs to show more flexibility in finding a new status to accommodate Belarus's expressed interest in its work.

A further strengthening of subregionalism along Russia's western front could also reduce some of the psychological resistance to similar 'both-and' solutions for the 'Southern Tier'. Russian perception of how Turkish strategic motives are mediated or constrained by the BSEC could be one obvious bridging factor. However, the bottom-up dynamics for actors in the 'Southern Tier' will remain significantly different from those in the west. Recent ceasefires and the containment, rather than solution, of the Chechnya situation may have opened up some space for people to think about more positive relations, but the leap into real-time economic integration still hinges upon the resolution of political conflicts. To maintain its statehood, the Georgian leadership must tackle irredentism from breakaway republics, coup attempts and assassinations, and Russian interference. Armenia's development is predicated upon the resolution – or continued prosecution – of the war over Nagorno-Karabakh. Kazakhstan must accept direct political compromise with Russia on a host of basic security issues for any near-term hope of substantial oil export. In each of these cases, economic development – international investment, pipeline construction and the rebuilding of infrastructure – will not be free to follow its own non-zero-sum logic until fundamental political problems have been resolved.

Any advance here towards a 'Southern Tier'-wide cooperative security structure with appropriate subregional elements is bound to be painfully slow, but it is also going to have to accommodate a kind of variable geometry beyond anything known in western Eurasia. Russia's more-than-equal status cannot be ignored and the real balances to it will come from other large powers' economic involvement – plus, ideally, some strengthening of the OSCE's normative overview – rather than any structural solution native to the 'Southern Tier'. Russia's various ties with Belarus, Kazakhstan, Iran and India will be a part of the pattern for the foreseeable future, and pragmatism would suggest accepting them for whatever genuine (voluntary or quasi-voluntary) integrative elements they contain. What the West can try to add, while avoiding further polarization of NIS choices, are options and elements of subregionalism which supplement and diversify these relations rather than compete with them.

For example, the presence of Armenia and Azerbaijan in the BSEC could be more consciously exploited as an opportunity for these states to work in a multilateral setting on practical issues that unite them, compartmentalizing the Nagorno-Karabakh issue at least to the extent that other BSEC members (Greece-Turkey, Russia-Ukraine) have done with their respective quarrels. The potential of the BSEC 'corridors', and of other member states' assistance in 'proximity talks' mode, could be particularly fruitful. Elsewhere in the 'Southern Tier', the West's limited political and economic levers could bring multiplier effects if they were directed to strengthening emergent habits of bottom-up cooperation on the functional agenda – new threats and the environment – most appropriate to the subregion. Wherever possible, the issue of Russian participation in such initiatives should be discussed in terms of practical need, not strategic side-taking, and where Russia is involved the formalization and transparency of cooperative regimes should bring protection against misuse. Any schemes which engage Russian provincial authorities (or other non-state actors) in their own right will have special value for stabilizing the Russian side of the frontier as well as transfrontier relations; but they must be approached with full consciousness of their delicacy for Moscow (which increases as the areas concerned grow more remote, so that optimism about reproducing the smooth engagement of Murmansk and Arkhangelsk in the BEAC would be misplaced).

Another useful touchstone for policy on NIS cooperation would be: does it promote openness to global processes, and the chances of success in digesting them, or not? Many of the benign effects of transfrontier cooperation meet this criterion, but it would also imply paying greater attention to factors like English language training, introduction of new information technologies, the nature of financial/fiscal systems and (however difficult to actualize) the rule of law.

An interesting consequence of this results-oriented approach would be a reassessment of the interplay between NIS subregional links and CIS integration. In the first place, it is not a good idea for the West to stimulate inter-NIS groups based only on resistance to CIS integration. The de facto alliance in this regard of Georgia, Moldova, Ukraine and Uzbekistan may be a political fact but formalizing it would bring no benefit in terms of economic integration, functional cooperation, internal democratization or transfrontier ties. It would merely harden the lines between these states and their immediate neighbours, and strengthen the reservations which the more pro-CIS states are bound to have about joining any new, non-Russia-driven subregional processes. The same test would, by contrast, bring out the value of new alignments which might develop within the existing subregional frames and in pursuit of positive shared interests, such as Moldovan-Ukrainian-Romanian cooperation in the CEI or the BSEC or an emergent dialogue between all three Caucasian states.

On this philosophy and with many mutandis to be mutatis, subregional ties could come to convey some of the same value in overcoming intra-CIS divisions and strains as the Barents-Black Sea groups do already between NATO's members, non-members and critics in the West. In the NIS sphere, as in Central and Eastern Europe, subregional cooperation will never replace other mechanisms for states' direct defence protection nor do anything directly to resolve their political disputes. Similarly, subregional cooperation will never have the normative impact, let alone economic significance, of the 'vision' of EU-style integration. For a region in the early stages of transition, needing more modest, evolutionary and messy prescriptions, however, that is precisely the secret of subregionalism's appeal and potential.

THE MEDITERRANEAN

Within the post-Cold War international system, there is a slow but steady shift towards a North-South geostrategic axis. It is likely, although by no means inevitable, that the evolving North-South 'confrontation' will escalate, with negative consequences for both sides. A glance at the map shows that the Mediterranean – NATO's southern flank – is perhaps the most important faultline between those two 'worlds'.

Many analysts discern an 'arc of crisis' in the wider Mediterranean subregion, extending from the Balkans/South-Eastern Europe, to the Middle East and the Caucasus/Central Asia. The majority of regimes in these areas face or will soon face crises of political legitimacy. The rapid evolution of societies and the defeat or exhaustion of traditional ideologies have produced extremist socio-political and national movements. Socio-economic crises provide fertile ground for these extremist ideologies. As with other subregions, defining the boundaries of the Mediterranean is a contentious, political issue. Nevertheless, there appears to be general agreement that the Mediterranean is geographically defined as including all Mediterranean Sea littoral states, but excluding the other South-Eastern European states (Albania and the states of former Yugoslavia) – although it is difficult to examine the Mediterranean, from a security perspective, in complete isolation from the surrounding areas of the Caucasus/Central Asia, South-Eastern Europe and the Middle East, including the Persian Gulf.

The states on the southern shore of the Mediterranean face a long list of problems – many of which constitute threats to security in themselves or have consequences which could easily undermine stability in the subregion. These include: slow or negative economic growth; a demographic explosion in many countries; the spread of religious extremism; the absence of democracy and respect for human rights; scarcity of water resources; drug trafficking and transnational crime; and the pollution of the Mediterranean Sea (which threatens economies, especially tourism, and the quality of life of the subregion's people). One particular concern is Islamic radicalism: different versions of Islamic radicalism are supported and funded by Saudi Arabia and Iran; Islamic regimes already exist in Sudan and in Iran; and Algeria faces an Islamic insurgency, while there are similar problems in Egypt and other countries, including Libya. Many of these problems, further, may have synergistic effects, exacerbating their cumulative impact. In addition to these problems, there are also more 'traditional' threats. These include a large number of conflicts, particularly the Kurdish problem, the occupation of Cyprus, the Greek-Turkish dispute, and the persistent and enduring Arab-Israeli conflict. The continuing (relative) isolation of Iran and Iraq and their possible re-emergence as military threats compound security problems in the Mediterranean. The Mediterranean is also characterized by the proliferation of sophisticated conventional weapons and (potentially) of weapons of mass destruction.

The Mediterranean is also strongly affected by the changing dynamics of security and so-called 'new' threats. The traditional definition of security in military terms is inadequate in the Mediterranean. There is no direct military threat from the south towards the north. Economic, social, demographic and environmental problems, however, have a considerable impact on national security in the Mediterranean. Most security challenges and problems in the Mediterranean are of a non-military nature and therefore cannot be dealt with by military means. Security problems in the Mediterranean are also largely transnational: they are likely to affect the security of many states and their resolution will require the cooperation of many states. Understanding and addressing Mediterranean security, therefore, requires a broader concept of security encompassing not only the political-military aspects (so-called 'high politics'), but also 'low politics' (economic, social, demographic and environmental factors). In this context, the Mediterranean constitutes a 'security complex' characterized by a high degree of interdependence, making close cooperation a necessity for addressing various common problems. Within this security complex, there are two sub-systems: the eastern Mediterranean and the western Mediterranean.

As a consequence, the Mediterranean security system is a combination of power politics with interdependence. Bilateral relations are conducted along realist lines, but on a multilateral level it is becoming clear that interdependence is increasing and many problems cannot be solved unilaterally. Although many threats and problems are common for the entire Mediterranean, the eastern Mediterranean nations are principally concerned with the spillover of subregional conflicts and the western Mediterranean states are likely to be more concerned about domestic problems of an economic, social or political nature.

Although Mediterranean states are members of various regional or subregional groups – the EU, the WEU, NATO, the OSCE, the Arab Maghreb Union – there is no single group/organization encompassing all Mediterranean states. Since at least the 1970s, but especially since the 1980s, there have been various attempts to establish subregional cooperation in the Mediterranean, particularly between the northern and southern shores. A Euro-Arab Dialogue was initiated by the Arab League in 1974, after the Yom Kippur war and the first oil crisis. The Euro-Arab dialogue made little progress, however, and was abandoned after Iraq's invasion of Kuwait in 1990. A 'five-plus-five' dialogue (bringing together France, Italy, Portugal, Spain, Malta, and the five Arab Maghreb Union states, Algeria, Libya, Morocco, Tunisia and Mauritania) was first proposed in 1983 by French President Francois Mitterand, but the first, informal meeting did not take place until 1988. The objective was to create a framework for dialogue on economic issues, EU-Maghreb relations, and intra-Maghreb relations. Disagreements among the European states and among the Maghreb states, the 1990-91 Gulf War, Algeria's internal crisis and the embargo against Libya, however, resulted in the 'neutralization' of the initiative.

In 1990 Italy and Spain proposed the establishment of a Conference for Security and Cooperation in the Mediterranean (CSCM), modelled on the then CSCE, as a forum for consultation and cooperation among all Mediterranean countries. All CSCM members would endorse the principles that the international frontiers should not be changed by force and force should not be used in resolving international disputes. The full range of security issues could theoretically be dealt with within a CSCM. States from outside the subregion (such as the United States and Russia) would participate, a crisis prevention/management centre would be created and emphasis would be given to CSBMs. The CSCM proposal, however, never received wider support and no progress was made.

The Mediterranean Forum was initiated by Egypt and created in July 1994, bringing together 11 states (Algeria, Egypt, Malta, Morocco, Tunisia, Turkey, France, Greece, Italy, Portugal and Spain). The Forum has a rather 'informal' character and focuses on three 'baskets' of issues (political, economic and cultural). Its effectiveness has been limited by disagreement over future enlargement (with European members opposing Libya's inclusion, the Arab members opposing Israel's inclusion and Turkey opposing Cyprus's inclusion) and a lack of funds.

With the failure/limitations of these various initiatives, by the mid-1990s most attention was focused on the EU's efforts to promote Mediterranean cooperation through the Barcelona Process. The EU sponsored Barcelona conference of November 1995, brought the EU together with 12 Mediterranean partners (Algeria, Cyprus, Egypt, Israel, Jordan, Lebanon, Malta, Morocco, Syria, Tunisia, Turkey and the Palestinian Authority), only Libya being excluded. The Barcelona conference resulted in a declaration on cooperation and a Work Programme. According to the Barcelona Declaration:

> The participants solemnly affirm their intention to work towards the creation of an area of peace, stability and security in the Mediterranean basin in an incremental way, through the structures of dialogue and cooperation established in this Charter. Their practical cooperation will be concentrated first on measures to promote democracy, the rule of law and the respect for human rights, and to build confidence between them.[9]

The EU-led Euro-Mediterranean Partnership has three dimensions: political and security, economic and financial; and social, cultural and human affairs. Each is implemented in two separate but complementary ways: via 'bilateral' agreements between the EU and individual Mediterranean states and subregionally. The Partnership embraces governments, economic actors and non-governmental groups. The EU's June 1995 Cannes European Council allocated the Euro-Mediterranean Partnership a budget for 1995-99 of 4.685 million ECU, essentially from the MEDA Programme, plus loans from the European Investment Bank.[10] Euro-Mediterranean Association Agreements have so far been signed with Tunisia, Israel and Morocco and similar agreements are being negotiated with Egypt, Jordan and Lebanon. An Interim Agreement has been negotiated with the Palestine Liberation Organization for the benefit of the Palestinian Authority. Negotiations with Algeria should start shortly, and exploratory talks are under way with Syria. Three other Mediterranean partners already have special ties with the EU, Cyprus and Malta in the form of Association Agreements and Turkey in the form of a Customs Union. A second Euro-Mediterranean Conference took place in Malta in

April 1997. Although the Euro-Mediterranean Partnership has made positive progress one wonders whether the effort may be 'too little, too late', given the multiple economic demands on the EU (internally and from Central and Eastern Europe, the former Soviet Union and Africa, as well as the Mediterranean itself).

A number of other cooperation efforts overlap with these initiatives. In the framework of the Arab-Israeli peace process, subregional efforts for economic cooperation were undertaken with the Casablanca and Amman conferences. There were initially high hopes for economic spin-offs from the Arab-Israeli peace process; for the creation of a 'common market' between Israel, the Palestinians and Jordan; and that economic cooperation would act as a confidence-building measure and strengthen the peace process. However, although intra-regional trade is at a very low level, not much progress has been achieved, mainly because of the setbacks in the peace process. Furthermore, suspicion, regional instability (which discourages investment), the centrally planned character of Arab economies, and Arab fears of Israeli economic domination are considerable obstacles to subregional economic cooperation.

The Maghreb states (Algeria, Libya, Morocco, Tunisia and Mauritania) also cooperate with each other in the Arab Maghreb Union created in February 1989. The main objectives of the Arab Maghreb Union are economic. Although the Union also offers the possibility of political consultations, it has made a rather limited contribution to subregional security. One should also briefly mention other subregional groups in the vicinity of the Mediterranean, such as the BSEC, the Gulf Cooperation Council (GCC), and the Economic Cooperation Council (ECO, which brings together Turkey, Iran, Pakistan and other Islamic states), although these groups have not had a major bearing on the Mediterranean.

A number of other international organizations and arms control regimes have relevance for the Mediterranean. NATO has launched a dialogue with selected Mediterranean countries, which is a far more constructive approach than cries about the existence of an 'Islamic threat'. In the near future, NATO could contemplate PfP-type agreements with specific countries, taking into consideration the 'special' circumstances of the Mediterranean. The WEU has also launched a 'Mediterranean Dialogue', which is informal and mainly bilateral. The OSCE has not been very active in the Mediterranean, and more attention should be paid to the subregion in the framework of the OSCE 'Security Model'. Mediterranean NATO members have signed the CFE Treaty and the Wassenaar Arrangement (which replaced COCOM). Most Mediterranean states have signed and ratified the Chemical Weapons Convention (although Egypt, Syria and Libya have not signed, linking the issue to Israel's nuclear capability), the Biological Weapons Convention and the Nuclear Non-Proliferation Treaty. Some states participate in the United Nations Register of Conventional Arms. Subregional arms control efforts (such as the ongoing talks in the framework of the Arab-Israeli peace process and discussions on a Middle Eastern Nuclear Weapons-Free Zone) have not been successful. In the Mediterranean and the Middle East, progress in arms control is only likely to follow the resolution of larger political problems.

The lack of success in efforts for subregional cooperation in the Mediterranean can be attributed to a number of factors. The Arab-Israeli conflict (and to a much lesser extent other conflicts such as the Greek-Turkish and the Kurdish conflicts) and overlapping rivalries and conflicts from outside the Mediterranean have made cooperation inherently difficult. The absence of two clear-cut blocs, with a leader in each bloc able to drag the states into cooperation (as in Europe during the Cold War), hinders cooperation. In the post-Cold War world, the leading power, the United States, has not so far pushed for Mediterranean subregional cooperation. The lack of homogeneity and absence of shared values between the northern and southern Mediterranean shores and the great differences in the level of development, size of states and military capabilities of the Mediterranean countries also hamper cooperation. Colonial memories in the south of the Mediterranean make cooperation all the more difficult.

Concerning the future prospects for subregional cooperation in the Mediterranean, one could make the following remarks. It is difficult to examine the Mediterranean, from a security perspective, in complete isolation from the surrounding subregions of the Caucasus/Central Asia, the Balkans and the Middle East, including the Persian Gulf. A 'bottom-up' approach appears to be the most promising means of promoting Mediterranean cooperation. In the past, there have been efforts to promote functional cooperation, such as the Mediterranean Action Plan for environmental protection launched by the United Nations Environmental Programme in 1975 (although this achieved only limited success). While it may be easier to agree upon and implement specific functional agreements, however, the synergistic effect of many subregional problems (for instance, the inter-relationship between population growth, economic underdevelopment, mass migration and environmental pollution) means that a more comprehensive policy may be necessary.

Given the significant economic, religious, political and security differences within the Mediterranean, there is a need for external pressure and leadership to promote cooperation. In this context, the moving force has to be the EU. While EU expansion is likely to include Malta and Cyprus, other Mediterranean states are unlikely to be admitted into the EU (or NATO) and will therefore have interests in subregional cooperation with the EU.[11] The application of UN/OSCE principles should be a main objective. The mechanical application of a model designed for Europe to the Mediterranean (as with the CSCM proposal) should be avoided. Keeping open lines of communication and dialogue should be a high priority. There should also be a strong emphasis on cultural and, especially, religious dialogue and activities. In order to promote economic cooperation, the European Mediterranean states and the EU should put more emphasis on joint ventures that on sales per se. There should not be high expectations for arms control and crisis management mechanisms in the near future, so attention should perhaps focus on 'soft arms control' measures (transparency, advance notification and other constraints on military activity) and 'soft security' issues.

If the developed countries sincerely wish to avoid the replacement of the military competition between East and West with an economic and social competition between North and South, the North must provide generous economic support for the South's economic development. The Mediterranean is a case in point. The European Union is the only international actor which can play a major role in this context, and this makes the success of the comprehensive EU Mediterranean policy agreed at the Barcelona Conference vital.

CONCLUSION

This chapter has examined the prospects for subregional cooperation in South-Eastern Europe, the NIS and the Mediterranean. It began by noting that – in the context of NATO and EU enlargement – the prospects for subregional cooperation could be particularly important in these 'boundary zones' sensitively located between various major powers. The existence of on-going, only recently resolved and possible future conflicts adds further to the importance of these subregions. This chapter suggests a number of initial conclusions. Most obviously, there are already significant efforts at building cooperation in all these subregions. These various processes are, however, less robust than those in the Barents-Black Sea belt – partly because they have been more recently established, but also because they face significant obstacles to their further development. A second feature of the attempts to build subregional cooperation in South-Eastern Europe, the NIS and the Mediterranean is the existence of multiple, overlapping institutional frameworks within each subregion, rather than a single relatively well-defined subregional group. Given the problems of defining the boundaries of any subregion and the diverse states and interests involved in these subregions, this is – at least in part – probably inevitable. However, it also raises the question of whether such multiple, overlapping processes are mutually re-inforcing and improve the prospects for subregional cooperation, or whether they reflect competing dynamics, risk unnecessary duplication and/or indicate a triumph of form over substance. If subregional cooperation is to develop further, this question will need to be answered.

The emerging subregional cooperation processes in South-Eastern Europe, the NIS and the Mediterranean also lack, at least so far, the substantive content in practical areas – economics, management of the environment, transfrontier cooperation – which has characterized the more successful of the groups in the Barents-Black Sea belt. This lack of substance reflects a number of problems. Serious political differences and disputes exist in all these subregions. In South-Eastern Europe, the far from resolved future of Bosnia-Herzegovina, as well as potential conflicts in Kosovo, Macedonia and Cyprus, make subregional cooperation difficult. In the Caucasus, the continuing – even if for the time-being non-violent – conflict over Nagorno-Karabakh is a major obstacle to subregional cooperation. In the Mediterranean, serious differences over democracy and human rights between the states of the northern and southern shores, as well as the Arab-Israeli and Algerian conflicts, have hampered progress. Thus, one of central question facing subregional cooperation in these areas is whether further progress must await the resolution of some very serious disputes or whether it can be achieved by by-passing or ignoring more contentious issues.

Subregional cooperation in South-Eastern Europe, the NIS and the Mediterranean is also hampered by a lack of resources. The countries in these subregions are relatively poor and have more urgent national priorities. They also lack the rich neighbours – the Nordic countries and Germany – who have underpinned the achievements of the BEAC and the CBSS. As a consequence, Western, particularly EU, political and financial support is likely to be very important for the further development of cooperation. This, however, poses dilemmas. For the West, unresolved conflicts and disputes over democracy and human rights raise the issue of how far support (especially economic support) for subregional cooperation should be conditional on progress in these areas. The West faces a difficult and on-going dilemma between using the 'carrot/stick' of economic aid to secure progress and providing aid in the hope that it will facilitate cooperation and conflict resolution in the longer term. There are also certain tensions between subregional cooperation and NATO and the EU's own outreach and enlargement policies. Countries seeking integration with the West may be reluctant to be 'consigned' to a non-integrated subregion and the 'bilateral' character of NATO and the EU's policies may inadvertently encourage such reluctance. If NATO and the EU are to encourage cooperation in these subregions, they will need to maximize their efforts to resolve these tensions. In short, while the further development of subregional cooperation in South-Eastern Europe, the NIS and the Mediterranean is important, it will not be easy to achieve and will pose difficult dilemmas for policy-makers in these subregions, neighbouring states and the West.

Part IV
Conclusion

12 Conclusion

Andrew Cottey

The 1990s have witnessed enormous changes in Europe. One of the more remarkable and positive, but not always widely recognized, developments has been the emergence of the new subregional groups in the Barents-Black Sea belt. From the late 1940s to the late 1980s, these subregions were the front-lines of the Cold War. They were characterized by political division, military confrontation and minimal economic and human ties between the two blocs. The end of the Cold War made the emergence of the Barents-Black Sea groups possible: patterns of cooperation which were previously unthinkable became political reality in a very short space of time.

While the Barents-Black Sea subregional groups are a product of Europe's new, more benign environment, a strong argument can be made that they also contribute positively to the continent's security. Europe is in a transitional period and the final outcome of that transition is unclear. By the late 1990s certain trends were apparent, but many issues remained open: the future character of the European Union (EU) and the North Atlantic Treaty Organization (NATO); how far and in what ways these organizations would extend eastwards; the status of those states lying between an enlarged EU/NATO and Russia; Russia's role in Europe; and the ability of the major powers and organizations to prevent, manage and resolve conflicts such as those in the former Yugoslavia. In this context, the subregional groups in the Barents-Black Sea belt contribute to security and cooperation by bringing together groups of states who cannot easily cooperate in other frameworks, bridging both the old Cold War divide and the potential dividing lines of the new Europe.

All the states in the Barents-Black Sea groups are members of the Organization for Security and Cooperation in Europe (OSCE) and thus engage in various forms of cooperation at the pan-European level. The OSCE's pan-European character and largely consensus decision-making, however, limit the possibilities for practical cooperation amongst its members, particularly when they face issues which inevitably do not affect all of them equally. Subregional groups such as those in the Barents-Black Sea belt, in contrast, allow their members to engage in more practical and sometimes more intensive forms of cooperation than are possible at the pan-European level. The larger subregional groups – the Barents Euro-Arctic Council (BEAC), the Council of Baltic Sea States (CBSS), the Central European Initiative (CEI) and the Black Sea Economic Cooperation (BSEC) – bring together EU and NATO members, aspiring members of these organizations, those states unlikely to join these organizations (at least at an early stage) and those states wary of the NATO/EU enlargement (particularly Russia). The smaller subregional groups – the Visegrad group and the Central European Free Trade Agreement (CEFTA) – allow smaller groups of Central and Eastern European states to cooperate with one another in ways that were not possible during the Cold War. This has strengthened them diplomatically vis-à-vis their larger neighbours (Russia and the West), helped them to put the issues of NATO and EU enlargement on the political agenda, helped them to prepare for integration with NATO and the EU and may play a role in averting or managing tensions between them as they are integrated with NATO and the EU at different speeds. The Barents-Black Sea groups also contribute to security in a variety of different ways: by their very existence they facilitate communication and dialogue; they help in the management of a wide range of non- and 'soft' security problems; and they sometimes play a more overt role in addressing particular political or security issues.

The relative success of the subregional groups in the Barents-Black Sea belt raises the question of how they are likely to develop in future. For the most part, these groups have been relatively low profile, focusing on practical cooperation in non- or 'soft' security areas. Even if they only continue to follow this pattern, the arguments above suggest that they may continue to make a positive contribution to European security. Arguably, however, at least some of these groups could increase their contribution to security through the intensification of cooperation and the development of more substantive, practical projects (perhaps not always involving all their members). In the cases of the BEAC and the CBSS, substantive cooperation was quite far advanced in some areas by 1997. Within the BSEC, by contrast, there was growing recognition by the same juncture that further progress would be difficult unless a breakthrough was made into concrete, jointly financed projects. Much the same could be said of the CEI. In all cases, however, further strides in this kind of practical cooperation clearly depended not just on common consent but also on the availability of financial resources. While member states may invest further resources, the relative poverty of most of the members of the BSEC and the CEI suggests that support from external powers and institutions (particularly the EU and international financial institutions) will be important.

Beyond this, is the issue of whether and how far the Barents-Black Sea groups should attempt to develop more overt or direct security roles. One of the defining features of these groups to date is that – with the partial exception of the Visegrad group – they have had little or no overt security role and have not usually discussed explicit security issues. Indeed, this is arguably one source of their success: by 'turning a blind eye' to overt security issues they have been able to develop and sustain cooperation despite the existence of serious bilateral disputes and very differing views on Europe's 'security architecture' (particularly NATO enlargement) amongst some of their members. Nevertheless, some observers argued that, now that some of these groups were quite well established, they should begin to contribute more directly to security and develop more overt security roles. They might consider organizing peacekeeping, mine clearance or other similar military exercises under their auspices or adopting specific military confidence-building measures on a subregional basis. They could provide a framework for discussing particular political issues in their subregion – for example, the situation of Kaliningrad (the Russian exclave located between Poland and Lithuania on the Baltic coast) in the case of the CBSS. They might engage more directly in conflict prevention or post-conflict peace-building activities in their subregions – the CEI might, for example, play a greater role in the former Yugoslavia. They could also consider discussing larger European security issues (for example, NATO/EU enlargement and the OSCE), exploring whether they could play any constructive role in relation to these issues (by stating their political will to sustain cooperation at the subregional despite differences on larger issues, by helping member states to prepare for integration with the EU or by supporting the implementation of OSCE decisions/activities). The more narrowly focused CEFTA faced the question of whether it should remain purely a free trade area or whether it should broaden its remit to become a framework for its members to discuss some other shared issues (such as integration with the EU). By these sorts of steps, the direct contribution of the subregional groups to security might gradually be expanded.

There were, however, also arguments for subregional groups to refrain from engaging too directly with security issues. Bringing potentially contentious security issues into these frameworks could highlight disputes between members states, undermining the groups' ability to sustain cooperation in other areas. In the worst case, clumsy attempts to bring security issues into a subregional group might trigger an irreparable break-down in cooperation. Further, if larger security issues – NATO enlargement, the conflict in the former Yugoslavia – cannot be resolved by the larger European security organizations and/or direct discussions between the parties concerned, subregional groups were probably unlikely to be able to make much further progress. It might also be argued that explicit security issues could be better handled in other frameworks designed for that purpose. Military cooperation and exercises, for example, might be better undertaken with the framework of NATO's Partnership for Peace (PfP). The issue, however, was one of striking the appropriate balance between avoiding potentially divisive issues which might disrupt cooperation and making a more explicit or direct contribution to security. The appropriate balance was obviously likely to differ for each group. If the issue were handled sensitively and incrementally, at least some of the groups in the Barents-Black Sea belt might gradually come to play a larger and more explicit security role. Equally, they might determine that such a role was not desirable or not possible.

The transitional nature of the current period in Europe also raises the question of whether the subregional groups in the Barents-Black Sea belt may themselves be transitional phenomenon, likely to decline as the particular circumstances which gave birth to them fade. By 1996-97, the Visegrad group had effectively ceased to exist, as the strategic situation which had given birth to it had changed and its strategic goals were close to being achieved. The experience of the Visegrad group suggested that those subregional groups whose goals were primarily related to their members desire for integration with the West were likely to be abandoned as their members joined NATO and/or the EU. CEFTA would clearly face questions about its future when some but not all of its members joined the EU and therefore had to leave CEFTA's separate trade arrangements. In the medium term, the likely accession of all CEFTA members to the EU would almost certainly result in the group's demise. Similarly, if most of the CEI's members joined the EU and/or NATO in the longer term, the same fate might befall that group. Certain 'echoes' of such groups might remain in the form of loose Central and Eastern European caucuses in an enlarged EU and NATO. As of 1996-97, however, there was little interest in retaining any more formal Central and Eastern European cooperation once those countries had joined NATO or the EU.

The larger subregional groups, with more diverse memberships – the BEAC, the CBSS and the BSEC – appear likely to have a longer term, more permanent role to play. Their inclusion of former Soviet states unlikely to join NATO or the EU in anything but the longest term, means that they have the potential to sustain cooperation between members of an enlarging NATO/EU and their eastern neighbours. In particular, the membership of Russia in these groups makes them useful frameworks for sustaining and developing cooperation with Russia. Although direct bilateral relations between NATO/EU/United States and Russia will be of primary importance, the BEAC, the CBSS and the BSEC may provide useful multilateral frameworks for managing relations with Russia in their particular subregions (where there are issues of importance to Russia and Western states in those subregions, but which have less relevance for the West as whole). More broadly, it may be argued that the Barents, Baltic Sea and Black Sea are more 'natural' subregions than those defined by the Visegrad group, CEFTA or the CEI, with deeper and more sustainable subregional identities. These subregions are defined in significant part by geography. This geography in turn creates substantial interdependence, particularly in terms of the environment, which means that the countries of the subregion face certain shared problems (environmental degradation, infrastructure and transport) which can only be resolved through cooperation. Some analysts argue further that the Barents, Baltic Sea and Black Sea are 'natural' economic subregions, where trade and economic cooperation make obvious sense. The Barents and Baltic (and to some extent Black Sea) subregions have also developed substantial 'bottom-up', non-governmental cooperation which should probably help to sustain cooperation and a general senses of shared interests in the longer term. Finally, certain historical traditions of a common identity and cooperation – even if deliberately used by political leaders rather than purely spontaneous phenomenon - underpin cooperation in these subregions. While the exact weight which should be attached to any of these arguments may be contentious, in combination they suggest a reasonably solid basis for longer term cooperation in the Barents, Baltic Sea and Black Sea subregions. The one obvious factor which could disrupt cooperation would be a return to confrontation between Russia and an enlarged West and resulting a re-polarization of Europe. In these circumstances, akin to a new Cold War, it would be difficult – if not impossible – for groups such as the BEAC, the CBSS and the BSEC to survive in any meaningful sense.

The relative success of the Barents-Black Sea groups also raised the question of the possible role of subregional cooperation elsewhere in Europe. By 1996-97, it was clear that the enlargement of NATO and the EU would be a phased process, taking some years and including only relatively small numbers of countries in the first instance. In this context, South-Eastern Europe, the western former Soviet Union (Ukraine, Belarus and Moldova), the Caucasus, Central Asia and the Mediterranean were likely to become Europe's new 'boundary zones' – subregions excluded (at least initially) from the integrative processes of NATO and EU enlargement, lying between an enlargement NATO/EU and other major powers (Russia, Turkey, Iran, China) and vulnerable to pressure from their more powerful neighbours. By the mid-1990s, various efforts at establishing subregional cooperation had been initiated in these areas, but these initiatives were less well established than the subregional groups in the Barents-Black Sea belt and had yet to generate more substantive, practical cooperation. The experience of the groups in the Barents-Black Sea belt suggested a number of lessons for these emerging subregional cooperation processes. High-level political initiatives and support had been important in establishing all of the groups in the Barents-Black Sea belt. Once established, however, the success of these groups seemed to depend more on their ability to develop practical cooperative projects in functional areas (economics, the environment, infrastructure), in order to sustain the momentum of cooperation. Elements of 'bottom-up' non-governmental and transfrontier cooperation were important in developing and sustaining cooperation. Political and financial support from the West, particularly the EU and/or wealthy neighbouring Western states, was also central.

The groups in the Barents-Black Sea belt additionally indicated some of the limits and problems of subregional cooperation which might have important implications elsewhere in Europe. The Barents-Black Sea groups have not been able (or, indeed, even attempted) to resolve serious disputes or conflicts between their members, instead developing cooperation by by-passing or ignoring such disputes. In South-Eastern Europe, the former Soviet Union and the Mediterranean there are even more serious disputes and conflicts. One central question for these subregions, therefore, was whether subregional cooperation could be built (for example, in economic, environmental or infrastructural areas) by by-passing or ignoring existing disputes and conflicts, whether such cooperation might play a more direct role in resolving such disputes (which the experience of the Barents-Black Sea groups suggested was unlikely) or whether it would depend on the prior resolution of at least the most serious disputes.

By 1996-97, the larger European security organizations – the OSCE, the Council of Europe, the EU, NATO and the Western European Union (WEU) – were also showing increasing interest in and support for subregional cooperation. There appeared to be opportunities for the larger organizations to support subregional cooperation and develop practical cooperation and divisions of labour with individual subregional groups. Substantive policies to achieve these goals, however, were only beginning to emerge. The OSCE had the potential to act as a pan-European normative framework and to encourage subregional cooperation by endorsing such cooperation generally and providing an institutional framework for regular discussion of and exchange of information on such cooperation. The OSCE might also development more practical cooperation with individual subregional groups and devolve certain elements of democracy-support and conflict management activities to them. The EU was already a member (through the Commission) of the BEAC and the CBSS and was engaged in various forms of more practical support for the BEAC, the CBSS, the CEI and the BSEC (as well as its own Royaumont Initiative in South-Eastern Europe). Through its general political and economic influence and the specific economic and other instruments at its disposal, the EU has the potential to be a driving force for subregional cooperation. It needs to explore, however, how it can provide further practical support for such cooperation. The democracy and human rights promotion activities of the Council of Europe also had certain subregional dimensions which might be expanded or involve useful cooperation with subregional groups.

NATO and the WEU, in contrast, were less directly engaged with the existing subregional groups in the Barents-Black Sea belt. NATO's – and to a lesser extent the WEU's – eastern outreach policy had significant subregional dimensions (for example, through subregional peacekeeping exercises within the framework of PfP). The subregional elements of NATO and the WEU's outreach policies, however, had no direct connection with the more formal groups in the Barents-Black Sea belt, nor did the states involved exactly parallel those in the Barents-Black Sea groups. There was, however, a good case for maintaining this separation. Developing a direct connection between NATO (and perhaps also the WEU) and the subregional groups in the Barents-Black Sea belt might risk undermining successful cooperation in non- or 'soft' security areas by bringing more contentious political-military issues into these frameworks. Such a step might also fuel Russian fears of an attempt by NATO to dominate Europe's security architecture and encircle it.

While the EU and NATO sought to support subregional cooperation, there were also certain tensions between that support and their own eastern outreach and enlargement policies. The 'bilateral' nature of the EU and NATO's outreach policies and the (inevitable) assessment of candidates for membership on a case-by-case basis encouraged Central and Eastern European states to emphasize their individual relationships with the West and to compete for membership of the EU/NATO, thereby discouraging subregional cooperation. Central and Eastern European states were concerned that successful subregional cooperation might be seen as an alternative to NATO/EU membership. They also feared that being treated as part of a specific group might delay their integration, by condemning them as part of a 'backward' subregion or making their membership of NATO/EU dependent on the progress of their 'least advanced' subregional partner. By 1996-97, NATO and the EU were beginning to address these problems, signalling their political support for subregional cooperation and seeking to develop more practical means of supporting such cooperation. Nevertheless, particularly in South-Eastern Europe, there seemed likely to be further tensions between some states desires for rapid integration with the West and the development of subregional cooperation.

The development of the subregional groups in the Barents-Black Sea belt, the various initiatives to establish subregional cooperation elsewhere in Europe and the growing interest of the larger European security organizations in such cooperation raises the issues of how far there is a more general dynamic towards the subregionalization of post-Cold War European security and what the longer term implications of this dynamic might be. Aside from specific subregional groups discussed here, a more general trend towards the subregionalization of European security can seen in a number of other areas. As noted above, the EU and NATO's outreach policies are developing significant – and growing – subregional dimensions. The internal dynamics of the EU and NATO are also characterized by elements of subregionalization. Although the EU and NATO have for some time be characterized by informal internal caucuses on a subregional basis, this trend has grown with the end of the Cold War. The Nordic/Scandinavian states and Germany share certain common interests and have taken a leading role in promoting EU/NATO engagement in the Barents and Baltic subregions. Germany and Austria have common interests in Central Europe and have taken a leading role in promoting EU/NATO engagement in that subregion. The Mediterranean members of the EU/NATO have shared interests and have taken a leading role in promoting EU/NATO engagement in that subregion. The conflicts of the post-Cold War era have also been characterized by their subregional rather than pan-European character - and efforts at conflict prevention, management and resolution have correspondingly reflected this. The policies of the OSCE, the EU and NATO have been directed towards these conflicts, often on the basis of ad hoc groups of states engaging in activities ranging from diplomatic missions to peace enforcement. NATO's adoption of the Combined Joint Task Force concept confirmed that this trend extends also into the military sphere – implicitly recognizing that most future military operations are likely to be undertaken on the basis of ad hoc groups of interested NATO/WEU members and non-members (often perhaps with a subregional character).

How far this wider dynamic of the subregionalization of European security will develop and what its implications may be are far from clear. The main force driving this dynamic is clear. With the end of the Cold War, many of the security problems facing Europe are subregional in character and the extent to which they impact on different states varies very greatly. In this context, it is hardly surprising – and, indeed, probably inevitable - that states direct their political and economic energies and resources to those issues which affect them most directly.

Almost all European states, however, see subregional relationships or cooperation not as an alternative to the larger organizations of which they are members and/or the bilateral relationships they have with other states and organizations, but rather as a complement to these organizations and relationships. The existing members of NATO and the EU, while supporting subregional cooperation and seeking to make NATO and the EU more flexible, nevertheless emphasize that NATO and the EU remain vital and the unity on which they are built remains central. Those Central and Eastern European states aspiring to join NATO and the EU similarly stress that, while they support subregional cooperation, such cooperation cannot for them be an alternative to full integration with NATO and/or the EU. Russia, while an active supporter of subregional cooperation, clearly sees such cooperation as a complement rather than an alternative to its more direct relations with its neighbours and the West. In particular, all the states engaged in the Barents-Black Sea groups have emphasized that they do not think that such cooperation should attempt to replicate the defence guarantees and military integration of NATO or the political solidarity and economic integration of the EU. For NATO and the EU's members and those states seeking to join these organizations, NATO and the EU are 'tried and tested' forms of cooperation, based on well established political relationships and institutional mechanisms. Given the diverse membership of groups such the BEAC, the CBSS, the CEI and the BSEC and the small size of the Visegrad group and CEFTA, it is difficult to see how they could credibly be alternatives to NATO or the EU. More generally – and one of the central reasons why states emphasize that subregional cooperation must be seen as a complement not an alternative to larger organizations and relationships – a greater subregionalization of European security could result in a growing fragmentation of Europe's international relations, with states pursuing narrowly defined interests, collective approaches to security breaking down and institutions such as NATO and the EU undermined as a consequence.

Nevertheless – and despite the political commitment of NATO/EU members and aspirants to maintain the unity of these bodies – the realities of differing national interests are leading to a greater subregionalization of

European security. The real issue, therefore, is how far this dynamic will extend and what its implications will be. There are obvious reasons why subregionalization may proceed further and arguments to suggest that such a trend, if well managed, could be beneficial. With Europe facing an increasingly diverse range of security problems which affect different states to very different degrees, there are obvious advantages to subregional groups of states engaging with the problems that affect them most directly. Similarly, there are good arguments for the larger organizations to develop more flexibility through the subregionalization of elements of their outreach policies and the development of role specialization and new divisions of labour within each organization and between the various organizations (often, perhaps, on a subregional basis). With the emergence of a quite large number of relatively small conflicts (or potential conflicts), further, it is unrealistic to expect all states to be engaged equally in all conflict management activities. In sum, the development of a 'variable geometry' of subregional cooperation – comprising established subregional groups such as those in the Barents-Black Sea belt, subregional dimensions of NATO/EU and their outreach policies, and subregional conflict management efforts under OSCE aegis or in more ad hoc forms – may play an increasing and broadly positive role in the management of Europe's security problems in the future.

As noted above, however, an increasing subregionalization of European security could also risk a growing fragmentation of Europe's international politics. In the worst case, this could lead to the narrow pursuit of national interests (often defined in subregional terms), unilateral action by interested states, disengagement by states without obvious interests, the breakdown of collective approaches to the management of European security problems and a serious weakening of the political unity on which NATO and the EU are based. Indeed, elements of all these dangers can be seen in the international community's failures in the former Yugoslavia. In the longer term, therefore, European states may face a difficult task in balancing the inevitable and often positive subregionalization of European security with the need to maintain broader, collective approaches to the management of European security and the unity of NATO and the EU.

Looking beyond Europe, the emergence of subregional cooperation can be seen also as part of a global trend. Groups such as the Association of South East Asia Nations (ASEAN), the North American Free Trade Area (NAFTA) and the Southern African Development Community (SADC) are broadly similar to the European subregional groups, contributing to the development of cooperation between their members, but with limited security agendas. In various ways, these and the European subregional groups also reflect some larger global trends and problems. They represent attempts to re-establish cooperation in areas where the Cold War – and other factors – previously made such cooperation impossible. They are, in part, a response to the growth of free trade, the globalization of much economic activity and the resulting need for states to find new economic partners and markets. They are also a response to the more localized dimensions of global problems – environmental degradation, mass migration, transnational crime – which because of their transnational character can only be dealt with through international cooperation (whether at the subregional, regional or global level). The growth of subregional cooperation, therefore, seems likely to be a feature not only of post-Cold War Europe, but also of post-Cold War international politics as a whole. The European subregional groups and similar groups elsewhere might benefit from beginning to explore what lessons their mutual experiences may hold for each other's future development.

The emergence of new forms of subregional cooperation, stretching from the Barents in the far north to the Black Sea in the south, is one of the more positive developments in Europe since the end of the Cold War. The groups in the Barents-Black Sea belt bridge the old Cold War divide, sustain cooperation between an enlarging NATO and EU and the states to their to east, facilitate the management of a wide range of non- and 'soft' security problems, and (even when they have no direct security role) have a positive spill-over into their members wider relations. Some of these groups – the Visegrad group, CEFTA and perhaps the CEI – are likely to decline as their historic missions are fulfilled. The BEAC, the CBSS and the BSEC, however, seem likely to have a longer term role. Newer initiatives are also developing in South-Eastern Europe, parts of the former Soviet Union and the Mediterranean. European subregional cooperation seems likely to raise a number of challenging issues in the future. Established and emerging subregional cooperation processes will face the task of sustaining and giving more substance to their cooperation and the question of how far they should attempt to develop more direct security roles. The larger European security organizations – especially the OSCE, the EU and NATO – must address the issues of how they can best promote subregional cooperation and how they might usefully cooperate with subregional groups. In the longer term, the subregionalization of European security may raise important questions about the balance between subregional approaches to security issues and wider collective approaches – with potentially major implications for the future of NATO, the EU and European security as a whole.

Appendix 1
Membership of the Barents-Black Sea Subregional Groups

(August 1997)

Barents Euro-Arctic Council
- Denmark
- European Commission
- Finland
- Iceland
- Norway
- Russia
- Sweden

Council of Baltic Sea States
- Denmark
- Estonia
- European Commission
- Finland
- Germany
- Iceland
- Latvia
- Lithuania
- Norway
- Poland
- Russia
- Sweden

Visegrad Group
- Czech Republic
- Hungary
- Poland
- Slovakia

Central European Free Trade Agreement
- Czech Republic
- Hungary
- Poland
- Romania
- Slovakia
- Slovenia

Central European Initiative
- Albania
- Austria
- Belarus
- Bosnia-Herzegovina
- Bulgaria
- Croatia
- Czech Republic
- Hungary
- Italy
- Moldova
- Poland
- Romania
- Slovakia
- Slovenia
- The Former Yugoslav Republic of Macedonia
- Ukraine

Black Sea Economic Cooperation
- Albania
- Armenia
- Azerbaijan
- Bulgaria
- Georgia
- Greece
- Moldova
- Romania
- Russia
- Turkey
- Ukraine

Appendix 2
Members of the Steering Board of the EWI Project 'Multi-Layered Integration: The Subregional Dimension'

Ambassador Anders Bjurner
  Steering Board Chair
  Deputy State Secretary
  Ministry of Foreign Affairs
  Sweden

Dr. Christopher Cviic
  Associate Fellow
  European Programme
  Royal Institute of International
  Affairs (Chatham House)
  London

Dr. Arndt Freytag von Loringhoven
  Policy Planning Staff
  Ministry of Foreign Affairs
  Germany

Ambassador Istvan Gyarmati
  Deputy State Secretary
  Ministry of Defence
  Hungary

Dr. Ihor Kharchenko
  Director of Policy Analysis
  and Planning
  Ministry of Foreign Affairs
  Ukraine

Dr. Guido Lenzi
  Director
  Institute for Security Studies of
  Western European Union
  Paris

Ambassador Jutta Stefan-Bastl
  Austrian Permanent
  Representative to the
  Organization for Security and
  Cooperation in Europe
  Vienna

Ambassador Justas Paleckis
  Lithuanian Ambassador to the
  United Kingdom

Dr. Andrzej Towpik
  Undersecretary of State
  Ministry of Foreign Affairs
  Poland

Ambassador Nikolai N Uspensky
  Deputy Director
  International Security Department
  Office of the Security Council of
  the Russian Federation

Notes and References

1 Introduction

1. Charter of the United Nations, Chapter VIII Regional Arrangements, Appendix B, in A. Roberts and B. Kingsbury, Eds., *United Nations, Divided World: The UN's Roles in International Relations*, 2nd ed., (Oxford: Clarendon Press, 1993) p. 514.
2. *CSCE Helsinki Document 1992: The Challenges of Change*, (CSCE: Helsinki, 1992) p. 9. The UN also concluded an agreement on cooperation with the CSCE in 1993 – see 'Framework for Cooperation and Coordination Between the United Nations Secretariat and the Conference on Security and Cooperation in Europe, New York, 26 May 1993', in Stockholm International Peace Research Institute, *SIPRI Yearbook 1994*, (Oxford: Oxford University Press/SIPRI, 1994) pp. 240–1.
3. Other analysts have used the term subregional to describe similar groups outside Europe, such as the Association of South-East Asian Nations, the Gulf Cooperation Council, the Organization of East Caribbean States, the Southern African Development Community and the South Pacific Forum. See W. T. Tow, *Subregional Security Cooperation in the Third World*, (Boulder and London: Lynne Rienner Publishers, 1990) and G. Cawthra, 'Subregional Security: The Southern African Development Community', *Security Dialogue*, 28 (2) (1997) 207–18.
4. The UN also seems to have accepted this logic. When UN Secretary-General Boutros Boutros-Ghali convened a meeting with the heads of regional organizations in 1994, the European organizations invited included the CSCE, the EU, NATO and the WEU, but none of what are referred to in this book as subregional groups. See A. K. Henrikson, 'The United Nations and Regional Organizations: "King Links" of a "Global Chain"', *Duke Journal of Comparative & International Law*, 7 (1) (1996) 61.

3. The Barents Euro-Arctic Council

1. F. Griffiths, 'Defence, Security and Civility in the Arctic Region', *Arctic Challenges, Report from the Nordic Council's Parliamentary Conference in Reykjavik, 16–17 August 1993*, p. 135.
2. A. Kjolberg, 'The Barents Region as a Security-Building Concept', in O. S. Stokke and O. Tunander, Eds., *The Barents Region: Cooperation in Arctic Europe*, (London: Sage, 1994) p. 21.
3. S. Jervell, 'Barentssamarbeidet februar 1996: Hvor star vi, hvor gar vi nu?' (Barents Cooperation in February 1996: Where do We Stand and Where are We Heading?), Presentation at Pax Nordica, Umea, February 1996.

4. E. Hansen, Ed., *Cooperation in the Baltic Sea Region, the Barents Region and the Black Sea Region: A Documentation Report*, Commissioned by the Royal Norwegian Ministry of Foreign Affairs, Fafo-paper 1997: 4, (Oslo: Fafo Institute of Applied Social Science, 1997) p. 27.
5. Hansen, Ed., *Cooperation in the Baltic Sea Region, the Barents Region and the Black Sea Region*, p. 26.
6. O. Stokke and R. Castberg, 'The Barents Region: Dimensions and Institutions', *International Challenges: The Fridtjof Nansen Institute Journal*, 12 (4) (1992) 22.
7. Barentsregionen: Et regionaliseringprosjekt i det nordligaste Europa, Det Kgl, *Utenriksdepartementet*, No. 1/93 (April 1993) p. 23.
8. Jervell, 'Barentssamarbeidet februar 1996', p. 5.
9. See P.K. Baev, 'Russian Perspectives on the Barents Region', in Stokke and Tunander, Eds., *The Barents Region*, p.180; and T. Tveito, 'The Barents Region – A Region of Cooperation in Europe and its Challenges', in Common Security in Northern Europe after the Cold War: The Baltic Sea and Barents Sea Region, (Stockholm: The Olof Palme International Centre, 1994) p. 37.
10. Hansen, Ed., *Cooperation in the Baltic Sea Region, the Barents Region and the Black Sea Region*, p. 12.
11. R. Castberg, O. S. Stokke and W. Ostreng, 'The Dynamics of the Barents Region', in Stokke and Tunander, Eds., *The Barents Region*, p. 74.
12. Castberg, Stokke and Ostreng, 'The Dynamics of the Barents Region', in Stokke and Tunander, Eds., *The Barents Region*, p. 80.
13. O. Tunander, 'Inventing the Barents Region: Overcoming the East-West Divide in the North', in Stokke and Tunander, Eds., *The Barents Region*, p. 40.
14. H. Haavisto, 'EU: lla huomattava merkitys Barentsin alueella', (The EU is a Significant Actor in the Barents Region), in L. Heininen, Ed., 'Pohjoinen Suomen politiikassa', (The North in Finland's Policy), *Lapin yliopiston hallintoviraston julkaisuja*, 27 (1994) 157.
15. H. Aalbu, E. Hoidahl, H. Jussila and U. Wiberg, 'A velge sina naboer - Barentsregionen som utrikespolitisk og regionalpolitisk prosjekt', *NordREFO*, 4 (1995) 50–2.
16. Castberg, Stokke and Ostreng, 'The Dynamics of the Barents Region', in Stokke and Tunander, Eds., *The Barents Region*, p. 78.
17. E. Hansen, 'Living Conditions in the North: The New Divide', in Stokke and Tunander, Eds., *The Barents Region*, pp. 69–70.
18. A. Kozyrev, 'Cooperation in the Barents Region: Promising Beginning', in Stokke and Tunander, Eds., *The Barents Region*, p. 29.
19. Baev, 'Russian Perspectives on the Barents Region', in Stokke and Tunander, Eds., *The Barents Region*, p. 180.
20. Hansen, Ed., *Cooperation in the Baltic Sea Region, the Barents Region and the Black Sea Region*, p. 28.
21. W. Ostreng, 'The Northern Sea Route and the Barents Region', in Stokke and Tunander, Eds., *The Barents Region,* p. 171.
22. Aalbu, Hoidahl, Jussila and Wiberg, 'A velge sina naboer', 51.

23. Hansen, Ed., *Cooperation in the Baltic Sea Region, the Barents Region and the Black Sea Region*, p. 31.
24. Jervell, 'Barentssamarbeidet februar 1996'.
25. Aalbu, Hoidahl, Jussila and Wiberg, 'A velge sina naboer', 78.
26. N. Uspensky, presentation on the Barents Euro-Arctic Council, summarized in *Multi-Layered Integration: The Sub-Regional Dimension – Report of an Inter-Governmental Conference, Bucharest, 7-8 October 1996*, (Warsaw: Institute for EastWest Studies, 1996) pp. 8–9.
27. Ostreng, 'The Northern Sea Route', in Stokke and Tunander, Eds., *The Barents Region.*
28. Aalbu, Hoidahl, Jussila and Wiberg, 'A velge sina naboer', 86.
29. Castberg, Stokke and Ostreng, 'The Dynamics of the Barents Region', in Stokke and Tunander, Eds., *The Barents Region*, p. 75.
30. See Griffiths, 'Defence, Security and Civility in the Arctic Region'; Kjolberg, 'The Barents Region as a Security-Building Concept'; and A. Nokkala, 'Turvallisuuden jatkuvuus ja muutoshaasteet Euroopan pohjoisessa', (The Continuity and Incentives for Change of Security in Northernmost Europe), *Kide*, 5 (1996).
31. S. Chaturvedi, 'The Arctic Today: New Thinking, New Visions, Old Power Structures', in J. Kakonen, Ed., *Dreaming of the Barents Region: Interpreting Cooperation in the Euro-Arctic Rim*, Research Report No. 73, (Tampere: Tampere Peace Research Institute, 1996) p. 34.
32. J. Eriksson, 'Euro-Arctic Insecurity: The Polity Puzzle', in *Common Security in Northern Europe after the Cold War: The Baltic Sea and Barents Sea Region*, (Stockholm: The Olof Palme International Centre, 1994).
33. See J. J. Holst; A. Kozyrev, 'Cooperation in the Barents Region: Promising Beginning', p. 28; and T. Stoltenberg, 'Foreword', in Stokke and Tunander, Eds., *The Barents Region*.
34. P. Joenniemi, 'Security in Northern Europe: The Contest between Different Understandings', *Osterreichische Aeitschrift fur Politikwissenschaft*, 25 (4) (1996).
35. T. Stoltenberg, Opening Speech at the Foreign Ministers' Conference on 'Cooperation in the Barents Euro-Arctic Region', Kirkenes, 10–11 January 1992.
36. Jervell, 'Barentssamarbeidet februar 1996'.
37. Jervell, 'Barentssamarbeidet februar 1996'.
38. See Kjolberg, 'The Barents Region as a Security-Building Concept', in Stokke and Tunander, Eds., *The Barents Region*.

4. The Council of Baltic Sea States

1. *Declaration of the Foreign Ministers of the Baltic Sea States*, Copenhagen, 5-6 March 1992.
2. As disclosed by Mrs. Thatcher in her memoirs, Germany was sometimes said

to be a de-stabilizing force manifested in a Drang nach Osten, to be contained by close relations between the UK and France and a sustained American commitment to Europe. M. Thtacher, *The Downing Street Years*, (London: HarperCollins Publishers, 1993).

3. The subject has been much discussed in the theoretical literature, see K. Goldmann and G. Sjostedt, *Power, Capabilities, Interdependence*, (London: SAGE International, 1979).

4. R. Falkenrath, *Shaping Europe's Military Order*, (Cambridge, Massachusetts: MIT Press, 1997) Chapter 6.

5. The distinction is elaborated in K. Mottola, 'Security around the Baltic Rim: Concepts, Actors and Processes', in Hedegaard and Lindstrom, Eds., *North European and Baltic Sea Integration Yearbook*, (Heidelberg: Springer International , 1997).

6. A. Skrzydlo, 'Transfrontier and Regional Cooperation in Poland', in P. Joenniemi and C. E. Stalvant, Eds., *Baltic Sea Politics: Achievements and Challenges*, (Copenhagen: Nordic Council, 1995) p. 35.

7. *Declaration of the Ronneby Baltic Sea meeting*, Ronneby, 2-3 September 1997. On Polish attitudes to the Baltic subregion see A. Kuklinski, Ed., *Baltic Europe in the Perspective of Global Change*, (Warsaw: Oficyna Naukowa, 1995).

8. A. A. Sergounin, 'Security in the Baltic Region: Russia's Perceptions and Search for New Identity', in Hedegaard and Lindstrom, Eds., North European and *Baltic Sea Integration Yearbook*.

9. P. Carlsen, *Confidence and Security Building Measures*, Workshop on Conflict and Security in the Baltic Region in a Long View, Conflict Studies Centre, Military Academy, Sandhurst (Mimeo, 1997).

10. Statement of the Russian Foreign Minister Andrei Kozyrev, 19 Janauary 1994.

11. D. Trenin, Untitled Mimeo, Workshop on Conflict and Security in the Baltic Region in a Long View, Conflict Studies Centre, Military Academy, Sandhurst (Mimeo, 1997).

12. The mechanisms of the 'Nordic balance' are much discussed in academic writing. See J. J. Holst, *Five Roads to Nordic Security*, (Oslo: Universitetsforlaget, 1974).

13. The restraint on the Nordic Council not to deal with foreign policy was a precondition for Finland's accession in 1954. Only in 1974 was this taboo broken in an open debate. In 1988 the first systematic overview of the Council's international cooperation activities was undertaken. The dual forces of European integration and subregionalization resulted in an overhaul of the Council's committee system in 1995.

14. The Aaland islands are close to the wealthiest region within the EU (Hamburg), while Mecklenburg-Vorpommern is at the opposite end of the spectrum with only 56 per cent of the average per capita EU income. Income disparities between Central and Eastern European countries and the West are tenfold in nominal measurements, although real purchasing power compar-

isons are apt to give better estimates. The hazardous redistribution of incomes and widening gaps in living standard in Russia show the rough type of 'Klondyke capitalism' which has emerged there.
15. Iver Neumann argues that 'the Baltic experience of the second half of the 1980s is a blatant example of the key role of intellectuals in region-building'. I. B. Neumann, 'A Nordic and/or a Baltic Sea Region? The Discursive Structure of Region-building', in C. Wellmann, *The Baltic Sea Region: Conflict or Co-operation?*, (Hamburg: Lit Verlag, 1992).
16. Various actors representing elected assemblies were also invited to the first Baltic Sea parliamentary conference in 1990.
17. Communication, former Soviet Foreign Minister Boris Pankin.
18. *Council of the Baltic Sea States*, (Tallinn: CBSS Monitor, 1994).
19. L. Kristoffersson and C. E. Stalvant, *Creating a Baltic Sea Agenda 21*, (Stockholm: Stockholm Environment Institute, 1996).
20. For an overview see C. E. Stalvant, *Actors Around the Baltic Sea*, (Stockholm: Swedish Ministry of Foreign Affairs, 1996).
21. Terms of reference point 20. One could compare this unexploited option with the practices of the EU's Council of Ministers and the Nordic Council.
22. The list of seminars and conferences held under the auspices of the CBSS or its committees comprised the following: Cross-border meetings (Helsinki, November 1993); Local self-government and democracy/relations betwen local and central government (Stockholm, October l994); Baltic Sea port and maritime transport (Naantali, November l994); Legal regulations and draft making (Helsinki, February l995); Networks and communication (Tampere, March l995); Status and functioning of non-governmental organizations (Tallinn, September 1995); Meeting of energy experts on the Baltic Ring (Tallinn, March l995); Customs and maritime transport (Bjornholm, May l995); Prospects and perspectives for the future development of maritime transport (Copenhagen, May l995); Trade related legislation to promote increased trade and investment (Stockholm, 1995); Combatting negative social consequences during the transition period to a market economy (Vilnius, November l993); and Cross-border cooperation (Karlskrona, March 1996).
23. E. Hansen, Ed., *Cooperation in the Baltic Sea Region, the Barents Region and the Black Sea Region: A Documentation Report*, Commissioned by the Royal Norwegian Ministry of Foreign Affairs, Fafo-paper 1997: 4, (Oslo: Fafo Institute of Applied Social Science, 1997) p. 13.
24. Communiquè, Helsinki, 1993.
25. *Declaration of the Foreign Ministers of the Baltic Sea States*, Copenhagen, 5–6 March l992.

5 The Visegrad Group and Beyond

1. The Speech of the President of the Czechoslovak Socialist Republic to the Polish Sejm and Senate, (25 January 1990) pp. 3–4.
2. A. Sabbat-Swidlicka, 'Havel in Poland: Beyond Bilateral Relations', *Report on Eastern Europe*, 1 (7) (16 February 1990) 37; and, 'Dienstbier Visit', Weekly Record of Events, 10–11 January 1990, Report on Eastern Europe, 1 (4) (26 January 1990) 52.
3. P. Moore, 'Bratislava and Bonn: Two Conferences on Europe's Future', *Report on Eastern Europe*, 1 (19) (11 May 1990) 43-4; and, J. B. Spero, *The Warsaw-Prague-Budapest Triangle: Central European Security After the Visegrad Summit*, Occassional Papers No. 31 (Warsaw: Polish Institute of International Affairs, 1992) p. 8.
4. 'Walesa Meets Havel', Weekly Record of Events, 17 March 1990, *Report on Eastern Europe*, 1 (13) (30 March 1990) 54; and, 'Hungarian Premier on his proposal for a Central-East European Union', *BBC Summary of World Broadcasts*, SWB EE/0862 (1990) A1/1.
5. I. Traynor, 'Moscow Defers Critical Summit', *The Guardian*, (24 October 1990); and S. Crow, 'International Department and Foreign Ministry Disagree on Eastern Europe', *Report on thhe USSR*, 3 (12 June 1991) 4–8.
6. R. L. Tokes, 'From Visegrad to Krakow: Cooperation, Competition, and Coexistence in Central Europe', *Problems of Communism,* XL (6) (Nov-Dec 1991) 104.
7. D. L. Clarke, 'Central Europe: Military Cooperation in the Triangle', *RFE/RL Research Report*, 1 (2) (10 January 1992) 42–3.
8. Spero, 'The Warsaw-Prague-Budapest Triangle', p. 7.
9. J. Obrman, 'Czechoslovakia: Putting the Country Back on the Map', *Report on Eastern Europe*, 1 (52) (28 December 1990) 13.
10. A. Reisch, 'Hungary: The Hard Task of Setting Relations with the USSR on a New Footing', *Report on Eastern Europe*, 2 (21) (24 May 1991) 9 and 11.
11. F. Harris, 'Czechs call for talks on quitting Warsaw Pact', *The Daily Telegraph*, (14 January 1991); and, I. Traynor, 'Central Europeans threaten to quit Warsaw Pact', *The Guardian,* (15 January 1991).
12. R. Boyes, 'East Europe split on Baltic unrest', *The Times*, (18 January 1991).
13. J. Warr, 'Three nations set deadline to quit the Warsaw Pact', *The Daily Telegraph*, (23 January 1991); S. R. Burant, 'Polish-Lithuanian Relations: Past, Present, and Future', *Problems of Communism*, XL (3) (May-June 1991) 76; and, Spero, 'The Warsaw-Prague-Budapest Triangle', p. 8.
14. V. V. Kusin, 'Gorbachev Agrees to Warsaw Pact Meeting on Military Structures', *Report on Eastern Europe*, 2 (22 February 1991) 44.
15. Text of the Visegrad Summit Declaration, *Report on Eastern Europe*, 2 (9) (1 March 1991) 31.
16. Text of the Visegrad Summit Declaration, 32.
17. Tokes, 'From Visegrad to Krakow', 111.

18. Tokes, 'From Visegrad to Krakow', 112; and, D. M. Perry, 'The Attempted Coup in the USSR: East European Reactions', *Report on Eastern Europe*, 2 (35) (30 August 1991) 2; 'Poland, Czechoslovakia, and Hungary Discuss Crisis', Weekly Record of Events, 20 August 1991, *Report on Eastern Europe*, 2 (35) (30 August 1991) 46; L. Vinton, 'The Attempted Coup in the Soviet Union: East European Reactions – Poland', *Report on Eastern Europe*, 2 (35) (30 August 1991) 12; and, 'President Urges Faster EC Association', Weekly Record of Events, 25 August 1991, *Report on Eastern Europe*, 2 (36) (6 September 1991) 40.
19. Tokes, 'From Visegrad to Krakow', 112; and, Perry, 'The Attempted Coup in the USSR: East European Reactions', 2; 'Poland, Czechoslovakia, and Hungary Discuss Crisis', 46; Vinton, 'The Attempted Coup in the Soviet Union: East European Reactions – Poland'; and, 'President Urges Faster EC Association', 40.
20. 'Partnership with the Countries of Central and Eastern Europe', Statement issued by the North Atlantic Council meeting in Ministerial Session in Copenhagen on 6 and 7 June 1991, *NATO Review*, 39 (June 1991) 28.
21. 'NATO Tells Moscow Not to Interfere', *The Times*, (4 July 1991).
22. 'The Situation in the Soviet Union', Statement issued by the North Atlantic Council meeting in Ministerial Session at NATO Headquarters, Brussels, on 21 August 1991, *NATO Review*, 39 (August 1991) 9. (Emphasis added).
23. I. Traynor, 'Fledgling Market Economies look to EC to End Trade Curbs', *The Guardian*, (21 August 1991).
24. Clarke, 'Central Europe: Military Cooperation in the Triangle', 44-5; and, '"State of Military Readiness" Maintained during Soviet Coup', Weekly Record of Events, 28 August 1991, *Report on Eastern Europe*, 2 (36) (6 September 1991) 41.
25. 'Walesa Views "Mutual Interdependence" With West', *Foreign Broadcast Information Service*, FBIS-EEU-91-196, (9 October 1991) 20.
26. 'Cracow Summit', Weekly Record of Events, 6 October 1991, *Report on Eastern Europe*, 2 (42) (18 October 1991) 41-2; J. B. de Weydenthal, 'The Cracow Summit', *Report on Eastern Europe*, 2 (43) (25 October 1991) 27; and, 'Statement Made at Cracow on 5 October 1991 by the Three Ministers for Foreign Affairs Concerning Cooperation with the North Atlantic Treaty Organization', Annex II, UN General Assembly Document A/C.1/46/7, (United Nations, 1991) p. 7.
27. 'Swifter Integration with EC Sought', Weekly Record of Events, 3 December 1991, *Report on Eastern Europe*, 2 (50) (13 December 1991) 37; 'Aid for the former USSR', RFE/RL Research Report, 1 (5) (31 January 1992) 72.; '"Triangle" Defense Ministers Meet', *RFE/RL Research Report*, 1 (12) (20 March 1992) 49–50; '"Triangle" Countries Seek Faster NATO Links', *RFE/RL Research Report*, 1 (15) (10 April 1992) 46; and, 'East European Recognition for Bosnia and Herzegovina', *RFE/RL Research Report*, 1 (16) (17 April 1992) 69.
28. Summit of the Visegrad Triangle, Prague, 5–6 May 1992, *Zbior*

Dokumentow/Receil De Documents, (Warsaw: Polish Institute of International Affairs, January-June 1992) pp. 173–81; and, 'Visegrad Triangle Foreign Ministers Meet EC Counterparts Before Prague Summit', and 'Conclusions of Visegrad Triangle Summit: Joint Application to Join EC', BBC Summary of World Broadcasts, SWB EE/1375 8, (May 1992) A2/1–1.

29. A. A. Reisch, 'No Plans for a Military Pact by the Visegrad Three', *RFE/RL Research Report*, 1 (40) (9 October 1992) 55; 'Visegrad Triangle Chiefs of Staff Meet', Military and Security Notes, *RFE/RL Research Report*, 1 (48) (4 December 1992) 59; and, 'Visegrad Defence Officials Meet', Military and Security Notes, *RFE/RL Research Report*, 1 (49) (11 December 1992) 64.

30. K. Okolocsanyi, 'The Visegrad Triangle's Free-Trade Zone', *RFE/RL Research Report*, 2 (3) (15 January 1993) 19–22.

31. D. J. Bartyzel, 'Knocking on the EC Door', *The Warsaw Voice*, (8 November 1992).

32. J. B. de Weydenthal, 'EC Keeps Central Europe at Arm's Length', *RFE/RL Research Report*, 2 (5) (29 January 1993) 31.

33. 'CSFR Politicians Reportedly See No Future in Visegrad Three Cooperation', *Summary of World Broadcasts – Eastern Europe*, SWB EE/1374 (7 May 1992) A2/2.

34. J. Obrman, 'The Central European Triangle: Czechoslovakia Overcomes Its Initial Reluctance', RFE/RL Research Report, 1 (23) (5 June 1992) 20; and, A. A. Reisch, 'The Central European Triangle: Hungary Sees Common Goals and Bilateral Issues', *RFE/RL Research Report*, 1 (23) (5 June 1992) 26.

35. M. A. Vachudova, 'The Visegrad Four: No Alternative to Cooperation?', *RFE/RL Research Report*, 2 (34) (27 August 1993) 41–2.

36. 'Visegrad Group Appeals for EC Membership', *RFE/RL News Briefs*, 2 (7–11 June 1993) 13.

37. 'Visegrad Defense Officials Meet in Poland', *RFE/RL News Briefs*, 2 (6–10 September 1993) 13–14.

38. G. Kolankiewicz, 'Consensus and Competition in the Eastern Enlargement of the European Union', *International Affairs*, 70 (July 1994) 484.

39. I. Traynor, J. Borger, and S. Tisdall, 'East European quartet out of synch over NATO', *The Guardian*, (7 January 1994).

40. 'Czechs opt to Act Alone on NATO Issue', *International Herald Tribune*, (7 January 1994).

41. A. LeBor, 'Poles accuse Czechs of hijacking prestige visit', *The Times*, (12 January 1994).

42. 'Klaus on Czech Republic's EU Membership', *RFE/RL News Briefs*, 3 (7–11 March 1994) 19.

43. Kolankiewicz, 'Consensus and Competition in the Eastern Enlargement of the European Union', 480.

44. S. Fisher, 'Slovakia is Falling Behind', *The Wall Street Journal*, (20–21 December 1996).

45. NATO's September 1995 study on the rationale and modalities of its enlarge-

ment made clear that decisions on which countries to invite to join the Alliance would be made on the basis of countries individual merits rather than on a group basis. NATO, *Study on NATO Enlargement*, (Brussels: NATO, September 1995) p. 4 and p. 27.
46. 'Poland, Hungary, CSFR to Sign Treaty with EEC', *Foreign Broadcast Information Service – Eastern Europe*, 91–218 (12 November 1991) 1.
47. Vachudova, 'The Visegrad Four: No Alternative to Cooperation?', 41.
48. Thus, Poland signed bilateral cooperation treaties with Czechoslovakia and Hungary at the October 1991 Cracow summit, but the Hungarian-Czechoslovak treaty remained unsigned because of the disputes over the Hungarian minority in Slovakia and the Gabcikovo-Nagymaros dam.
49. Clarke, 'Central Europe: Military Cooperation in the Triangle', 44.
50. On the concept of a security community, se K. W. Deutsch et al, *Political Community in the North Atlantic Area: International Organization in the Light of Historical Experience*, (New York: Greenwood Press, 1969).
51. For a good discussion of the prospects for the emerging security community in Central and Eastern Europe, see I. Gambles, Ed., *A Lasting Peace in Central Europe?*, Chaillot Paper 20 (Paris: Institute for Security Studies Western European Union, October 1995).
52. Text of the Visegrad Summit Declaration, 32.
53. A. Hyde-Price, *The International Politics of East-Central Europe*, (Manchester and New York: Manchester University Press, 1996) p. 124.
54. B. Nahaylo, 'Ukraine and the Visegrad Triangle', *RFE/RL Research Report,* 1 (23) (5 June 1992) 28-9.
55. P. Dunay, O. Pavliuk and W. Zajaczkowski, *The Effects of Enlargement on Bilateral Relations in Central and Eastern Europe*, Chaillot Papers 26 (Paris: Institute for Security Studies Western European Union, June 1997).
56. J. Pehe, 'Improving Czech-Polish Relations', *OMRI Analytical Brief*, 67 (15 April 1996) 3; and, 'Deal makers, not pilots, will decide fighter jet race', NATO in Focus, *Warsaw Business Journal*, (14–20 July 1997) S7.
57. 'Poland and Hungary on the path towards Euro-Atlantic Integration', Lecture by Aleksander Kwasniewski, President of the Republic of Poland, Budapest, 21 January 1997, pp. 3–4.

6. The Central European Free Trade Agreement

1. D. Rosati, *After the CMEA Collapse: Is the Central European Payments Union Really Necessary?*, (Warsaw: Foreign Trade Research Institute, 1991).
2. Text of formal declaration as cited in *Materialy i Dokumenty* BSE, No.7, (Warsaw: Office of the Polish Parliament, March 1992).
3. 'The Cracow Declaration' (6 October 1991) in *European Security*, 1 (1) (Spring 1992) pp.104–8.
4. J. Kaczurba, *The Impact of CEFTA*, mimeo, (Warsaw: November 1996).
5. *Poland's Foreign Trade Results in 1995: Annual Report*, (Warsaw: Ministry of

Foreign Economic Relations, 1996) p. 51.
6. See P. Bocyk, 'Kraje Grupy Wyszehradzkiej, Razem czy osobno do Unii Europejskiej', *Rynki Zagraniczne*, 12 (1996); A. Kupich, 'Problemy rozwoju pozahandlowych form wspupracy godpodarczej paostw CEFTA', *Gospodarka i Przyszoúe*, 2 (1996); A. Rudka and K. Mizsei, *East Central Europe Between Disintegration and Reintegration: Is CEFTA the Solution?*, (New York: Institute for EastWest Studies, 1995); and proceedings of a conference on 'The Future Development of CEFTA: Institutionalization, Deepening, Widening', organized by the Friedrich Ebert Foundation, Warsaw, 28–30 November 1996.
7. See A. Kupich, *Partnerstwo dla transformacji*, (Warsaw, Polish Institute of International Affairs, 1994); and Z. Madej, *Rynki wschodnie w handlu zagranicznym krajuw CEFTA: CEFTA a integracja ekonomiczna w Europie*, (Warsaw: Warsaw School of Economics, 1996).
8. 'Slovak Cabinet...', *OMRI Daily Digest II*, 32 (14 February 1996) 3.

7 The Central European Initiative

1. Research for this chapter is chiefly based on CEI documents, but also on (mostly unattributable) conversations with CEI officials.
2. F. Herre, *Kaiser Franz Joseph von Osterreich: Sein Leben-Seine Zeit*, (Koln: Verlag Kiepenheuerig, 1978).
3. C. Magris, *Danube,* (London: Collins-Houwill, 1989).
4. On Italian interest in Central and Eastern Europe see V. Mastny, Ed., *Italy and East Central Europe: Dimensions of the Regional Relationship*, (Boulder: Westview Press, 1995).
5. P. Moore, 'New Dimension of the Alpine-Adria Project', *Report on Eastern Europe*, 1 (9) (2 March 1990) 53–6.
6. V. V. Kusin, 'The Initiative from Venice', *Report on Eastern Europe*, 1 (33) (17 August 1990) 26–9; and, 'The Empire Strikes Back', *The Economist*, (25 August 1990).
7. *Report from the Commission to the Council on European Union Cooperation with the Central European Initiative*, COM (96) 601 Final, (Brussels: European Commission, 4 December 1996).
8. A. Unterberger, *Die Presse*, (9 November 1996).
9. For a similar assessment of the CEI see A. A. Reisch, 'The Central European Initiative: To Be or Not to Be?', *RFE/RL Research Report*, 2 (34) (27 August 1993) 30–7.
10. Mastny, Ed., *Italy and East Central Europe*.

8 The Black Sea Economic Cooperation

1. The author would like to thank the BSEC Permanent Secretariat for assistance in obtaining BSEC materials and documents and Mr. Andrii Kononenko,

Notes and References 267

Acting Director of the Department for International Economic Cooperation of the Foreign Ministry of Ukraine for his advice and assistance.

2. See E. Fuller, 'The Tussle for Influence in Central Asia and the Transcaucasus', *Transition*, (14 June 1996) 11–16.
3. See 'Summit Declaration on Black Sea Economic Cooperation' and 'The Bosphorus Statement', Istanbul, 25 June 1992, in *Black Sea Economic Cooperation: Handbook of Documents*, Volume One, (Istanbul: Black Sea Economic Cooperation Permanent International Secretariat, July 1995) pp. 3–10.
4. See Rules of Procedure of the Black Sea Economic Cooperation, in *Black Sea Economic Cooperation: Handbook of Documents*, Volume One, pp. 517–31.
5. See T. Bukkvoll, 'The Black Sea Region', in E. Hansen, Ed., *Cooperation in the Baltic Sea Region, the Barents Region and the Black Sea Region: A Documentation Report*, Commissioned by the Royal Norwegian Ministry of Foreign Affairs, Fafo-paper 1997: 4, (Oslo: Fafo Institute of Applied Social Science, 1997) pp. 40–1.
6. Declaration on the Establishment of the Parliamentary Assembly of the Black Sea Economic Cooperation, in *Biannual Bulletin of the PABSEC*, (1994) p. 7.
7. *Document File, Meeting of the Senior Officials of the BSEC Participating States, Moscow, 22–4 October 1996*, (Istanbul: Black Sea Economic Cooperation Permanent International Secretariat, 1996) p. 22.
8. *Meeting of the Ministers of Foreign Affairs, Moscow, 25 October 1996, Resolutions, Decisions and Recommendations* (Istanbul: Black Sea Economic Cooperation Permanent International Secretariat, 1996), p. 9.
9. T. Bukkvoll, 'The Black Sea Region', p. 43.
10. V. Aleksandrov, 'Chernoie more. Na povestke dnia – ekologicheskaia bezopasnost', *Mezhdunarodnaia zhyzn'*, 1 (1997) 25–36.
11. Summit Declaration on Black Sea Economic Cooperation, Istanbul, 25 June 1992, in *Black Sea Economic Cooperation: Handbook of Documents*, Volume One, p. 5.
12. Author's interviews with Ukrainian Foreign Ministry officials, December 1996 and January 1997.
13. See *The Progress Report on the Operations and Activities of the BSEC Permanent International Secretariat* (27 April – 25 October 1996), (Istanbul: Black Sea Economic Cooperation Permanent International Secretariat, 1996) p. 3.
14. O. F. Genckaya, 'The Black Sea Economic Cooperation Project: A Regional Challenge to European Integration', *International Social Science Journal*, XLVI (1993) 551.
15. D. B. Sezer, 'Balance of Power in the Black Sea' in M. Drohobycky, Ed., *Post-Cold War Era: Russia, Turkey, and Ukraine in Crimea: Dynamics, Challenges, and Prospects,* (American Association for the Advancement of Science, 1995) p. 163.
16. M. Drohobycky, Ed., *Post-Cold War Era: Russia, Turkey, and Ukraine in Crimea*, pp. 549–56.
17. See E. Fuller, 'The Tussle for Influence in Central Asia and the

Transcaucasus', 11–15.
18. For further information on Turkish-Russian tensions in the Black Sea see D. B. Sezer, 'Balance of Power in the Black Sea', pp. 155–94.
19. *Izvestiia*, (3 October 1996).
20. See, for example, V. Nadein-Raievsky, 'Turtsiia, Rossiia i tiurkoiazychnyie narody poslie raspada SSSR', *Mirovaia ekonomika I mezhdunarodnyie otnosheniia*, IV (1994) 39-50 and D. Trenin, 'Komu prinadliezhyt Chornoie more?', *Novoie vriemia* XVIII-XIX (1996) 31–7.
21. E. Fuller, 'The Tussle for Influence in Central Asia and the Transcaucasus', 15.
22. See H. Poulton, 'Playing the Kinship Card in the Balkans', *Transition*, (14 June 1996) 16–20.
23. Author's interviews with Ukrainian Foreign Ministry officials, December 1996 and January 1997.
24. S. Berindei, 'Cooperarea in Zona Marii Negre, un act politic', *Natiunea*, XXVII (1995).
25. The fact that the BSEC contributes to the 'deepening of all-European integration' was emphasized by President Kuchma in his address to the International conference on 'New Possibilities in the Black Sea Region' held on 28 April 1997 in Istanbul, see *Uriadovyi Kurier*, (6 May 1997).
26. *Moscow Declaration of the Heads of State and Government of the Participating States of the Black Sea Economic Cooperation.*
27. *Moscow Declaration of the Heads of State and Government of the Participating States of the Black Sea Economic Cooperation.*
28. *Report of the Meeting of the Ministers of Internal Affairs of the BSEC Participating States*, Yerevan, 17 October 1996, pp. 2–8.
29. *The Report of the Seventh Meeting of the Ministers of Foreign Affairs of the BSEC, Bucharest, 27 April 1996*, (Istanbul: Black Sea Economic Cooperation Permanent International Secretariat, 1996) pp. 103–4.
30. *Moscow Declaration of the Heads of State and Government of the Participating States of the Black Sea Economic Cooperation.*
31. O. Waever and H. Wiberg, 'Baltic Sea/Black Sea: Regionalization on the Fringes of the 'New Europe', in *Regionalism –Concepts and Approaches at the Turn of the Century*, (Bucharest: Romanian Institute of International Relations, 1995) p. 220.
32 *Meeting of the Ministers of Foreign Affairs*, Bucharest, 27 April 1996, p. 104.
33. *Report of the Eighth Meeting of the Ministers of Foreign Affairs, Moscow, 25 October 1996*, (Istanbul: Black Sea Economic Cooperation Permanent International Secretariat) p. 4.
34. See the address of the President of Georgia Eduard Shevardnadze at the BSEC summit in Bucharest on 30 June 1995, in *Romania Business Journal*, (1995) 8.
35. T. Bukkvoll, 'The Black Sea Region', p. 45.

9. The Role of Subregional Cooperation in Post-Cold War Europe

1. The opinions expressed in this chapter are the author's own and should not be construed as representing official British policy. Parts of this material are adapted, by permission, from a lecture delivered at Leangkollen, Norway in March 1997 and published by the Norwegian Foreign Policy Institute.
2. On the range of security policy options open to the countries of Central and Eastern Europe after 1989 see A. Cottey, *East-Central Europe after the Cold War: Poland, the Czech Republic, Slovakia and Hungary in Search of Security*, (Houndmills and London: Macmillan, 1995) chapter 2, pp. 13–26; C. Gasteyger, 'The Remaking of Eastern Europe's Security', *Survival*, XXXIII (1991) 111–24; J. M. O. Sharp, 'Security Options for Central Europe in the 1990s', in B. Crawford, Ed., *The Future of European Security*, (University of California, Berkeley: Center for German and European Studies, 1992) pp. 54–78; A. G. V. Hyde-Price, 'After the Pact: East European Security in the 1990s', *Arms Control*, 12 (September 1991) 279–302; and J. Orme, 'Security in East Central Europe: Seven Futures', *The Washington Quarterly*, 14 (Summer 1991) 91–105.
3. See chapter 5 on the Visegrad group in this volume.
4. See chapter 3 on the BEAC in this volume.
5. This was most obviously the case with CEFTA, but also applied to varying degrees to the other subregional groups in the Barents-Black Sea belt.
6. See chapters 6, 7 and 8 on CEFTA, the CEI, and the BSEC in this volume.
7. See A. J. K. Bailes, 'Subregional Organizations: The Cinderellas of European Security', *NATO Review*, 45 (2) (March 1997) 29.
8. On Finnish and Swedish debates on Baltic cooperation and their relations with the Baltic states and NATO, see R. D. Asmus and R. C. Nurick, 'NATO Enlargement and the Baltic States', *Survival*, 38 (2) 126–7 and 132–3.
9. NATO's 1995 study on enlargement stated that 'each invitation to join the Alliance will be decided on its own merits, case by case'. NATO, *Study on NATO Enlargement*, (Brussels: NATO, September 1995) p. 27.
10. The OSCE's December 1996 Lisbon Summit statement encouraged 'bilateral or regional initiatives aimed at developing relations of good neighbourliness and cooperation'. OSCE, *Lisbon Document 1996*, (OSCE: Lisbon, 1996) p. 7. Reflecting its growing interest in this area, the OSCE held an official seminar on 'Regional Security and Cooperation' in Vienna in June 1997 – for more on this see chapter 10 in this volume.
11. See chapters 5 and 6 on the Visegrad group and CEFTA in this volume.
12. The four Visegrad states were systematically consulted by NATO in the run-up to the formal CFE Treaty revision discussions in 1997.
13. See chapters 5 and 6 on the Visegrad group and CEFTA in this volume.
14. In 1996, for example, Finland and Sweden submitted a joint proposal on the EU's future military/peacekeeping role – see A. Bailes, 'Europe's Defense Challenge', *Foreign Affairs*, 76 (1) (January/February 1997) 17–18.

15. See chapter 3 on the BEAC in this volume.
16. The OSCE's 'Framework for Arms Control' was adopted at its December 1996 Lisbon summit – see OSCE, *Lisbon Document 1996*, pp. 13–7.
17. The related issue of subregionalism within NATO's own outreach programmes is examined in more detail in chapter 10 of this volume.
18. S. Jervell, '"Top-down" and "Bottom-up" Region Building: Some Notes on Barents Cooperation', paper presented at the Institute for EastWest Studies conference 'Multi-Layered Integration: The Subregional Dimension', Bucharest, 7–8 October 1996.
19. See chapter 8 on the BSEC in this volume.
20. See, for example, the statement from the CBSS's 1996 Visby summit – *Baltic Sea States Summit 1996 – Presidency Declaration*, (Visby: 3–4 May 1996).
21. See chapter 3 on the BEAC in this volume.
22. See chapters 5 and 6 on the Visegrad group and CEFTA in this volume.
23. On Kaliningrad see L. D. Fairlie, 'Kaliningrad: NATO and EU Enlargement Issues Focus New Attention on Russia's Border with Central Europe', *Boundary and Security Bulletin*, 4 (Autumn 1996) 61–9.
24. *A Future Security Agenda for Europe*, Report of the Independent Working Group established by the Stockholm International Peace Research Institute, (Stockholm: SIPRI, October 1996).
25. On the various 'bottom-up' elements of subregional cooperation see E. Hansen, Ed., *Cooperation in the Baltic Sea Region, the Barents Region and the Black Sea Region: A Documentation Report,* Commissioned by the Royal Norwegian Ministry of Foreign Affairs, Fafo-paper 1997: 4, (Oslo: Fafo Institute of Applied Social Science, 1997).
26. On the Transcarpathian Euroregion see M. F. Bukovetski, 'Case Study of the Carpathian Euroregion', in V. Hudak, Ed., *Building a New Europe: Transfrontier Cooperation in Central Europe*, (Prague: Institute for EastWest Studies, 1996) pp. 83–88.
27. On transfrontier cooperation generally see Hudak, Ed., *Building a New Europe*.
28. When substantive BEAC cooperative activities began in 1996 the Norwegian government committed approximately ten million ECU to support them. See E. Hansen, 'The Barents Region' in Hansen, Ed., *Cooperation in the Baltic Sea Region, the Barents Region and the Black Sea Region*, p. 31.
29. The Council of Europe's role in supporting subregional cooperation, in particular transfrontier cooperation, is explored in more detail in chapter 10 of this volume.
30. V. Hudak, 'Transfrontier Cooperation in Central Europe: Current Status and Future Challenges', in Hudak, Ed., *Building a New Europe*, pp. 8–10.
31. Council of Europe, *Explanatory Report on the European Outline Convention on Transfrontier Cooperation between Territorial Communities or Authorities*, No. 106, (Strasbourg: Council of Europe, 1980).
32. The Institute for EastWest Studies, for example, itself guided the early years

Notes and References 271

of the Transcarpathian Euroregion and is now working to transfer relevant expertise for new transfrontier regimes being planned inter alia in the Baltic.

10 Subregional Cooperation and the New European Security Architecture

1. The author would like thank Alyson Bailes for helpful comments on and contributions to this chapter.
2. *CSCE Helsinki Document 1992: The Challenges of Change*, p. 7, p. 11 and p. 61.
3. *Budapest Summit Declaration: CSCE Budapest Document 1994, Towards a Genuine Partnership in a New Era*, Budapest, 1994, (London: HMSO, Cm 3182, April 1996), p.24 and p. 6.
4. *CSCE Helsinki Documnt 1992: The Challenges of Change*, p. 36, p.41 and p.42.
5. Organization for Security and Cooperation in Europe, *Lisbon Document 1996*, (OSCE: Lisbon, 1996), p. 13, p. 16 and pp. 19–20; and *Budapest Summit Declaration*, p. 5, p.2, p.13 and p. 14.
6. Author's discussions with representatives of various OSCE delegations in Vienna.
7. For example, seeking to counter-balance tensions with its neighbours over border disputes and minority rights, Hungary has been particularly active in this area (– see A. Cottey, *East-Central Europe After the Cold War: Poland, the Czech Republic, Slovakia and Hungary in Search of Security*, (Houndmills and London: Macmillan, 1995), chapter 6 and pp. 93–125. Most Central and Eastern European states have concluded various military cooperation and confidence building measures with their immediate neighbours.
8. Organization for Security and Cooperation in Europe, *Vienna Document 1994 of the Negotiations on Confidence – and Security-Building Measures*, (Vienna: OSCE, 1994).
9. On the Stability Pact see C. Guicherd, *Securing Central Europe: Will the Stability Pact Do?*, Paper for Institute for Public Policy Research Conference on 'The Root Causes of Forced Migration', London, 27–8 November 1995; and 'Whose Stability Pact?', *The Economist*, (18 March 1995).
10. Author's discussions with representatives of various OSCE delegations in Vienna.
11. *Lisbon Document 1996*, p. 2 and pp. 7–8.
12. *OSCE Seminar within the framework of the Common and Comprehensive Security Model for Europe for the Twenty-First Century, 'Regional Security and Cooperation', Vienna, 2–4 June 1997, Chairman's Summary*, (Organization for Security and Cooperation in Europe, Permanent Council, REF.PC/502/97, 4 June 1997).
13. *OSCE Seminar... 'Regional Security and Cooperation'... Chairman's Summary*, pp1–3. (The author attended the seminar as a representative of the Institute for EastWest Studies).
14. The December 1996 Lisbon summit declaration mandated OSCE delegations in Vienna to continue work on the Security Model and referred to the possibility of a new OSCE Charter. The relationship between the two was,

however, not clear. See *Lisbon Document 1996*, pp. 8–9.
15. These ideas are based on discussions at the OSCE's seminar on 'Regional Security and Cooperation' and proposals submitted to the OSCE by the Institute for EastWest Studies in autumn 1996. See *OSCE Seminar... 'Regional Security and Cooperation'... Chairman's Summary; OSCE Seminar within the framework of the Common and Comprehensive Security Model for Europe for the Twenty-First Century, 'Regional Security and Cooperation', Vienna, 2–4 June 1997, Report on the discussion in Working Group I: Institutional Framework*, (Organization for Security and Cooperation in Europe, Permanent Council, REF.PC/499/97, 4 June 1997); *OSCE Seminar within the framework of the Common and Comprehensive Security Model for Europe for the Twenty-First Century, 'Regional Security and Cooperation', Vienna, 2–4 June 1997, Report on the discussion in Working Group II: Measures in Support of Regional Security and Cooperation*, (Organization for Security and Cooperation in Europe, Permanent Council, REF.PC/467/97, 4 June 1997); and Institute for EastWest Studies, *Multi-Layered Integration: The Sub-Regional Dimension –An Interim Report with Recommendations Addressed to the Chairman-in-Office of OSCE and OSCE Participating States*, (IEWS: Warsaw, October 1996).
16. *Lisbon Document 1996*, pp. 7–8.
17. *Lisbon Document 1996*, p. 7; and 'A Menu of Sub-Regional CSBMs: Enjoy Your Meal!!!', Keynote address by Jacques Werner, Security Policy Department, Ministry of Foreign Affairs, The Netherlands, Working Group II: Measures in Support of Regional Security and Cooperation, OSCE Seminar on Regional Security and Cooperation, Vienna, 2–4 June 1997 (OSCE: REF.PC/483/97, 3 June 1997).
18. Author's discussions with members of OSCE delegations, Vienna.
19. *OSCE Seminar... 'Regional Security and Cooperation'... Chairman's Summary*, p. 3.
20. In 1993, the OSCE concluded a formal cooperation agreement with the United Nations which defined means of liaison between the two organizations and possible areas for cooperation. In 1997, any similar agreement between the OSCE and any of the European subregional groups seemed premature. For the OSCE-UN agreement, see 'Framework for Cooperation and Co-ordination Between the United Nations Secretariat and the Conference on Security and Cooperation in Europe, New York, 26 May 1993', in Stockholm International Peace Research Institute, *SIPRI Yearbook 1994*, (Oxford: Oxford University Press/SIPRI, 1994) pp. 240–1.
21. Council of Europe, *Explanatory Report on the European Outline Convention on Transfrontier Cooperation between Territorial Communities or Authorities*, No 106, (Strasbourg: Council of Europe, 1980).
22. See K. Schumann and N. Levrat in V. Hudak, Ed., *Building a New Europe: Transfrontier Cooperation in Central Europe*, (Prague: Institute for EastWest Studies, 1996).

23. *Additional Protocol to the European Outline Convention on Transfrontier Cooperation between Territorial Communities or Authorities*, (Strasbourg: Council of Europe, 1995).
24. The Council of Europe's priorities for action in Bosnia-Herzegovina include the reconstruction and training of local authorities and the creation of ties between them and 'model' European partners from outside. See *Council of Europe action in Bosnia and Herzegovina: Priority Areas*, (Strasbourg: Council of Europe, November 1996).
25. *Baltic Sea Region Initiative, Communication from the Commission*, (Brussels: European Commission, 10 April 1996) SEC (96) 608 Final.
26. J. Declerck (DG1A, European Commission), 'Baltic Sea Region Cooperation', (Mimeo, 18 November 1996); and, J. Declerck, 'The Baltic Sea Cooperation', Euopean Conference, Petersberg Bonn, 16 December 1996.
27. *Report from the Commission to the Council on European Union Cooperation with the Central European Initiative,* (Brussels: Commission of the European Communities, 4 December 1996) COM (96) 601 Final.
28. *INTERRG II: Barents Region 1995-1999*, European Regional Development Fund/European Social Fund (Brussels: European Commission, Directorate General for Regional Policies and Cohesion) No. FEDER: 950010017/No. ARINCO: 95EU16017.
29. *European Council in Edinburgh – 11 and 12 December 1992, Conclusions of the Presidency*, DN: DOC/92/8 (13 December 1992) (European Commission web-site: http://europe.eu.int/rapid/cgi/rapcgi.ksh?reslist).
30. On the Commission's 'opinions' see 'Joining the Club', *The Economist*, (12 July 1997) 23–4.
31. 'NATO's Woerner Discusses East European Security', *Foreign Broadcast Information Service – Eastern Europe*, 91–218, (12 November 1991) 21.
32. 'Work Plan for Dialgoue, Partnership and Cooperation', Documentation, *NATO Review*, 40 (April 1992) 34; and, 'Statement Issued at the Meeting of Defence Ministers at NATO Headquarters, Brussels on 1st April 1992', Documentation, *NATO Review*, 40 (April 1992) 32.
33. M. Ruhle and N. Williams, 'Partnership for Peace after NATO Enlargement', *European Security*, 5 (4) (Winter 1996) 524.
34. NATO, *Study on NATO Enlargement*, (Brussels: NATO, September 1995) p. 4 and p. 27.
35. *Basic Document of the Euro-Atlantic Partnership Council*, Press Release M-NACC-EAPC-1(97)66, (30 May 1997) (NATO web-site: http://www.nato.int/docu/pr/p97–066e.htm).
36. *Final Communique, Meeting of the North Atlantic Council in Defence Ministers Session, Press Release M-NAC-D-1(97)71*, Brussels, (12 June 1997) (NATO web-site: http://www.nato.int/docu/pr/p97-071e.htm).
37. *Madrid Declaration on Euro-Atlantic Security and Cooperation, Issued by the Heads of State and Government, Press Release M–1(97)81, Meeting of the North Atlantic Council*, Madrid, (8 July 1997) (NATO web-site:

http://www.nato.int/docu/pr/p97-081e.htm).
38. *Summary, Press Release S-APHSG–1(97)84, Meeting of Allied and Partner Heads of State and Government under the Aegis of the Euro-Atlantic Partnership Council, Madrid,* (9 July 1997) (NATO web-site: http://www.nato.int/docu/pr/p97-084e.htm); and, *Press Statement of the Secretary General, Following the Meeting of Allied and Partner Heads of State and Government, Madrid,* (9 July 1997) (NATO web-site: http://www.nato.int/docu/speech/s199709e.htm).
39. Declaration of the Heads of State and Government participating in the meeting of the North Atlantic Council held at NATO Headquarters, Brussels, on 10–11 January 1994, *NATO Review*, 42 (1) (February 1994) 30–31.
40. *Ministerial Meeting of the North Atlantic Council in Berlin, 3 June 1996,* Press Communique M-NAC-1 (96) 63 (3 June 1996) 11.
41. *Final Communique, Meeting of the North Atlantic Council in Defence Ministers Session, Press Release M-NAC-D-1(97)71, Brussels,* (12 June 1997) (NATO web-site: http://www.nato.int/docu/pr/p97-071e.htm).
42. R. D. Asmus and F. S. Larrabee, 'NATO and the Have-Nots: Reassurance After Enlargement', *Foreign Affairs*, 75 (6) (November/December 1996) 18–9.
43. L. Tindemans, et al, *Unfinished Peace: Report of the International Commission on the Balkans,* (Berlin/Washington, DC: Aspen Institute/Carnegie Endowment for International Peace, 1996) p. 168.
44. *Extraordinary Meeting of the WEU Council of Ministers with States of Central Europe, Bonn, 19 June 1992, Declaration.* (NATO website: gopher://marvin.nc3a.nato.int/00/Other_International/weu/PRESS/1992/19-06-92.e%09%09%2B); and *Western European Union, Kirchberg Declaration, 9 May 1994*, pp6–8. (NATO website: gopher://marvin.stc.nato.int/00/Other_International/weu/COM/com0905.94).
45. Western European Union, *European Security: A Common Concept of the 27 WEU Countries*, WEU Council of Ministers, Madrid, 14 November 1995, p27. (NATO website: gopher://marvin.stc.nato.int/00/Other_International/weu/COM/concepte.txt).
46. Presentation by Dr. Monika Wohlfeld (Institute for Security Studies Western European Union) on WEU and Sub-Regional Cooperation, summarised in A. Cottey and A. J. K. Bailes, *Sub-Regional Cooperation in the New Europe: Current Issues and Future Prospects – Summary of an Intergovernmental Conference, Bratislava, 7–8 April 1997*, (Warsaw: Institute for EastWest Studies, 1997).
47. Some analysts have suggested that WEU membership might be offered to Central and Eastern European states as an alternative to NATO membership, but this never appears to have been seriously considered within WEU. See S. Rogov, 'Russia, NATO and Western European Union', Chapter 6 in A. Deighton, *Western European Union 1954–1997: Defence, Security, Integration,* (Oxford: European Interdependence Research Unit, St. Anthony's College, 1997), pp. 79–91.

48. *Western European Union, Council of Ministers, Bonn, 19 June 1992, Petersberg Declaration*, II. On Strengthening WEU's Operational Role, p. 1.

11 Emerging Subregional Cooperation Processes

1. The section of this chapter on South-Eastern Europe was written by Sophia Clement, that on the Newly Independent States by Ian Bremmer, that on the Mediterranean by Thanos Dokos and the introduction and conclusion by Andrew Cottey.
2. This scenario assumes that over the next decade or so (approximately 1997 to 2010) the majority of the current Central and Eastern European Associates of the EU will join the EU and/or NATO. It remains conceivable that the processes of NATO and EU enlargement could be more limited and slower (or could even collapse entirely) or, alternatively, that NATO and the EU could enlarge more widely and more quickly. As of 1997, however, the middle path between these two extremes seemed more likely. For a good summary of the overall dynamics of the EU and NATO enlargement processes by 1997, see W. Wallace, 'On the Move – Destination Unknown', *The World Today*, 53 (4) (April 1997) 99–102.
3. Called the 'Stoica Plan', after the then Romanian Prime Minister, the initiative seems to have been driven both by Romania's wish to pursue a more independent foreign policy and, directly or indirectly, by the Soviet Union.
4. In the 1980s, under Prime Minister Constantine Karamanlis, these attempts aimed at enhancing Greece's record of good neighbourliness in the subregion in view of its application for membership of the European Union. In the 1980s, the Papandreou government, trying to have a more independent policy with regard to the United States and the European Union, initiated an 'equal distance policy' at the subregional level. It was also trying to balance tense relations with Turkey over the Aegean and Cyprus.
5. *Sofia Declaration on Good-Neighbourly Relations, Stability, Security and Cooperation in the Balkans*, Conference in Sofia on 6–7 July 1996, of the Ministers of Foreign Affairs of seven countries of South Eastern Europe (Albania, Bosnia-Herzegovina, Bulgaria, Federal Republic of Yugoslavia, Greece, Romania and Turkey); and *Thessaloniki Declaration on Good-Neighbourly Relations, Stability, Security and Co-operation in the Balkans*, Conference of the Ministers of Foreign Affairs of countries of South Eastern Europe, 9–10 June 1997.
6. S. Economides, *The Balkan Agenda: Security and Regionalism in the New Europe*, London Defence Studies, (London: Center for Defence Studies/Brassey's, 1992).
7. J. Gow, 'Enlargement in the Balkan Mirror', *War Report*, (June/July 1997).
8. S. Calleya, *Navigating Regional Dynamics in the Post-Cold War World*, (Dartmouth, 1997).
9. *Barcelona Declaration*, November 1995.

10. Examples of projects include the South East Mediterranean Development/SEMED, the Jordan Rift Valley, the Taba-Eilat-Aqaba-Macro Area/TEAM, and the Regional Economic Development Working Group/REDWG.
11. J. Redmond and R. Pace, 'European Security in the 1990s and Beyond: The Implications of the Accession of Cyprus and Malta to the EU', *Contemporary Security Policy*, 17 (3) (December 1996).

Index

"Agenda 21", 14, 60
Alpe-Adria Working Group, 113-4, 115
Andersson, Sven, Swedish Foreign Minister, 56
Antall, Joszef, Hungarian Prime Minister, 71, 72, 73, 77
Arctic subregion, 8, 23, 24, 26, 32, 39
Asia, 26, 128

Baltic Sea subregion/region, 5, 32, 38, 46-68
  Comprehensive Environmental Action Programme, 58
  and European Union, 65-6, 198
  Nuclear weapon free zone, 57
Baltic states, 49, 50, 51, 52, 53, 54, 55, 58, 63
  and Nordic States, 51, 53, 68
  Baltic peacekeeping battalion, 52
Barents subregion, 23-45, 51, 53
Barents Euro-Arctic Council (BEAC), 3, 5, 6, 8, 23-45, 52, 244, 246
  and European Union, 199-200
  Regional Council, 25, 26, 27-8, 29, 36
Belarus, 67
Benelux cooperation, 6, 10, 112
Black Sea subregion, 8, 32, 128-50
Black Sea Economic Cooperation (BSEC), 3, 5, 6, 8, 128-50, 244, 246
  Black Sea Trade and Development Bank (BSTDB), 130, 136-7, 140, 146, 147
  enlargement, 131-2
  and European Union, 136, 140, 145-6, 199
  free trade area, 135
  future prospects, 147-50
  history, 128-32
  Parliamentary Assembly, 130-1, 135
  Permanent International Secretariat (PERMIS), 130, 136, 145, 149
  political/security dimension, 141-4, 150
  and Russia, 139-40
  and Turkey, 139-40
Bulgaria, 101

Canada, 24
Caspian Sea, 132, 226

Caucasus, 5, 213, 226, 228, 231, 247
Central and Eastern Europe, 3, 18, 19, 36, 50, 51, 54, 55, 69, 80, 88-9, 184, 151
  economic links, 92-8, 111-2
  and subregional cooperation 153-7
  and transfrontier cooperation, 177-81
Central Asia, 5, 213, 226, 227-8, 247
Central Europe, 5, 31, 38, 51, 73
  and European Union, 72, 77, 81-2, 85
  military cooperation, 75, 78, 82-3
  Visegrad group and security, 80-4
Central European Free Trade Agreement (CEFTA), 3, 4, 5, 6, 8, 70, 90-112, 158, 244, 246
  Brno Heads of Government meeting, September 1995, 101-2
  enlargement, 109
  and European Union, 101, 109-10, 200-2
  future prospects, 106-11
  Poznan Prime Ministers meeting, November 1994, 101
  trade liberalization, 99-100, 102-6
Central European Initiative (CEI), 3, 5, 6, 8, 113-27, 172-3, 244, 246
  and European Union, 124-5, 198-9
  future prospects, 125-7
  Graz summit, November 1996, 113, 118, 120
  history, 113-6
  "Instrument for the Protection of Minorities", 122, 127
  Secretariat, 116
  structure and activities, 116-24
  Warsaw summit, October 1995, 117, 124
  Working Groups, 118, 120-4
Chernomyrdin, Victor, Russian Prime Minister, 33
Clinton, Bill, US President, 78
Cold War, 3, 6, 8, 11, 12, 23, 30, 38, 42, 46, 48, 52, 128, 219, 243, 247
COMECON, 90, 91
Commonwealth of Independent States (CIS), 6, 7, 12, 95, 107-8, 224, 231
Conference on Security and Cooperation in Europe (CSCE), see Organization for

Security and Cooperation in Europe (OSCE)
Confidence (and Security)-Building Measures, 12-13, 14, 16, 143
Conventional Armed Forces in Europe (CFE) Treaty, 38, 49, 51, 76, 188, 203, 224
Council of Baltic Sea States (CBSS), 3, 5, 6, 8, 16, 24, 26, 30, 33, 46-68, 244, 246
  Action Programmes, June 1996, 59
  Commissioner on Democratic Institutions and Human Rights, 58-9, 172
  Committee of Senior Officials, 61
  and European Union, 65-6, 198
  Kalmar Meeting, June 1996, 59
  and security, 61-5
  Visby Summit, May 1996, 47, 59, 61, 65
Council of Europe, 7, 12, 79, 127, 180-1, 184, 249
  and subregional cooperation, 195-7, 249
Croatia, 53, 115, 126-7
Czech Republic, 58, 77

democracy, 7, 11, 12, 232
  and subregional cooperation, 175-81
Denmark, 33, 34, 47, 52, 53, 54
  Barents subregion/cooperation, 25

East-West conflict/divide, 10, 11, 23, 30, 35, 38, 41, 44, 125
Ellemann-Jensen, Uffe, Danish Foreign Minister, 47, 57
Engholm, Bjorn, Minister-President, Schleswig-Holstein, 56
Estonia, 47, 48, 51, 53, 54, 59
European Bank for Reconstruction and Development (EBRD), 37, 115, 118, 119, 120
European Commission, 18, 26, 27, 34, 47, 51, 54, 58, 65, 197
  Baltic cooperation, 198
  Barents cooperation, 24
  Black Sea cooperation, 136
European Economic Area, 53, 202
European Free Trade Association (EFTA), 99, 201
European Union (EU), 3, 4, 5, 6, 7, 12, 13, 15, 28, 30, 31, 32, 33, 34, 36, 37, 40, 45, 46, 48, 49, 50, 51, 52, 53, 54, 55, 58, 184, 243, 249
  Association Agreements, 51, 54, 75, 80, 197, 200
  and Baltic subregion, 54, 65-6
  Barcelona Process, 235

Barents cooperation, 24, 199-200
and BSEC, 140, 145-6, 199
and CBSS, 198
and CEFTA, 109-10, 200-2
and CEI, 124-5, 198-9
and Central Europe, 72, 77, 85, 90
enlargement, 4, 5, 7, 13, 18, 47, 54, 87, 160-4, 179, 182, 183, 185, 200-1, 211, 213, 216-7, 247
Euro-Mediterranean Initiative/Partnership, 147, 235, 238
EU-Russia Partnership and Cooperation Agreement, 51, 54
Interreg, 66, 197, 198
PHARE, 66, 197, 198
and subregional cooperation, 197-203, 249
TACIS, 33, 197, 198
and Visegrad group, 78, 80, 81-2, 200-1
"Euro-regions", 5, 60

Finland, 24, 26, 30, 31, 32, 33, 34, 35, 36, 37, 45, 47, 49, 51, 52, 53, 54, 55
  and Russia, 50
former Soviet states/Union (see also Newly Independent States), 3, 5, 52, 224, 247
France, 24

Gabcikovo-Nagymaros dam, 77, 78-9
Genscher, Hans-Dietrich, German Foreign Minister, 47, 56
Germany, 24, 30, 47, 49, 50, 54, 55, 63, 70, 71, 91
  unification of, 48
  Nazi, 49
  and Russia, 49
  East Germany, 52
Gorbachev, Mikhail, Soviet President, 40, 56

Hansa, 55, 56, 156
Hapsburg empire, 114, 156
Havel, Vaclav, Czechoslovak President, 70, 72, 73, 77, 78
High North, 23, 31, 36, 38, 39, 40, 42, 43
Hungary, 79, 127

Iceland, 52
Italy, 24, 86, 126-7

Japan, 24
Kaliningrad, 48, 51, 174, 245
Karelia, 53
Kirkenes Declaration, 24, 39
Klaus, Vaclav, Czech Prime Minister, 77, 87
Kohl, Helmut, German Chancellor, 49, 61, 65

Index

Kola Peninsula, 53
Kwasniewski, Aleksander, 85

Lapland, 24
Latvia, 47, 48, 53, 54, 59, 62
Lithuania, 47, 48, 53, 54, 101

Meciar, Vladimir, Slovak Prime Minister, 77, 79
Mediterranean, 5, 7, 213, 232-8, 239, 240, 247
  Arab Maghreb Union, 234
  Barcelona Process, 235
  Euro-Arab Dialogue, 234
  Euro-Mediterranean Initiative/Partnership, 147, 235, 238
  Conference on Security and Cooperation in the Mediterranean, 234
  Maghreb states, 236
  Mediterranean Forum, 234
Mitteleuropa, 114

Netherlands, 24
Newly Independent States (see also former Soviet states/Union), 7, 213, 224-32, 239, 240
Nordic states, 36, 41, 48, 49, 52, 53, 54, 56, 57, 58, 63, 64
  cooperation, 6, 10, 36, 53, 112
  Nordic Council, 49, 53, 55
  and Baltic states, 50, 51, 53
North Atlantic Treaty Organization (NATO), 3, 4, 5, 6, 7, 12, 13, 16, 31, 32, 45, 48, 49, 50, 51, 52, 55, 63, 184, 243, 249
  Combined Joint Task Forces (CJTFs), 206, 250
  enlargement, 4, 5, 7, 13, 47, 87, 160-4, 179, 182, 183, 185, 205-6, 211, 213, 216-7, 247
  Euro-Atlantic Partnership Council (EAPC), 12, 16, 18, 205-6, 207, 208, 210
  NATO-Russia Founding Act, 55, 137
  North Atlantic Cooperation Council (NACC), 203
  Partnership for Peace (PfP), 12, 16, 18, 51, 52, 55, 64, 187, 204-5, 206, 207, 208, 210, 246, 249
  and subregional cooperation, 203-8, 249
  and Visegrad group, 78, 81-2, 204
Northern Europe, 11, 25, 30, 31, 32, 33, 48, 51, 56, 68, 183
Northern Sea Route, 26, 35, 37

Norway, 24, 26, 27, 28, 30, 31, 32, 35, 36, 37, 44, 45, 47, 48, 51, 52, 53, 58, 178
nuclear weapons, 28, 38, 51

Organization for Security and Cooperation in Europe (OSCE), 3, 4, 5, 6, 11, 12, 15, 16, 17, 19, 20, 50, 55, 64, 71, 142, 184, 243, 248-9
  Budapest summit, December 1994, 186, 187, 191
  Charter, 191
  Confidence and Security-Building Measures (CSBMs), 12, 64, 125, 188, 193-4
  Forum for Security Cooperation (FSC), 187
  Helsinki summit, July 1992, 186, 189, 191
  High Commissioner on National Minorities, 59, 172, 186, 194
  Lisbon Summit, December 1996, 15, 187, 188, 190, 191, 192, 194
  Security Model, 190, 191, 192
  and subregional cooperation, 186-95, 248-9
  Vienna Document 1990/1994, 12, 188

Poland, 24, 47, 49, 50, 52, 53, 54, 55, 63
prevention of conflicts, 9

region (terminology), 5
Romania, 79, 84, 90, 101, 178
Royaumont Initiative/Process, 220-1
Russia, 3, 4, 5, 18-9, 23, 26, 28, 29, 30, 31, 33, 35, 36, 37, 41, 44, 45, 47, 48, 49, 50, 51, 52, 54, 55, 57, 58, 62, 70, 108, 243, 246
  and Baltic Sea subregion, 51
  Barents subregion/cooperation, 25
  and BSEC, 139-40
  and Finland, 50
  and former Soviet Union, 224-6, 227
  and Germany, 49
  EU-Russia Partnership and Cooperation Agreement, 51

security, 38, 39, 42, 154-5, 164-75
  and Baltic subregion, 54-55, 61-5
  "civic" security, 47, 63, 65
  "civilian" security, 40
  "existential" security, 168
  "hard" security, 14, 41, 44, 63, 64, 143, 150, 173, 215
  military security, 9, 13-14

non-military security, 15, 227-8
"soft" security, 7, 39, 40, 141-2, 169-72, 185, 196, 211, 249
and subregional cooperation, 164-75
threats/risks, 9, 233
Slovakia, 58, 77, 79, 127, 178
Slovenia, 86, 90, 101, 115, 126-7
Sofia process, 221
South-Eastern Europe, 5, 7, 8, 19, 213, 217-224, 239, 240, 247
and NATO/EU enlargement, 219-20, 250
Southeast European Cooperation Initiative (SECI), 221
Soviet bloc, 4, 54
Soviet Union, 30, 48, 56
"Stability Pact", 188-9, 202
Stoltenberg, Thorvald, Norwegian Foreign Minister, 24, 40
subregion (terminology), 4-5, 6
subregional cooperation and democracy, 175-81
subregional cooperation and integration, 157-64
subregional cooperation and security, 164-75
subregionalization of European security, 4, 250-3
Sweden, 26, 30, 31, 32, 33, 34, 35, 36, 47, 49, 50, 52, 53, 54, 55, 61

Transcarpathian Euroregion, 177
transfrontier cooperation, 7, 177-81, 196, 214, 248
Turkey, 128, 139-40
and BSEC, 128, 139-40

Ukraine, 4, 127, 224
United Kingdom, 24
United Nations (UN), 5, 11
Charter of the, 5
United States, 19, 24, 30, 64, 246

Vayrynen, Finnish Foreign Minister, 57
Visegrad group, 3, 4, 5, 6, 69-89, 90, 244, 246
Bratislava summit, April 1990, 71
Cracow summit, October 1991, 75-6, 98
and European Union, 78, 80, 81-2, 200-1
military cooperation, 75, 78, 82-3
and NATO, 76, 81-2, 204
Prague summit, May 1992, 76-7
Prague summit, January 1994, 78
and security, 80-4
Visegrad summit, February 1991,72-4, 98

Walesa, Lech, Polish President, 71, 73, 77
Warsaw Pact, 52
"Weimar Triangle", 86
Western European Union (WEU), 3, 4, 12, 16, 62, 75, 184, 249
Associate Partners, 208
enlargement, 209
"Petersberg tasks", 210
and subregional cooperation, 208-10, 249
Woerner, Manfred, NATO Secretary-General, 75, 203-4

Yeltsin, Boris, Russian President, 33, 225
(former) Yugoslavia, 113, 116, 184, 243